LATE ESSAYS

ALSO BY J. M. COETZEE

J. M. COETZEE

Late Essays

2006–2017

VIKING

VIKING

An imprint of Penguin Random House LLC

375 Hudson Street
New York, New York 10014
penguin.com

First published in Great Britain by Harvill Secker, an imprint of Penguin
Random House UK.

Acknowledgments to earlier publishers of these essays appear on pages 295–7.

ISBN: 9780735223912 (hardcover)
ISBN: 9780735223936 (e-book)

Printed in the United States of America
1   3   5   7   9   10   8   6   4   2

Set in Bembo

Contents

1. Daniel Defoe, *Roxana*

Daniel Defoe was born in 1660 into a family of Dissenters, that is to say, fringe Protestants of Calvinist orientation. Universities being closed by law to Dissenters as to Roman Catholics, he was educated at a Dissenting academy on the outskirts of London. This was not a bad thing. English universities were at a low point in their history, whereas academies like the one he attended were open to new currents in philosophy and natural science. They taught not the classical curriculum of grammar and rhetoric but practical subjects like history and geography, and trained students to write in their native English.

On graduating Defoe looked forward to a career in commerce; but his restless, sometimes headstrong involvement in national affairs, complicated by his minority status as a Dissident, made life as a businessman hard to realize. Though he prudently retreated from the radically egalitarian views of his early years, his standpoint remained, broadly speaking, progressive, particularly on relations between the sexes. As a journalist and political commentator he decried arranged marriages and agitated for reform of the marriage laws. Being married to someone you do not love, he wrote, was like the variety of capital punishment practised in ancient Rome in which the homicide was bound to the corpse of his victim and left to die of slow putrefaction. He advocated education for women according to a modern curriculum that would equip them to manage their own affairs. His own marriage was notably happy.

Because he wrote freely (promiscuously, his critics said) on every subject under the sun, and with (apparently) careless haste, Defoe has been accorded a peculiar position in the history of literature: as an unwitting, accidental pioneer of the novel of realism. Here is the French critic Hippolyte Taine, writing in 1863:

> [Defoe's] imagination is that of a man of business rather than an artist, packed with facts, almost crammed full with them. He presents them as they come to him, without arrangement or style, as if conversing, not trying to achieve effects or compose a proper sentence, employing technical terms and vulgar turns of phrase, repeating himself if need be, saying the same thing two or three times.

To Taine, Defoe seems simply to be exposing the contents of his mind without the intervening agency of art. Because the resulting jumble is much like the jumble of everyday life, we take it to be in some vague sense 'real' or 'true'.

> It is in [avoiding the appearance of fiction] that his talent lies. In this way his imperfections serve his interest. His oversights, his repetitions, his prolixity contribute to the illusion: we cannot claim that such and such a detail, so petty, so dull, could be invented – an inventor would have left it out, it is too tedious to have been put in on purpose.

Art makes choices, embellishes, engages our interest; art could not possibly have piled up this load of dull, vulgar particulars; therefore it must be the truth.[1]

Taine's verdict on Defoe is a harsh one, yet in essence it persists to the present day. As a writer Defoe did not know what he was doing, therefore could have had no idea of the importance of what he was doing. Instead, following intuitions that, in retrospect, we concede may have flowed from a certain inborn genius, he gave us, under a series of disguises, a representation of the mind of his age, or rather, the mind of an important social actor: the inquisitive, acquisitive man or woman of the ascendant Protestant middle class.

One of the things about Defoe that irritated the people around him was his self-confidence. There was nothing he believed he could not do. In an age that did not lack for men of high intellect (Isaac Newton was a contemporary), Defoe was a supreme exemplar of a different kind of intelligence: of practical intelligence, of knowing or working out how to do things. Here follows a partial list of things he did during his seventy years on earth.

He conducted, at various times and with varying degrees of success, trading operations in wines and spirits; in riding-horses; in linen textiles; in woollen textiles and hosiery; in commercial seed; in tobacco and lumber; in cheese, honey, and shellfish. He engaged in the financing of commercial fishing and ran a factory that made bricks and roofing tiles. He ploughed money into two failed projects: raising civet cats for the perfume trade; and building a diving bell to search for sunken treasure on the seabed. He was twice declared bankrupt and imprisoned.

In a parallel career in journalism he edited a journal of

opinion, the *Review*, which he brought out three times a week from 1704 until 1713. Specializing in foreign affairs and economic forecasting, it was unmatched in its day for the acuity and intelligence of its reporting, for all of which Defoe himself was responsible. Republished in full for the benefit of scholars in 1938, it runs to twenty-two fat volumes.

In 1703 Defoe was prosecuted and found guilty of what would today be called hate speech, on the basis of a pamphlet he wrote in which, impersonating a fanatical Church of England preacher, he argued that the best way of dealing with troublesome Dissenters was to crucify them. He spent five months in prison, followed by public exposure on the pillory.

He was employed by successive government administrations as what we would today call an intelligence officer but in his day was called a spy. In the course of his duties he crossed the length and breadth of the country sounding out popular opinion and reporting his findings to his bosses in London. He used this experience to set up a nationwide network of informers run from Whitehall.

His close knowledge of national affairs provided the basis of a three-volume work he published after he had left state employment and was making a living as a professional writer (a profession which, if he did not invent it, he certainly pioneered). *A Tour through the Whole Island of Great Britain* is at the same time a guidebook for travellers, an analysis of the state of British society, and an account of Britain's economic prospects, the most authoritative such survey of its day.

Then, beginning in 1719, when he was nearing the age of sixty, Defoe wrote and published in rapid succession a series of books that pretended to be the life stories of adventurers and criminals, as narrated by themselves – books which did much to define the shape and style of the modern novel. The first of these fictions, *The Life and Strange Surprising Adventures of Robinson Crusoe, of York, Mariner: Written by Himself,* gripped the public imagination and was a great commercial success.

The last of Defoe's string of book-length fictions was *Roxana: The Fortunate Mistress,* published in 1724. *Roxana* bears all the marks of hasty production. It is repetitive (it could safely be cut by a third); it seems not to have been revised at all (there are two versions of the heroine's landing at Harwich after the storm-tossed voyage from the Continent); and the passages in which she expresses her remorse for a life of sin read suspiciously like late insertions intended for the censor's eye.

Roxana (a pseudonym: it is implied that she has a 'real' name but we never learn it) is a beautiful and intelligent woman who trades on her looks (on which the passage of time seems to have little effect – she uses no cosmetics, yet at the age of fifty men still find her alluring) to win for herself what she most deeply craves: material independence. In the course of an eventful erotic life she has two marriages and one quasi-marriage as well as two significant affairs, one in France, one in England. Regarding the English affair she is tight-lipped, leaving us to infer that the lover in question must have been the reigning monarch. (This is of course a writer's trick: if this were a made-up story, we are supposed to reason, the author would not have drawn a veil over so juicy an episode, therefore the story cannot be made up, it must be 'true'.)

Apart from her first husband, whom she marries early and who abandons her with no money and five young children to feed, the men in Roxana's life are deeply attached to her, even in thrall to her. To prove his devotion, her aristocratic French lover breaks off relations with his other mistresses; all her lovers lavish money and jewels on her.

Given how central Roxana's sexual allure is to the action of the book, it is surprising how little we discover about her erotic psychology. Is sexual pleasure important to her or does she use sex simply as a means to an end? She is silent on the question. Are we to presume that she has little sexual feeling; or does she lack the kind of narcissism that would enable her to enjoy seeing herself as the object of another's desire; or does her silence simply mean that she is too modest to broach the subject?

What Roxana's silence certainly does not mean is that Defoe, her creator, is too prudent or prudish to explore the workings of sexual desire. One has only to think of the extended erotic game he describes between Roxana, her second (pseudo) husband, and her maidservant Amy, a game in which the two women excite each other and goad each other on until copulation ensues.

This episode initiates an inquiry into the psychology of seduction – more specifically the psychology of being seduced – that is pursued in patches across the book. The key word here is 'irresistible'. After succumbing to her French lover for the first time, Roxana stills her unease by telling herself that the seduction was 'irresistible' and that a just God would not punish us for 'that which it was not possible for us to avoid'. In the case of the king, she again claims that she was not responsible: he laid siege to her 'in such an irresistible manner that . . . there was no withstanding it'.[2]

As with the earlier *Fortunes and Misfortunes of the Famous Moll Flanders* (1722), *Roxana* has at least the appearance of a confession, a contrite recounting of the story of an ill-spent past. It is thus to be expected that Roxana should present her various affairs as moral lapses rather than as personal triumphs. Her plea is that though she did not want to succumb she had to succumb because her seducer was irresistible; further, that one cannot be blamed for yielding to an irresistible force.

But the truth is that sexual seduction is always resistible: it is precisely its being resistible that distinguishes it from rape. One can be forced to do what one does not want to do but one cannot be persuaded to do it – not if one really does not want to do it. This is in essence the answer that Aristotle offers to the question of why we sometimes act against our own better interests: when we do so, he says, it is because we do not know what is good for us in such a way that we fully inhabit that knowledge. (That is why, according to Aristotle, mere adherence to a moral code does not qualify one as a good person.)[3]

Roxana does not pretend that the virtue whose loss she intermittently laments is something she deeply and sincerely believes in. On the contrary, she is happy to remain in a divided, ambivalent state in which she wants to resist seduction but equally wants her resistance to be swept away. She is well aware of this division or ambivalence within herself, and exploits it to evade blame. Thus she says to Amy, of one of her suitors: 'I believe I shall yield to him, if he should importune me . . . but I should be glad he would not do it at all, but leave me as I am.' (p. 74) Implicitly she recognizes that she finds being seduced more interesting (more engaging, more thrilling, more erotic, more seductive in prospect) than giving herself in a direct, unambiguous way; that the prelude to the sexual act can be more desirable, more erotically fulfilling, than the act itself. Seduction, the thought of seduction, the approach of seduction, the imagined experience of seduction, turns out to be profoundly seductive, even irresistible.

Sin and its devious machinations are a staple of Protestant moral psychology, one of the many fields of which Defoe had a close knowledge. He was certainly familiar with the most common excuse that people give for why they have fallen into sin: they were blinded by passion ('irresistible' passion), they say, which is beyond the reach of reason, since its basis is in our animal selves. Defoe was also aware of the crack in this argument, namely that, since we do not invariably give in to our passions, there must be some voice within us telling us when to give in and when not to give in, which seductions we should find irresistible and which we should find resistible. That voice belongs to ourselves, not to our animal being.

It is easy enough to dismiss as self-serving Roxana's resort to psychology to excuse her lapses from virtue ('something in me made me do it'). What is less easy to brush aside is the economic argument she puts forward in her defence, namely that a woman abandoned and left destitute by her husband has either to find male protectors or to prostitute herself; that the England of her day offers no other options.

No doubt Roxana overstates her case. One can imagine an alternative story in which an accomplished young woman like herself has the good fortune to be taken into the home of a wealthy merchant and asked to tutor the children of the family in French. But, through the story he actually invents, Defoe is concerned to plead for an easing of the divorce laws that make it impossible for an abandoned wife to remarry, and more generally to put the case for legal equality between the partners in a marriage. He is also eager to advocate a form of education for girls that will enable them to make an independent living. This joint case is made with a great deal of force. It comes to a head in the blazing attack that

Roxana launches on the institution of marriage when the amiable Dutch merchant with whom she has already slept has the temerity to ask for her hand. By marrying him, she says, she will lose her liberty, her estate and her autonomy, and become a servant for the rest of her days. 'Though I could give up my virtue . . . yet I would not give up my money'. (p. 186)

Money plays a key role in all of Defoe's fictions, nowhere more so than in *Roxana*. What Roxana admires most in a man is a good head for money; what she looks for in a husband is trustworthiness in financial matters. Respect for such quintessentially bourgeois qualities may seem odd in a woman whose highest dream is to be a grand courtesan. But beneath the glamorous exterior Roxana is a prudent, even avaricious hoarder. She spends money freely, but each expenditure is an investment calculated to bring in a future return. For the rest, the many 'gifts' she receives from men are locked away in an iron chest. Her lovers have no idea of the scale of her growing fortune. It is her greatest secret.

Moving from country to country as she is forced by circumstance to do, Roxana faces the problem of how to shift her assets. Travelling with quantities of jewellery and silver plate is too risky to contemplate, yet as a woman she has neither the competence nor the contacts to convert her valuables into safer and more easily transferable bills. What recommends the Dutch merchant to her, and eventually qualifies him as a marriage partner, is the deftness with which he handles the financial instruments of the new, mercantile age. Once she is settled in London, she takes lessons in financial management, making the crucial economic move from hoarding treasure to getting her capital to grow.

Although *Roxana* suffers from being too long and repetitive, in the last fifth of the book the flagging drama comes to life. Through an unlikely coincidence, the eldest child from Roxana's first marriage tracks down the mother who abandoned her years ago. Her sudden appearance on the scene, a veritable return of the repressed, throws Roxana into a terrible quandary. The child has discovered her secret past as a courtesan. If that becomes public knowledge, her happy marriage to the Dutchman will be wrecked. But even worse, the child is demanding that Roxana recognize her as her daughter, confess to the wrong she has done her, make reparation, and become the mother she has refused to be. It is a demand Roxana will not meet: she will not ruin her life for the sake of a stranger who is clearly unbalanced. It is also a demand Roxana *cannot* meet: as we begin to comprehend, there is a fundamental coldness in her emotional make-up which a lifetime of selfish calculation has only served to intensify, a lack of heart that makes her incapable of giving herself.

The novel ends in moral and formal chaos: the narrator who has so carefully and comprehensively chronicled the events of her life begins to lose control both of her life and of the narrative itself. Her companion Amy, who has for so long been so close that she seems to be Roxana's second self, offers to murder the child; Roxana either does or does not (we are not sure which, we are beginning to have doubts about her truthfulness) give Amy the nod; and the deed, it seems, is done – we do not know how or where or when because Roxana does not want to know.

Defoe had no models for the kind of extended fiction he was writing: he was not only making up the story as he went along, he was making up the form too. Although it cannot be proved, there is every reason to believe he wrote at speed and with little revision. It would be wrong to say that the last sixty or seventy pages of *Roxana* were written in a state of possession – Defoe was too clear-minded, too intelligent, too professional for that. But he was certainly writing beyond his powers, beyond what either he or his contemporaries thought him capable of.

2. Nathaniel Hawthorne, *The Scarlet Letter*

In 1694 the magistrates of the town of Salem in Massachusetts passed a law making adultery a crime for which the following punishment was prescribed: the guilty pair were to sit for an hour on the gallows with ropes about their necks, after which they were to be severely whipped; then for the rest of their lives they were to wear, cut out of cloth in a clearly visible colour and sewn onto their garments, the capital letter A, two inches in height.

Nathaniel Hawthorne came upon this singular fact in the course of exploring the annals of the early years of the New England settlement. The idea of writing a story about a woman sentenced to wear the mark of her crime like an identifying brand, going about her daily life under the constant censorious gaze of the community, held a unique interest to him. Although his family history qualified him eminently as a New Englander (a Hawthorne had been among the first settlers of Massachusetts), he had reason to think of himself as a traitor to his traditions, undetected because, unlike his heroine, he carried no distinguishing mark.

As his notebooks attest, Hawthorne had little sympathy with the policing of morals. On the scale of sinfulness, sexual transgressions seemed to him far outweighed by the inhuman cold-heartedness of the Puritan temperament in its New England manifestation, particularly when this expressed itself in intrusions into the private lives of others in the name of pastoral care.

The plot of *The Scarlet Letter* was devised by Hawthorne to bring together two concerns of his: the fate of the ostracized truth-bearer; and the intrusion of the scientific spirit, with its programmatic elision of sympathetic movements of the heart, into the exploration of human psychology. The first of these concerns was relevant to his sense of himself as critic of American society, the second to his vocation as a writer.

Hawthorne was in his mid-forties when he embarked on *The Scarlet Letter*. His literary output hitherto had been meagre: aside from children's stories, a mere two volumes of short fiction. To the literary public he was known, in his own ironic words, as 'a mild, shy, gentle, melancholic, exceedingly sensitive, and not very forcible man', a dabbler in literature who seemed to have adopted 'Hawthorne' as a pen name on account of the quaintness of the word.[1] *The Scarlet Letter* was at first meant to be a short story too, but as he worked on it in a state of total absorption it grew in length. He completed it in a brief seven months and published it in 1850. His spurt of creative energy was not exhausted: the novels *The House of the Seven Gables* and *The Blithedale Romance* followed in the next two years.

Hawthorne's publisher found *The Scarlet Letter* to be somewhat short for a book. At his prompting, Hawthorne added a rambling preface entitled 'The Custom-House', purporting to tell how, in the course of his duties as customs officer of the port of Salem, he had discovered, among odds and ends in a dusty corner of the customs house, a packet containing some fine though moth-eaten red cloth in the shape of a letter A embroidered in gold thread. In this way 'The Custom-House' dramatizes the moment when the germ of the novel occurred to him. It also spells out, more trenchantly than we read in the novel itself, the purpose (or one of the purposes) behind its writing:

The figure of that first ancestor [i.e., the first of the American Hawthornes], invested by family tradition with a dim and dusky grandeur, was present to my boyish imagination as far back as I can remember. It still haunts me, and induces a sort of home-feeling with the past, which I scarcely claim in reference to the present phase of the town. I seem to have a stronger claim to a residence here on account of this grave, bearded, sable-cloaked, and steeple-crowned progenitor – who came so early, with his Bible and his sword, and trode the unworn street with such a stately port, and made so large a figure, as a man of war and peace – a stronger claim than for myself, whose name is seldom heard and my face hardly known. He was a soldier, legislator, judge; he was a ruler in the Church; he had all the Puritanic traits, both good and evil. He was likewise a bitter persecutor; as witness the Quakers, who have remembered him in their histories . . .

His son, too, inherited the persecuting spirit, and made himself so conspicuous in the martyrdom of the witches [i.e., the witchcraft trials of 1692], that their blood may fairly be said to have left a stain upon him. So deep a stain, indeed, that his dry old bones, in the Charter-street burial-ground, must still retain it, if they have not crumbled utterly to dust.

I know not whether these ancestors of mine bethought

themselves to repent, and ask pardon of Heaven for their cruelties; or whether they are now groaning under the heavy consequences of them in another state of being. At all events, I, the present writer, as their representative, hereby take shame upon myself for their sakes, and pray that any curse incurred by them – as I have heard, and as the dreary and unprosperous condition of the race [i.e., the Hawthornes], for many a long year back, would argue to exist – may be now and henceforth removed.[2]

The writer cannot always tell the deepest motive behind his writing. But Hawthorne clearly believed or wanted his readers to believe that writing *The Scarlet Letter* was an act of expiation, meant to acknowledge inherited guilt and to put a distance between himself and his Puritan forebears.

Although voices were raised against the book (a commentator in the *Church Review* of January 1851 called it 'the nauseous amour of a Puritan pastor with a frail creature of his charge'), *The Scarlet Letter* was soon recognized as a landmark in the young literature of the United States.[3] Three decades after it appeared, Henry James was able to celebrate it as a book that might with pride be offered to the European gaze, 'exquisite . . . [yet] absolutely American'.[4]

The character in *The Scarlet Letter* who embodies the cold-hearted strain in the Puritan temperament is Roger Chillingworth, who chills whatever he touches. Back in England he had married young Hester Prynne but (it is delicately implied) had been unable to pay her her marital due. Years later Hester still shudders when she recalls his touch.

Chillingworth makes his appearance in the first scene of the book, when he observes Hester on the scaffold with the child in her arms that is proof of her adultery. At once he guesses that the pastor, Arthur Dimmesdale, is the father. His revenge takes the form of worming his way into Dimmesdale's confidence, pretending to tend to his health while secretly devouring his strength.

Chillingworth illustrates an element of Hawthorne's compositional method that has been termed *allegorical*. Although, in putting him together, Hawthorne drew on his reading of popular Gothic romances like *The Monk* by Matthew Lewis and *Melmoth the Wanderer* by Charles Maturin, he is meant to be a living illustration of the indifference to the integrity of the soul that underlies a loveless psychological science.

Another and more complex 'allegorical' character is Pearl, daughter of Hester and Dimmesdale. Pearl has a number of roles to fulfil in the moral scheme of the book. She needs to stand for the ideal of personal autonomy that has been claimed by the lovers (hence her wild antics and indifference to solitude). She also needs to stand for the principle that one should affirm the truth no matter what the consequences (hence her refusal to let Hester discard the scarlet letter and her pressure on Dimmesdale to confess). Finally she needs to embody the spirit of the scarlet letter (hence her fantastical garb). Since the first two roles are more than a little in conflict, and since the scarlet letter (this is the deep point of the book) always stands for more than we think we know, Pearl becomes a particularly difficult character to grasp as a whole: it is only by breaking her down into distinct roles that we can understand what function she is fulfilling at any moment in the text. Her cause is not helped by the cloying sentimentality with which Hawthorne sometimes treats her.

Dimmesdale and Hester, the other principal characters in the book, are not constructed 'allegorically' at all, though Dimmesdale has allegorical features grafted onto him, notably the gesture of shielding his breast, which may or may not be painfully imprinted with his own version of the scarlet letter.

The novel *The Scarlet Letter* is not an allegory – that is to say, it is not a story whose elements map closely onto the elements of another story taking place in some other, parallel realm. It does, however, rely on being read in an allegorical spirit: without the Judaeo-Christian tradition of allegorical reading behind it, it would be a bare little fable indeed. It is the scarlet letter itself, rather than the events of Hester's life, that signals to us we are moving in an allegorical world. The scarlet letter is the sign of meaningfulness: what the letter stands for, Adulteress or Angel or anything else, even Artist, is unimportant compared to the fact that it stands for something outside itself; also compared to the supremely ironic fact – on which the whole book pivots – that the meaning of the letter is mobile, does not always have to be what it was intended to be by those who brought it into existence.

Hester takes over a sign that was imposed on her as a mark of sin and shame and, by an effort all her own, gives it another meaning. That other meaning is articulated neither to her fellow citizens nor to the reader: it belongs to Hester alone and is not necessarily articulable. Similarly, we do not know what the consuming project of writing the book titled *The Scarlet Letter* – a three-word motto to which Hawthorne's person would thereafter always be linked – meant to Hawthorne himself. We can guess, however, that as Hester stands in relation to early Puritan society, so Hawthorne stood in relation to the New England of his day.

Henry James – whose 1878 book on Hawthorne has become

a classic of American criticism, not least for what it says about James's own ambitions as a novelist at the time of its writing – was not wholly approving of *The Scarlet Letter* or indeed of Hawthorne's general approach to fiction. At the heart of James's critique is his distaste for allegory. 'To my sense,' he writes, 'allegory . . . is quite one of the lighter exercises of the imagination . . . It has never seemed to me to be . . . a first-rate literary form.' (*Hawthorne*, p. 70)

James is here echoing Edgar Allan Poe, who in reviewing Hawthorne's stories had been similarly dismissive: 'In defence of allegory,' he wrote, 'there is scarcely one respectable word to be said . . . Under the best circumstances, [allegory] must always interfere with that unity of effect which, to the artist, is worth all the allegory in the world'.[5]

Hawthorne did not use the term *novel* for *The Scarlet Letter* or any of his other long fictions. The term he preferred was *romance*, by which he indicated that he was neither aspiring to nor attempting the denseness of social texture or the complexity of social relationships that we find in such English novelists as Charles Dickens.

James discusses at length the plight of Hawthorne and any aspiring American writer of Hawthorne's day – that is to say, of the generation or two before James himself:

> It takes so many things, as Hawthorne must have felt later in life, when he made the acquaintance of the denser, warmer, richer European spectacle – it takes such an accumulation of history and custom, such a complexity of manners and types, to form a fund of suggestion for a novelist. (*Hawthorne*, p. 55)

There is a degree of sympathy here toward his predecessor, but a degree of condescension too: the condescension of a cosmopolite who has sat at the feet of Turgenev and Flaubert toward a provincial forebear. Whether that condescension is merited is no longer as obvious as it must once have seemed. 'Romances' set on the western frontier (Fenimore Cooper) or in Puritan New England (Hawthorne) or on the high seas (Herman Melville) no longer seem to us inherently inferior to the 'novels' that James was learning to write.

The year after *The Scarlet Letter* appeared, Melville brought out *Moby-Dick*, the grandest of American fictions of its day in ambition and scale, a work which dips as unashamedly into allegory as Hawthorne ever did. Melville was a friend and admirer of Hawthorne, his senior by fifteen years. In the same year that *The Scarlet Letter* came out, Melville published what was nominally a book review but was in fact an inquiry into the mind of Hawthorne, drawing upon such mysterious earlier stories as 'The Minister's Black Veil', 'Wakefield', and 'Young Goodman Brown'. How true, how deeply felt, he asks, was Hawthorne's engagement with the Puritan past? Was he drawn to it merely by its quaintness and novelty as a subject for fiction; or was his writing desk an arena where he in secret wrestled with inherited demons?

Though the suspicion had already been in the air in the 1840s that Hawthorne drew on the Puritan past simply for its picturesque qualities, it was James who formulated the charge most clearly:

Nothing is more curious and interesting than [the] almost exclusively *imported* character of the sense of sin in

Hawthorne's mind; it seems to exist there merely for an artistic or literary purpose. He had ample cognizance of the Puritan conscience; it was his natural heritage; it was reproduced in him; looking into his soul, he found it there. But his relation to it was only, as one may say, intellectual; it was not moral and theological. He played with it and used it as a pigment; he treated it, as the metaphysicians say, objectively. He was not discomposed, disturbed, haunted by it, in the manner of its usual and regular victims . . . What pleased him in [his] subjects was their picturesqueness, their rich duskiness of colour, their chiaroscuro. (*Hawthorne*, pp. 67–8)

Melville reflects too on this key question, the question of Hawthorne's moral sincerity. At first his response is uncertain:

For spite of all the Indian-summer sunlight on the hither side of Hawthorne's soul, the other side – like the dark half of the physical sphere – is shrouded in a blackness, ten times black . . . Whether Hawthorne has simply availed himself of this mystical blackness as a means to the wondrous effects he makes it to produce in his lights and shades; or whether there really lurks in him, perhaps unknown to himself, a touch of Puritanic gloom – this I cannot altogether tell.

But then, more resolutely, he continues:

Certain it is, however, that this great power of blackness in him derives its force from its appeals to that Calvinistic sense of Innate Depravity and Original Sin from whose visitations, in some shape or other, no deeply thinking mind is always and wholly free . . . Perhaps no writer has ever wielded this terrific thought with greater terror than this same harmless Hawthorne . . . You may be witched by his sunlight, transported by the bright gildings in the skies he builds over you; but there is the blackness of darkness beyond . . . In one word, the world is mistaken in this Nathaniel Hawthorne. He himself must often have smiled at its absurd misconception of him. He is immeasurably deeper than the plummet of the mere critic. For it is not the brain that can test such a man; it is only the heart.[6]

Melville is surely right here in pointing toward the conflict out of which the action of *The Scarlet Letter* grows: between hopes that in the New World a free, happy, loving life ought to be possible, unencumbered by Old World guilts; and the countervailing intuition that there may be intractable and unappeasable forces within us that will forever thwart such revolutionary hopes. This conflict is played out in the lives of Hester and Dimmesdale, jointly and individually. Dimmesdale is clearly the figure of the artist whose secret wound is the source of his eloquence (his art) but also of his alienation from his fellow men. Although he twice falls under the sway of Hester (first during his liaison with her, then briefly when he allows himself to be persuaded that he and she and Pearl should run away to Europe), he is at heart unconvinced that the sense of sinfulness can be escaped from.

Hester is a more independent thinker (she is at one point compared explicitly with Anne Hutchinson, who in 1638 had been excommunicated and banished from the colony of Massachusetts for preaching that the intuitions of the soul took priority over dogma). At heart Hester never accepts the verdict of society on her; her every effort is devoted to overturning that verdict by undermining the prescribed meaning of the scarlet letter and giving it a meaning of her own. As she asserts during her secret meeting with Dimmesdale in the forest, the place where presumably they used to make love, 'What we did had a consecration of its own. We felt it so!' (p. 140) The moral intuitions of the individual (or of the loving couple) override doctrine.

Hester is a powerfully attractive character, not only in her boldness of thought but in her physical person. Her nature, which is at one point described as 'rich, voluptuous . . . Oriental' (p. 64), manifests itself in her dark, abundant tresses, which flow free in the first scene of the book, when she confronts her judges, but are then coiled away under her demure cap, to be set loose only one more time, in the forest scene with Dimmesdale. Here, tellingly, it is the child Pearl who compels her to imprison her hair again, as she also compels her to resume the scarlet letter and to stand with Dimmesdale on the scaffold.

Hester does not flee, but ends her days in the settlement, still wearing the scarlet letter while steadily labouring to transform its meaning by acts of selflessness and courage. It is difficult to know how much of a victory this is, for while much is achieved – her example must surely take the chill off the hearts of some of her neighbours – much too has to be renounced, including any life of the senses. It is significant that on attaining adulthood her daughter leaves the colony in quest of a better life and does not come back.

3. Ford Madox Ford, *The Good Soldier*

Although Ford Madox Ford has been dead for nearly eighty years, his place in the pantheon of British novelists has yet to be settled. The genealogy Ford claimed for himself, running from Turgenev, Flaubert and Maupassant through Henry James and Joseph Conrad, set him apart from the mainstream of the British novel, while his association with the literary avant-garde before and after the First World War, particularly with Ezra Pound, seemed to place him in the cosmopolitan modernist camp. Yet his two indubitable masterpieces, *The Good Soldier* (1915) and the tetralogy *Parade's End* (1924–8), are the work of a painstaking craftsman rather than an experimentalist, and express a social vision that is conservative, even backward-looking, rather than revolutionary.

Part of the reason for Ford's unsettled place in literary history is that he was born neither into the generation of the great modernists – in the English language, the generation of Pound, T. S. Eliot, and James Joyce – nor into the last generation of the great Victorians – the generation of Thomas Hardy – but in between. Thus, while he felt sympathetic toward the impatience of the young with settled social and artistic conventions, he was a little too old and cautious to give himself fully to their revolutionary enthusiasms.

Another complicating factor was his uncertain relationship with the land of his birth. Ford Madox Ford was born in 1873 as Ford Madox Hueffer, the son of a German father and an English mother; he changed his name after the Great War, when hostility toward everything German was sweeping through Britain. His father was a distinguished musicologist and advocate of the music of Wagner; his mother was the daughter of Ford Madox Brown, one of the school of avant-garde artists who called themselves the Pre-Raphaelite Brotherhood. A precociously brilliant child, Ford was educated partly at home, partly at a school that implemented the most advanced educational theories of the day. He never went to a university.

In a society in which class divisions were a deeply entrenched fact of life, the young Ford had no clearly recognizable class identity. His uneasy situation vis-à-vis the English nation, the English class system, and the English national church (he was born a Catholic), compounded by a very public marital scandal in which he was engulfed during his thirties – a scandal which made him somewhat of a pariah in polite society and lost him many friends – led him, after 1919, to withdraw from England and Englishness. He settled in France, where he made an insecure living as writer and journalist with occasional lecture tours to the United States. He died in 1939.

Ford was a prolific writer. By the time he sat down to write *The Good Soldier*, at the age of forty, he already had dozens of books behind him. Though some of these – principally a trilogy of novels set in the times of King Henry VIII and various memoirs – have their aficionados, the fact is that the bulk of his fiction has not stood the test of time. Wave after wave of scholars have revisited his oeuvre, hoping to discover unrecognized masterpieces, only to return empty-handed. Surprisingly, for a writer who revered Flaubert for his exhausting labours over *Madame Bovary* and his uncompromising quest for *le mot juste*, who in addition had had the privilege of collaborating with Conrad and seeing at first hand the agonies of doubt that Conrad underwent over his own writing and the massive revisions he undertook, Ford himself published one novel after another in which the construction is careless, the plot uninteresting, the characterization shallow, and the prose merely passable.

How could this have happened? Part of the reason was that Ford, chronically short of money, often had to write in a hurry for the market. Another part is that, having been encouraged as a youth to think of himself as a genius, he tended to believe that whatever his hand touched was bound to have merit. But the deeper reason is that, until *The Good Soldier*, Ford failed to plumb the obscurer, more personal sources of his urge to write.

Written before the Great War, *The Good Soldier* is a novel not about war (despite its title) but about the institution of marriage in Edwardian England and the ways in which infidelities were managed within that institution. More broadly, it is a novel about the pan-European class of 'good people' and the codes by which that class maintained itself. (That the Europe it portrays was about to go down in a welter of blood could not have been foreseen by its author.) The novel brings together a bitter critique of the sacrifices, both personal and moral, required for the maintenance of 'good' standards, with the remembered anguish of Ford's own marital crisis. It is an exploration of civilization and its discontents, and specifically an exposé of the psychic cost of married life in days when divorce was rare.

Here is the narrator of the novel explaining the unwritten rules by which 'good people' are to be recognized:

> The odd, queer thing is that the whole collection of rules applies to anybody – to the anybodies that you meet in hotels, in railway trains, to a less degree, perhaps, in steamers, but even, in the end, upon steamers. You meet a man or a woman and, from tiny and intimate sounds, from the slightest of movements, you know at once whether you are concerned with good people or with those who won't do.[1]

The speaker is John Dowell, an American, a New Englander, a wealthy but rather bloodless man who has spent much of his adult life squiring his wife around the fashionable vacation resorts of Europe's upper classes. As heirs to 'old' money, born into 'old' families with long genealogies, John and Florence Dowell qualify as 'good people' themselves. Yet as citizens of the New World the Dowells are to an extent outside the snobberies and rivalries of the Europeans, and to that extent John Dowell can be a dispassionate, objective observer of European manners.

Good people, as opposed to *people who won't do*, are of course euphemisms, part of the deliberately euphemistic vocabulary employed by 'good people', who have no need to say clearly what they tacitly agree upon. They have no need for clear words because they know how to interpret the minute sounds and gestures by which strangers either signal that they are 'good' or betray that they 'won't do'.

Edward Ashburnham, the good soldier, retired in the prime of life from the officer corps of the British army on the grounds of a heart condition, is the chief practitioner of this code or cult of wordlessness, and in the end its principal victim. For nine years, from the moment we first lay eyes on him in the dining room of the Hotel Excelsior in Nauheim until shortly before his death, Ashburnham utters not a single word in our hearing that is not conventional or platitudinous. Why? Because he and his wife Leonora accept a code which dictates that any public display of feeling, any expression that comes straight from the heart, risks being unseemly. The code dictates a strict separation of the public from the private. In public, says the code, civilized standards must be maintained. As for what goes on in private, that is a matter solely for the individuals concerned, or perhaps for the individuals concerned and their God.

Thus the marriage of the Ashburnhams, so well ordered in public that their friend Dowell admires them as a model couple, turns out to be, behind closed doors, a purgatory of rage and jealousy and shame and misery; while the marriage of the Dowells themselves, their distant imitators, is founded on practised deception on the one side and naive complacency on the other.

As young people Edward and Leonora had been brought together in the kind of arranged marriage which (we are given to understand) is not uncommon among the landed gentry into which they are born, a class to whom relations with their horses and dogs are at least as important as relations with other human beings. Leonora, as Edward's potential bride, is appraised in terms appropriate to horseflesh. Specifically, Edward approves her 'clean-run' looks. *Clean-run* is a term used by horse breeders to mean that a horse is well proportioned and of good pedigree (*clean-bred*). During its long history the English word *clean* has been as multifarious in use and as slippery in meaning as the word *good*. In olden times a virtuous woman was called *clean*.

In the Middle Ages an erotic code, the code of chivalry, grew up among the knightly class, the class of horsemen. It had a strong quasi-religious component, projecting onto the object of the knight's desire many of the attributes of the Virgin. It is this code, more or less, that Edward Ashburnham follows in relation to women. Thus, although he is systematically unfaithful to his wife, he nonetheless worships her and will say nothing that might sully her name.

Edward permits himself to be unfaithful to his wife because among 'good people' this is a normal way for a man to behave. At the same time he reveres his wife because this too is normal. As to his actual feelings – what he feels in his heart for his wife or his mistresses – he himself is largely in the dark: the code is of no help to him here. One of the subsidiary themes of *The Good Soldier* is that, since they do not read books or talk about their feelings, 'good people' tend to be ignorant about the emotions and to lead inchoate emotional lives. The library on Ashburnham's country estate is full of horse-racing memorabilia, empty of books. After his retirement from the army, if and when he has time to kill, Ashburnham sometimes dips into a popular novel. As might be expected, his reading only reinforces his romantic and wholly conventional notions about relations between the sexes.

The most direct commentary in the book on the love of a man for a woman comes from Dowell:

As I see it, at least, with regard to man, a love affair, a love for a definite woman – is something in the nature of a widening of the experience. With each new woman that a man is attracted to there appears to come a broadening of the outlook, or, if you like, an acquiring of new territory . . . Of the question of the sex instinct I know very little and I do not think that it counts for much in a really great passion. It can be aroused by such nothings – by an untied shoelace, by a glance of the eye in passing – that I think it might be left out of the calculation. I don't mean to say that any great passion can exist without a desire for consummation . . . But the real fierceness of desire, the real heat of a passion long continued and withering up the soul of a man is the craving for identity with the woman he loves. He desires to see with the same eyes, to touch with the same sense of touch, to hear with the same ears, to lose his identity, to be enveloped, to be supported . . .

So, for a time, if such a passion come to fruition, the man will get what he wants . . . But these things pass away . . . It is sad, but it is so. The pages of the book will become familiar; the beautiful corner of the road will have been turned too many times . . .

And yet . . . for every man there comes at last a time of life when the woman who then sets her seal upon his imagination has set her seal for good. He will travel over no more horizons; he will never again set the knapsack over his shoulders; he will retire from those scenes. He will have gone out of business. (pp. 105–7)

The man Dowell has in mind is Ashburnham, and the woman

who has set her seal upon Ashburnham's imagination is his young ward, Nancy Rufford. It is at this moment in the history of their marriage – in Dowell's reading – that Leonora turns against her husband. Hitherto Leonora has bitterly tolerated her husband's affairs, and even managed their disastrous consequences, in the knowledge that they will pass. Now she begins to fight in earnest for her interests; and now (in Dowell's reading) the story of the Ashburnhams ceases to be merely sad (*The Saddest Story* was the title Ford wanted for the novel, but his publisher vetoed it) and becomes tragic, culminating in Edward's suicide.

The Good Soldier is a virtuoso exercise in novelistic technique. It is narrated by the most deceived of the personages in the action, the one who, for a variety of reasons, is being kept in the dark by the others. The only voice that the reader hears is that of John Dowell. The constraints of the method of narration chosen by Ford dictate that when Dowell reports the speech of other actors, it is only the words they say to him or say in his hearing, or their words as reported to him, that he himself can report. Since he learns about the deception that has been acted out before him only late in the action, much of his understanding of the history of relations between the Dowells and the Ashburnhams, or between Edward and Leonora Ashburnham and their ward, must be retrospective, pieced together and reconstructed from remembered fragments.

The Good Soldier is rightly admired for the ingenuity of its construction and the rigorousness with which a limited point of view – Dowell's – is maintained. But there is more to Ford's choice of an ignorant man as narrator than a desire to set and solve a technical problem. Dowell is the only participant in the action who learns anything: the others simply enact their roles in life. Dowell is thus the representative of the reader in the novel, the one who learns by 'reading' what has been going on around him. What Dowell learns from the fate of the good soldier Edward Ashburnham is – one presumes – what the reader is meant to learn.

But is it so?

Among the host of deceived spouses in literature, one of the best known is Charles Bovary. Under his nose his wife Emma carries on two lengthy and passionate love affairs and runs up extravagant debts. Of all of this he is ignorant. Yet after her suicide and his own financial ruin Charles finds himself more in love with her than ever. He abandons his staid old ways and dresses fashionably, trying to be the kind of man she would have admired. 'He adopted her taste, her ideas; he bought patent leather boots and took to wearing white cravats. He waxed his moustache and, just like her, signed promissory notes. She corrupted him from beyond the grave.'[2] When, much later, he finds out about Emma's infidelities, his reaction is to wish that he had been one of her lovers.

There are echoes of *Madame Bovary* in *The Good Soldier*, and there is every reason to think they are deliberate. 'Yes, no doubt I am jealous,' says Dowell, summing up his position after the dust has settled. 'In my fainter sort of way I seem to perceive myself following the lines of Edward Ashburnham. I suppose that I should really like to be a polygamist; with Nancy, and with Leonora, and with Maisie Maidan and possibly even with Florence . . . At the same time I am able to assure you that I am a strictly respectable person . . . I have only followed, faintly, and in my unconscious desires, Edward Ashburnham'. (p. 204)

If, after tracing in such detail the history of the Ashburnhams, Dowell longs to imitate the life and habits of the deceased Edward, as Charles tries to follow the example of the deceased Emma, then we can only conclude that Dowell has been corrupted from beyond the grave. More to the point, if Dowell is the representative of the reader, then the reader has been misled, for Dowell has profoundly misread the story of the good soldier. Not only has Dowell been blinded throughout (by his wife, by his 'good' friends) but also, in a different sense, he remains blind even when his eyes have been opened.

Dowell reads Edward as a figure of tragedy, but Edward is not a tragic figure. It is a mark of the tragic hero that he should not simply be the victim of forces beyond his control, but should also be able to understand what those forces are. Edward has no such understanding, not because he is a fool but because the code by which he lives forbids him to inquire too closely into anything. Edward is not just a good, brave soldier and what his class would call 'a good chap' but a good man too: he is kind-hearted, he is generous, he is conscientious, he cares for the needy, there is every indication that he treats his mistresses chivalrously. Asked why he behaves and has always behaved well, he might resort to one of the inarticulate formulas of the code – for example, 'Oh, one tries to do the decent thing.' He would certainly not say, 'Oh, one tries to follow the example of Our Lord.'

As Dowell clearly sees, either the fate of Edward Ashburnham has a meaning or else everything is chaos. But there is every reason to be sceptical about the lesson that Dowell extracts in the passage quoted: that indulging one's passions, even at great cost, is better than repressing them. Though he never uses the word, what Dowell really admires about Ashburnham is his stoicism, in particular the stoicism with which (in Dowell's account) he bears the joint assault of Leonora and Nancy in his last months on earth:

> Those two women pursued that poor devil and flayed the skin off him as if they had done it with whips. I tell you his mind bled almost visibly. I seem to see him stand, naked to the waist, his forearms shielding his eyes, and flesh hanging from him in rags. I tell you that is no exaggeration of what I feel. It was as if Leonora and Nancy banded themselves together to do execution, for the sake of humanity, upon the body of a man who was at their disposal. They were like a couple of Sioux who had got hold of an Apache and had him well tied to a stake. I tell you there was no end to the tortures they inflicted upon him . . .
>
> And, all the while, that wretched fellow knew – by a curious instinct that runs between human beings living together – exactly what was going on. And he remained dumb; he stretched out no finger to help himself. (pp. 206, 208)

Of course it is a debased version of stoicism that Edward follows here, a version from which all intelligence has been excluded. Nevertheless, it represents a stance toward the world that Ford himself admired, if one is to look beyond *The Good Soldier* and take in the massive testimony of *Parade's End*, whose hero, Christopher Tietjens, lives as Ashburnham does by the code of 'doing the decent thing' without inquiring too deeply why one does so.

The haunting quality of *The Good Soldier* derives, in the end, from its author's divided feelings about the code by which

Ashburnham lives. It is a code whose tautologicality it is easy enough to expose: one does the right thing because one does the right thing; one doesn't talk about one's feelings because one doesn't talk about one's feelings. Although it ends on the most sombre of notes, *The Good Soldier* is not uniformly tragic in tone. On the contrary, in carrying out an exposé of the hypocrisies of the British ruling class, it has its satiric, comic moments. The mixture of tones suggests that Ford is aware that, once the code that holds together the ruling class unravels, the fibre of the whole social system might begin to unravel too; and his attachment to England – not the England of his day, certainly, but the England of his fantasy, the eighteenth-century England that he would have liked to belong to – was too strong for him to regard that prospect with unmixed pleasure.

4. Philip Roth's Tale of the Plague

Between 1894 and 1952 the United States suffered a series of epidemic outbreaks of poliomyelitis. The worst of these, in 1916, claimed 6,000 lives. For another forty years polio would remain a substantial threat to public health. The development of a vaccine changed all that. By 1994 the disease had been eradicated in the United States and the rest of the western hemisphere. It survives today only in a few pockets in Africa and Asia beyond the reach of public health agencies.

Polio has been around for millennia as a contagious viral disease. Before the twentieth century it was an endemic infection of early childhood, causing fever, headaches, and nausea, no worse. In only a tiny minority of cases did it assume full-blown form and attack the nervous system, leading to paralysis or even death.

The mutation of polio into a serious disease can be blamed on improved standards of hygiene. The polio virus is passed on via human faeces (the virus breeds in the small intestine). A regime of hand-washing, regular baths, and clean underwear cuts down transmission. The catch is that clean habits rob communities of resistance to the virus; and when non-resistant older children and adults happen to contract the disease, it tends to take an extreme form. Thus the very measures that subdued diseases like cholera, typhus, tuberculosis, and diphtheria have rendered poliomyelitis a threat to life.

The paradox that, while strict hygiene lessens the risk to individuals, it also weakens resistance and turns the disease lethal, was not widely grasped in the heyday of polio. In afflicted communities, eruptions of polio would trigger parallel and no less morbid eruptions of anxiety, despair, and misdirected rage.

The psychopathology of populations under attack by diseases whose transmission is ill understood was explored by Daniel Defoe in his *Journal of the Plague Year*, which pretends to be the journal of a survivor of the bubonic plague that decimated London in 1665. Defoe records all the moves typical of plague communities: superstitious attention to signs and symptoms; vulnerability to rumour; the stigmatization and isolation (quarantining) of suspect families and groups; the scapegoating of the poor and the homeless; the extermination of whole classes of suddenly abhorred animals (dogs, cats, pigs); the fragmenting of the city into healthy and sick zones, with aggressive policing of boundaries; flight from the diseased centre, never mind that contagion might thereby be spread far and wide; and rampant mistrust of all by all, amounting to a general collapse of social bonds.

Albert Camus knew Defoe's *Journal*: in his novel *The Plague* (*La Peste*), written during the war years, he quotes from it and generally imitates the matter-of-fact stance of Defoe's narrator towards the catastrophe unfolding around him. Nominally about an outbreak of bubonic plague in an Algerian city, *The Plague* also invites a reading as about what the French called 'the brown plague' of the German occupation, and more generally as about the ease with which a community can be infected by a bacillus-like ideology. It concludes with a sober warning:

The plague bacillus neither dies nor disappears for good . . . it can lie dormant for years and years in furniture and linen-chests . . . it bides its time in bedrooms, cellars, trunks, and bookshelves; and . . . perhaps the day [will] come when, for the bane and the enlightenment of men, it [rouses] up its rats again and [sends] them forth to die in a happy city.[1]

In a 2008 interview, Philip Roth mentioned that he had been rereading *The Plague*. Two years later he published *Nemesis*, a work of fiction set in Newark in the polio summer of 1944 (19,000 cases nationwide), thereby placing himself in a line of writers who have used the plague condition to explore the resolve of human beings and the durability of their institutions under attack by an invisible, inscrutable, and deadly force. In this respect – as Defoe, Camus, and Roth are aware – the plague condition is simply a heightened state of the condition of being mortal.

Eugene 'Bucky' Cantor is a physical education instructor at a public school. Because of poor eyesight he has been exempted from the draft. He is ashamed of his good fortune, and tries to pay for it by giving the children in his charge every care and attention. In return the children adore him, particularly the boys.

Bucky is twenty-three years old, level-headed, dutiful, and scrupulously honest. Though not an intellectual, he thinks about things. He is a Jew, but an indifferent practitioner of his religion.

Polio breaks out in Newark and is soon sweeping through the Jewish section. Amid the general panic Bucky stays calm. Convinced that what children need in time of crisis is stability, he organizes a sports programme for the boys, and continues to run it against the doubts of the community, even when some of the boys begin to sicken and die. To set an example of human solidarity in the face of the plague, he openly shakes hands with the local simpleton, who is shunned by the boys as a carrier ('Smell him! . . . He has shit all over him! . . . He's the one who is carrying the polio!'). In private Bucky rails against the 'lunatic cruelty' of a God who kills innocent children.[2]

Bucky has a girlfriend, Marcia, also a teacher, who is away helping run a summer camp in the mountains of Pennsylvania. Marcia puts pressure on Bucky to flee the infected city and join her in her haven. He resists. On the home front as much as in Normandy or the Pacific, he feels, these are extraordinary times calling for extraordinary sacrifice. Nonetheless, one day his principles inexplicably collapse. Yes, he says, he will come to her; he will abandon his boys and save himself.

'How could he have done what he'd just done?' he asks himself the moment he hangs up. He has no answer. (p. 135)

Nemesis is an artfully constructed, suspenseful novel with a cunning twist towards the end. The twist is that Bucky Cantor himself carries the polio virus. More specifically, he is that statistically rare creature, a healthy infected carrier. The boys in Bucky's care who sickened and died may well have been infected by him; the man whose hand he shook may be doomed. Furthermore, when Bucky flees the plague-ridden city he will be bearing the plague into an idyllic retreat where a party of inno-cents believed they were safe.

The rest of the tale of Bucky is quickly told. Shortly after his arrival at the camp, polio erupts there. Bucky has himself tested and the terrible truth emerges. He succumbs to the disease. After treatment he is discharged from the hospital a cripple. Marcia still wants to marry him, but he refuses, preferring bitter iso-lation. Marcia speaks:

'You're always holding yourself accountable when you're *not*. Either it's terrible God who is accountable, or it's ter-rible Bucky Cantor who is accountable, when in fact accountability belongs to neither. Your attitude toward God – it's juvenile, it's just plain silly'.

'Look [says Bucky], your God is not to my liking, so don't bring Him into the picture. He's too mean for me. He spends too much time killing children'.

'And that is nonsense too! Just because you got polio doesn't give you the right to say ridiculous things. You have no idea what God is! No one does or can!'
(pp. 260–1)

God is not accountable because God is above accountability, above mere human reckoning. Marcia echoes the God of the Book of Job, and the scorn expressed there for the puniness of the human intellect ('Canst thou by searching find out God?' Job 11:7). But Roth's novel evokes a Greek context more explic-itly than it does a biblical one. The title *Nemesis* frames the interrogation of cosmic justice in Greek terms; and the plot piv-ots on the same dramatic irony as in Sophocles' *Oedipus Rex*: a leader in the fight against the plague is unbeknown to himself a bringer of the plague.

What exactly is Nemesis (or *nemesis*, the abstract noun)? *Nemesis* (the noun) exactly translates the Latin word *indignatio*, from which we get the English word *indignation*; and *Indignation* happens to be the title of a book Roth published in 2008 (the plot thickens), a book that, together with *Everyman* (2006), *The Humbling* (2009), and *Nemesis*, belongs to a subgroup of his oeuvre that Roth calls 'Nemeses: Short Novels'.

Indignatio and *nemesis* are words of complex meaning: they refer to both unbefitting (unjust) actions and feelings of (just) anger at such actions. Behind *nemesis* (via the verb *nemo,* to distribute) lies the idea of fortune, good or bad, and how fortune is dealt out in the universe. Nemesis (the goddess, the cosmic force) sees to it that those who prosper beyond what is fitting are humbled. Thus Oedipus, conqueror of the Sphinx and great king, leaves Thebes a blind beggar. Thus Bucky Cantor, admired athlete – the most lyrical pages of *Nemesis* celebrate his prowess as a javelin thrower – ends up a cripple behind a desk in the post office.

Since he wittingly did no wrong, Oedipus is not a criminal. Nevertheless, his actions – parricide, incest – pollute him and pollute whatever he touches. He must leave the city. 'No man but I can bear my evil doom,' he says.[3] Bucky has likewise committed no crime. Yet even more literally than Oedipus, he is polluted. He too accepts his guilt and, in his own manner, takes the lonely road of exile.

At the core of the Oedipus fable, and of the archaic Greek world view enshrined in it, lies a question foreign to the modern, post-tragic imagination: How does the logic of justice work when vast universal forces intersect the trajectories of individual human lives? In particular, what is to be learned from the fate of a man who unwittingly carried out the prophecy that he would kill his father and marry his mother, a man who did not see until he was blind?

To respond that for one man to unwittingly ('by accident') kill his own father and then unwittingly ('by chance') marry his own mother is so statistically rare a sequence of events – even rarer than bearing the plague while seeming healthy – that it can hold no general lesson, or – to put it another way – that the laws of the universe are probabilistic in nature, not to be disconfirmed by a single aberrant individual case – to respond in this way would to Sophocles seem like evading the question. Such a man lived: his name was Oedipus. He experienced such a fate. How should his fate be understood?

Nemesis is not openly named by Sophocles, for which he doubtless had his reasons. Nevertheless, *nemesis* pervades Greek tragedy as a feared force presiding over human affairs, a force that redistributes fortune downward toward the middle or middling, and is in that sense mean, mean-minded: unkind, ungenerous, unrelenting. At one time all of Thebes envied Oedipus, says the chorus at the end of the play, yet look at him now! Greek tradition is full of cautionary tales of mortals who provoke the envy (*nemesis*) of the gods by being too beautiful or too happy or too fortunate, and are then made to suffer for it. The chorus, as an embodiment of received Theban opinion, is all too ready to package the story of Oedipus along these lines.

There is a Greek-chorus way of reading the story of Bucky Cantor too. He was happy and healthy, he had a fulfilling job, he was in love with a beautiful girl, he had a 4-F exemption from the army; when the plague struck the city (the plague of polio, the plague of paranoia) he was not cowed but battled against it; whereupon Nemesis took aim at him; and look at him now! Moral: Don't stand out from the crowd.

The story of Newark's polio summer comes to us, initially, via someone (male) from Newark's Jewish section who takes care not to name himself, uses 'we' at every turn instead of 'I', and is generally so unobtrusive that the question of who he is barely arises. After twenty pages, as we move into the story of Bucky, even the most minimal traces of an identifiable storyteller vanish. So familiar does the narrating voice turn out to be with what goes on in Bucky's mind that we might guess it is simply Bucky's own I-voice transposed into the third person; or if not that then the voice of some impersonal, bodiless narrator, neither inventor of the story nor participant in it. Though this being now and again lets fall a *mot juste* – 'He [began] to cry, awkwardly, *inexpertly*, the way men cry who ordinarily like to think of themselves as a match for anything' (my italics) – he is certainly not the Philip Roth we know, either in style or in expressive power or in intellect. (p. 49)

Only fleetingly is our assumption disturbed that this is Bucky's story – both the story of Bucky and a story that Bucky in some sense authorizes. 'Mr Cantor' seems an oddly formal name for oneself, yet that is how Bucky is more often than not referred to. After a hundred pages, in among a list of boys who came down with polio, there occurs the puzzling phrase 'me, Arnie Mesnikoff'. But having surfaced for a moment, 'me, Arnie' sinks away again, not to resurface until forty pages from the end, when he comes forward to announce himself as no less than the author – more specifically the as-told-to author – of the story we have been reading. In 1971, he explains, he encountered his ex-teacher Bucky Cantor in the street, greeted him, and eventually became a confidant close enough to now relate his history. ('Now' is given no date, but we infer that Bucky is deceased.)

Thus the narratorial device that we have assumed – the mask or voice with no mind of its own and no stake in the story – is thrust aside and a stranger, Arnie Mesnikoff, reveals himself to have been present all the time as a full-blooded interpreter between Bucky Cantor and ourselves. *Nemesis* thus continues Roth's long-running practice of complicating the line of transmission along which the story reaches the reader and putting in question the mediator's angle on it. The experience of reading *The Facts: A Novelist's Autobiography* (1988) or *Operation Shylock* (1993), to name only two examples, is dominated by uncertainty about how far the narrator is to be believed. Indeed, *Operation Shylock* is built on the Cretan-liar paradox of a narrator who asserts he is lying.

In Roth's recent fiction the question of how the story reaches us is as prominent as ever. Though neither *Everyman* nor *Indignation* is in any sense mystical, both novels turn out to be narrated from, so to speak, beyond the grave. *Indignation* even includes meditations, reminiscent of the Beckett of *The Unnamable* and *How It Is*, on post-mortem existence and what it is like to have to spend eternity going over and over the story of one's life on earth.

The revelation that Bucky has been refracted through the mind of another fictional character, someone about whose life we never learn much beyond that as a boy he was quiet and sensitive, that in 1944 he was struck down by polio, and that he later became an architect specializing in home modifications for the disabled, requires that we reconsider the whole story we have been reading. If it seems unlikely that the prickly Bucky would have confided to the younger man the details of his lovemaking with Marcia, then is Arnie making up that part? And if he is, may there not be other parts of Bucky's story that he has left out, misinterpreted, or simply not been competent to represent?

(Arnie puts it on record that the young Marcia had 'tiny breasts, affixed high on her chest, and nipples that were soft, pale, and unprotuberant'. (p. 166) What does a word like 'affixed' say about Arnie's sense of a woman's body, or, more to the point, about Arnie's sense of Bucky's sense?)

Arnie's attitude toward the post-polio Bucky is at the very least ambivalent. To an extent he can respect Bucky's single-minded devotion to his self-chosen task of punishing himself. But in the main he finds people like Bucky wrong-headed and excessive. Our lives are subject to chance, he believes; when Bucky rails against God, he is in fact railing against chance, which is stupid. A polio epidemic is 'pointless, contingent, pre-posterous, and tragic'; there is no 'deeper cause' behind it. In attributing hostile intent to a natural event, Bucky has exhibited 'nothing more than stupid hubris, not the hubris of will or desire but the hubris of fantastical, childish religious interpretation'. (p. 265) If he, Arnie, has made his peace with what befell him, then Bucky can do the same. The calamity of the summer of 1944 'didn't have to be a lifelong personal tragedy too'. (p. 269)

Arnie's life of Bucky culminates in a page-long summation in which Bucky's philosophical position is pretty much trashed. Bucky was a humourless soul with no saving sense of irony, a man with an overblown sense of duty and not enough intellect.

By brooding too long on the harm he had caused, he turned a quirk of chance into 'a great crime of his own'. (p. 263) Temperamentally unable to come to terms with unmerited human suffering, he took on the guilt for that suffering and used it to punish himself endlessly.

Though he sometimes wavers, this is in substance Arnie's verdict on Bucky. Sympathetic to the man, he is deeply unsympathetic, even uncomprehending, toward his view of life. A modern soul, Arnie has found ways of navigating a world beyond good and evil; Bucky, he feels, should have done the same.

Back in the 1940s, Bucky looked at what polio was doing to Newark (and what war was doing to the world), concluded that whatever force was running the show could only be malign, and vowed to resist that force, if only by refusing to bend his knee to it. It is this resistance on Bucky's part that Arnie singles out as 'stupid hubris'. On the same page that he writes of hubris he uses the word 'tragic' as if it belonged in the same semantic field as 'pointless', 'contingent', and 'preposterous'.

Since Arnie does not go ahead to reflect on ancient (elevated) versus modern (debased) conceptions of the tragic – from what we know of him we might suspect that he would not see the point – we may guess that it is the ironical author himself who is dropping these telling Greek terms into Arnie's discourse, and not without purpose. That purpose, one might guess further, might be to arm the hapless Bucky against his spokesman, to suggest that there may be a way of reading Bucky's resistance other than the dismissive way Arnie offers. Such a reading – briefly, so as not to build upon the lightest of authorial hints a mountain of interpretation – might commence with the emending of Arnie's characterization of polio epidemics – and by extension other destructive acts of God – as 'pointless, contingent, preposterous, and tragic' to 'pointless, contingent, preposterous, *yet nevertheless* tragic'.

God may indeed be incomprehensible, as Marcia says. Nonetheless, someone who tries to grasp God's mysterious designs at least takes humanity, and the reach of human understanding, seriously; whereas someone who treats the divine mystery as just another name for chance does not. What Arnie is unwilling to see – or at least unwilling to respect – is first the force of Bucky's *Why?* ('this maniac of the why', he calls him) and then the nature of Bucky's *No!*, which, pig-headed, self-defeating, and absurd though it may be, nevertheless keeps an ideal of human dignity alive in the face of fate, Nemesis, the gods, God. (p. 265)

The unkindest – and meanest – cut of all comes when Arnie disparages Bucky's transgression itself, the wellspring of all his woe. Just as God cannot be a great criminal masterminding the woes of humankind (because God is just another name for Chance), so carrying the polio virus cannot be a great crime, just a matter of ill luck. Ill luck does not call for remorse on a grand, heroic scale: best to pick yourself up and get on with your life. In wanting to be regarded as a great criminal, Bucky merely reveals himself as a belated imitator of the great-criminal pretenders of the nineteenth century, desperate for attention and ready to do anything, even commit the vilest of crimes, to get it (Dostoevsky dissected the great-criminal type in the person of Stavrogin in *The Possessed*).

In *Nemesis* we witness plenty of deplorable behaviour on the part of a plague- and panic-stricken populace, not excluding ethnic scapegoating. The Newark of *Nemesis* turns out to be a no less fertile breeding ground for anti-Semitism than the cities of Roth's dystopian fantasy *The Plot against America* (2004), set in the same time period. But in his narrative of the plague year of 1944 Roth's concern is less with how communities behave in times of crisis than with questions of fate and freedom.

It seems to be a rule of tragedy that only in retrospect can you see the logic that led to your fall. Only after Nemesis has struck can you work out what provoked her. In each of the four Nemeses novels there occurs a slip or fall from which it turns out the hero cannot recover. Nemesis has done her work; life will never be the same again. In *The Humbling* a famous actor inexplicably loses his power to hold an audience; this loss is followed by a failure of male sexual power. In *Everyman* the protagonist, looking forward to a comfortable retirement, feels his life-horizons shrink to nothing as without warning he falls into all-consuming dread. In *Indignation* the young hero's modest-seeming resolution to have sexual intercourse at least once before he dies leads by an inscrutable logic to his expulsion from college and his death in Korea, still, in a Clintonian sense, a virgin. His father's prophecy is fulfilled: 'The tiniest misstep can have tragic consequences'.[4]

In *Nemesis* the action pivots on what seems a tiny misstep that in retrospect turns out to be a fatal fall. It occurs at the instant when Bucky gives in to his girlfriend's pleas and agrees to quit Newark. Intuition warns him that he is betraying himself, acting against his higher interests. He is on some kind of moral brink; yet he does nothing to save himself from falling.

Bucky thus provides a textbook example of weakness or failure of the will, which as a moral/psychological phenomenon has attracted the attention of philosophers since Socrates. How is it possible that we can knowingly act against our own interests? Are we indeed, as we like to think of ourselves, rational agents; or are the decisions we arrive at dictated by more primitive forces, on whose behalf reason merely provides rationalizations? To Bucky the instant when he made his decision – the instant when he fell – remains opaque. The Bucky with whom Arnie does not sympathize is haunted by a suspicion that when he said 'Yes, I will flee the city', the voice that spoke was not that of his daytime self but of some Other within him.

Compared with works of such high ambition as *Sabbath's Theater* (1995) or *American Pastoral* (1997), the four Nemeses novels are lesser additions to the Roth canon. *Nemesis* itself is not really large enough in conception – in the inherent capacities of the characters it deploys, in the action it gives them to play out – to do more than scratch the surface of the great questions it raises. Despite its length (280 pages) it has the feel of a novella.

There is a further sense in which the four Nemeses novels are minor. Their overall mood is subdued, regret-filled, melancholy: they are composed, as it were, in a minor key. One can read them with admiration for their craft, their intelligence, their seriousness; but nowhere does one feel that the creative flame is burning at white heat, or the author being stretched by his material.

If the intensity of the Roth of old, the 'major' Roth, has died down, has anything new come in its place?

Toward the end of his life on earth, 'he', the protagonist of *Everyman*, visits the graveyard where his parents lie buried and strikes up a conversation with a gravedigger, a man who takes a solid, professional pride in his work. From him 'he' elicits a full, clear, and concise account of how a good grave is dug. (Among the subsidiary pleasures Roth provides are the expert little how-to essays embedded in the novels: how to make a good glove, how to dress a butcher's display window.) This is the man, 'he' reflects, who when the time comes will dig *his* grave, see to it that *his* coffin is well seated, and, once the mourners have dispersed, fill in the earth over *him*. He bids farewell to the gravedigger – *his* gravedigger – in a curiously lightened mood: 'I want to thank you . . . You couldn't have made things more concrete. It's a good education for an older person'.[5]

This modest but beautifully composed little ten-page episode does indeed provide a good education, and not just for older persons: how to dig a grave, how to write, how to face death, all in one.

5. Johann Wolfgang von Goethe, *The Sorrows of Young Werther*

In the spring of 1771 Werther (no first name), a young man of good education and comfortable means, arrives in the small German town of Wahlheim. He is there to attend to family business (an inheritance) but also to escape an unhappy love affair. To his friend Wilhelm back home he writes long letters telling of the joys of living close to nature as well as of his meeting with a local belle, Charlotte (Lotte), who shares his tastes in literature.

Unfortunately for Werther, Lotte is betrothed to Albert, an up-and-coming young bureaucrat. Albert and Lotte treat Werther with the utmost friendliness, but he finds the frustration of his undeclared love for Lotte increasingly hard to bear. He quits Wahlheim to take up a diplomatic post in a principality some distance away. Here he suffers a humiliating snub when, as a person of middle-class origin, he is asked to leave a reception for the diplomatic corps. He resigns, and for months drifts around before fatalistically returning to Wahlheim.

Lotte and Albert are now married; there is no hope for Werther. His letters to Wilhelm break off, and an unnamed editor appears on the scene, undertaking to put together a record of Werther's last days from his diaries and private papers. For, it emerges, having decided that there is no way out, Werther has borrowed Albert's duelling pistols and, after a last, stormy meeting with Lotte, shot himself.

Die Leiden des jungen Werthers, known in English as *The Sufferings of Young Werther* or *The Sorrows of Young Werther*, appeared in 1774. Goethe sent a synopsis to a friend:

> I present a young person gifted with deep, pure feeling and true penetration, who loses himself in rapturous dreams, buries himself in speculation, until at last, ruined by unhappy passions that supervene, in particular an unfulfilled love, puts a bullet in his head.[1]

This synopsis is notable for the distance Goethe seems to be putting between himself and a hero whose story was in important respects his own. He too had gloomily asked himself whether a self-defeating compulsion did not underlie his practice of falling in love with unattainable women; he too had contemplated suicide, though he had lacked the courage to do the deed. The crucial difference between himself and Werther was that he could call on his art to diagnose and expel the malaise that afflicted him, whereas Werther could only suffer it. As Thomas Mann put it, Werther is 'the young Goethe himself, minus the creative gift'.[2]

Two energies go into the making of *Werther*: the confessional, which gives the book its tragic emotional force, and the political. Passionate and idealistic, Werther is representative of the best of a new generation of Germans sensitive to the stirrings of history, impatient to see the renewal of a torpid social order. An unhappy love affair may precipitate his suicide, but the deeper cause is the failure of German society to offer young people like him anything but what Goethe would later call 'dull, spiritless citizen life'.[3]

The Sorrows of Young Werther was avidly read; its youthful author was lionized. A spate of unauthorized editions and translations followed (authors in Goethe's day had little protection against piracy). The gossip press soon uncovered who the characters in the book 'really' were: Lotte was Charlotte Kestner, née Buff, daughter of a bailiff in the town of Wetzlar; Albert was Johann Kestner; and of course Werther was Goethe himself.

Kestner was justifiably peeved at what he regarded as a betrayal of their friendship. Goethe shamefacedly pleaded that his book was 'an innocent mixture of truth and lies'; but Kestner continued to grumble that his wife had never been on such close terms with their visitor as was claimed, nor was he as cold a fish as Goethe made him out to be.[4]

If Goethe was now surrounded by a buzz of scandal in which art was hopelessly confused with life, he had only himself to blame. He had meant to maintain an ironic distance between himself as author and Werther as character; but for most readers the irony was too subtle. As a text ostensibly assembled from writings the dead man had left behind, *Werther* lacks a guiding authorial voice. Readers naturally identified with the point of view of Werther himself, the sole narrator until the late appearance of his 'editor' (Wilhelm's responses to Werther's letters are not reproduced). The excesses of Werther's language, the discrepancies between his idealized view of Lotte and Lotte's often coquettish behaviour, were passed over by all but the most attentive readers. *Werther* was read not only as a *roman-à-clef* about

Goethe and the Kestners, but as an endorsement of Romantic suicide.

In the fourth of his *Roman Elegies*, written 1788–9, in a suppressed draft, Goethe gives thanks that he has escaped from the endless interrogation – Was there really such a person as Werther? Was it all true? Where did Lotte live? 'How often I have cursed those stupid pages / that exposed my youthful suffering to the masses,' he writes. 'Even if Werther had been my brother and I had killed him, / it could not be worse than this: being vengefully pursued by his sad ghost'.[5]

The image of Werther as a twin or brother who has died or been killed and returns to haunt him recurs in a poem entitled 'To Werther', written when Goethe was near the end of his life. Between Goethe and his Werther self there was a complex, lifelong relationship that swung back and forth. In some accounts, Werther is the self he had to split off and abandon in order to live (Goethe spoke of the 'pathological state' out of which the book emerged); in others, Werther is the passionate side of himself that he sacrificed, to his own cost. He was haunted not only by Werther but by the story of Werther he had sent into the world, which called out to be rewritten or more fully written. He spoke at various times of writing another *Werther* and of writing a prequel to *Werther*; but it would seem he could not find his way back into Werther's world. Even the revisions he did to the book in 1787, masterly though they are, were done from the outside, and are not at one with the original inspiration.[6]

The history of Werther and his Lotte comes to an end with Werther's death on Christmas Day, 1772. But the story of Goethe and his model Charlotte Buff had yet a while to run. In 1816

Charlotte, then a widow of sixty-three, visited Goethe's home town of Weimar and contacted him. After their meeting she wrote to her son: 'I have made the acquaintance of an old man, who, if I had not known it was Goethe, and even then, made no very pleasing impression on me.' Coming across this sour remark, Thomas Mann made a note: 'I believe this anecdote could form the basis . . . of a novel'.[7]

In 1939 Mann published *Lotte in Weimar*, in which he dramatizes the 1816 encounter, bringing together the couple who, inextricably confused as they are in the national imagination with their fictional avatars, belong by now to the realm of myth. Goethe is as ungracious as can be ('Why could not the old woman have spared me this?'). Reluctantly he invites Charlotte and her daughter to his grand home, then pays more attention to the daughter than to her. Observing that she suffers from a nervous tremor, he shuts his eyes fastidiously. For her part, Charlotte recalls why she turned Goethe down in the old days: because he seemed 'inhuman, without purpose or poise'.[8]

In this novel about the transfiguring powers of art, Goethe the artist – or the human shell in which the artist resides – takes second place behind his model Frau Charlotte Kestner, who in Weimar can at last become who she truly is: Germany's sweetheart, the beautiful, dark-eyed heroine of *Werther*. Rumours of her presence cause a sensation. Fans camp outside her hotel hoping to catch a glimpse of her. She revels in her celebrity.

Having resolved to kill himself, Werther writes a farewell note to be handed to Lotte after his death. But then he cannot resist calling in person one last time.

Lotte is not thrilled to see the distracted young man. At a loss for how to deal with him, she produces a manuscript he has lent her and asks him to read to her. Werther proceeds to read aloud from his translation of *The Works of Ossian*, renderings into rhythmical English prose by James Macpherson, a young Scottish schoolmaster, of fragments of what he claimed to be epic poetry sung by the bard Ossian in the third century CE, passed down orally from one generation to the next of Gaelic-speaking Scots.

The poetry moves Lotte to tears, in which Werther joins. Their hands touch; they embrace; he tries to kiss her. She tears herself free. 'This is the last time, Werther! You will not see me again,' she cries, and hurries from the room.[9]

Werther's declamation from Ossian is no small affair: for page after page ancient bards raise their voices in lament over lost heroes. The taste for Ossian is a feature of early Romantic sensibility easy to mock. The fact is, however, that until well into the nineteenth century the poems were widely accepted as a great epic of northern European civilization. 'The Homer of the North', Madame de Staël called Ossian.[10]

The recovery of the Ossian epic in Scotland became a spur to the recovery – or invention – of other founding national epics: *Beowulf* in England, the *Kalevala* in Finland, the *Nibelungenlied* in Germany, the *Chanson de Roland* in France, the *Song of the Host of Igor* in Russia.

Macpherson was not a great poet (*pace* William Hazlitt, who set him alongside Dante and Shakespeare) nor even a dedicated one: his Ossian project concluded, Macpherson quit the Highlands for London, where he was feted, then took ship to Pensacola in the new British colony of West Florida, where he spent two years on the staff of the governor. Returning to England, he entered politics; he died a wealthy man.

As an historian of ancient times Macpherson was unreliable: much of his archaic Scotland was cribbed from Tacitus on the Gauls and Germans. His barbaric warriors behave like eighteenth-century gentlemen of sensibility, tempering pride of arms with generosity to fallen foes. Nonetheless, he was an innovator of genius. The wild popularity of his Ossian signalled the rise of a new, assertive nationalism in which each European people would demand not only its national independence but its national language and national literature and unique national past too.

Macpherson's most perceptive reader was Walter Scott. The Ossian poems were certainly not what they were claimed to be, namely the words of a blind bard from the third century, said Scott, yet Scotland might be proud that in modern times it had brought forth 'a bard, capable . . . of giving a new tone to poetry throughout all Europe'.[11]

Macpherson's signal achievement was to detect, ahead of anyone else, that the public was ripe not just for tales of clashing broadswords and keening women, but also – and more interestingly – for a new poetic speech that would sound convincingly like the way bards and heroes might have spoken in an archaic, if not mythical, British past. Brushed aside is John Dryden's ideal of making an ancient author 'speak such English as he would himself have spoken, if he had been born in England, and in this present age', that is, of rendering the classics in discreetly modern speech.[12] On the contrary, Macpherson's English carries echoes, sometimes lofty, more often merely quaint, of a barbaric foreign original conveyed to us by a strenuous labour of translation.

In Britain the Ossian poems were tainted by controversy over their authenticity. Were there indeed Highlanders who could recall and recite these ancient lays, or had Macpherson made them up? Macpherson did not help his case by seeming reluctant to produce his Gaelic originals.

In Europe the question of authenticity had no purchase. Translated into German in 1767, Ossian had a huge impact, inspiring an outpouring of bardic imitations. The young Goethe was so smitten that he taught himself Gaelic in order to translate directly into German the specimens of Scottish Gaelic he found in *The Works of Ossian*. The early Schiller is full of Ossianic echoes; Hölderlin committed pages of Ossian to memory.

Ossian is exactly the kind of poetry that we would expect a young man like Werther to go into raptures over; but it would be excessively subtle to say that the rendering of Ossian in *Werther* is designed to reflect the mind of Werther, as opposed to the mind of his author. Goethe claimed that he wrote the first draft of *Werther* in four weeks, in a somnambulistic trance. There is no reason to doubt him. But he achieved that feat only by absorbing into the text a body of pre-existing material: diaries, letters, and his own Ossian translations. At an aesthetic level, reproducing a monstrous slab of Ossian in so short a short novel is a misstep. The hold-up in the action while Werther delivers his aria is a steep price to pay for what the aria actually achieves: raising the emotional temperature, reducing Werther and Lotte to tears.

Goethe outgrew his taste for Ossian. If the public took Werther's enthusiasm for Ossian as an endorsement of Ossian, he remarked, the public should think again: Werther admired Homer while he was sane, Ossian when he was going mad.[13]

Germany in the mid-eighteenth century was a loose federation of states of various sizes nominally ruled by an emperor. Politically it was disunited and riven with strife. Culturally it was directionless. The literature of the courts was imported from France.

About 1770 a movement of young intellectuals coalesced under the name *Sturm und Drang*, rebelling against stifling social conventions as well as against French literary models. For his generation, said Goethe, 'the French way of life [was] too restricted and genteel, their poetry cold, their criticism destructive, their philosophy abstruse yet unsatisfying'. English literature, with its 'earnest melancholy', was more to their taste. They revered Shakespeare (*Hamlet* in particular) and Ossian. For their literary credo they relied upon Edward Young's *Conjectures on Original Composition*, in which the great soul, the genius, uses his semi-divine creative powers to transform experience into art.[14]

Sturm und Drang foreshadowed full-blown Romanticism in its emphasis on originality as against imitation, the modern as against the classical, inspiration as against learning, intuition as against rules, as well as in its enthusiasm for philosophical pantheism, the cult of genius, and a return to the Middle Ages. Goethe was never more than a fringe member of the group; Werther is a more representative camp follower.

Sturm und Drang did not last long: its social base was too narrow. But despite the twists and turns of his later career Goethe adhered to the core aspiration of the movement: to build a new national literature that would overturn ossified norms of conduct and thought. Even as he anatomized *Sturm und Drang* in the person of Werther, he offered, in *Werther*, a seminal contribution to that new national literature.

The strongest philosophical influence on the young Goethe was Johann Herder, to whose anthology of folk poetry he contributed his Ossian versions. To Herder the spirit of a language is the spirit of the people. Thus any renewal of national literature had to go back to native sources. Here again the British showed the way with Macpherson's Ossian and, in 1765, Bishop Thomas Percy's collection of folk ballads *Reliques of Ancient English Poetry*.

In the Germany of Goethe's youth there was still some reserve about the novel as a serious literary form. But Goethe grasped early on the potentialities of the novel of multiple perspectives perfected by Richardson and Rousseau; while from Sterne he absorbed the technique of illuminating the interior by bringing up fragments of involuntary memory. The first pages of *Werther* bear all the signs of Sterne's mercurial narrative style.

Rousseau, in particular the Rousseau of *La Nouvelle Héloïse*, was the shining exception to the strictures of *Sturm und Drang* on French literature of the day. Read simplistically as a plea for the rights of individual sensibility over convention, and generally for the privileging of feeling over reason, Rousseau's novel was popular among the German public, to whom it offered *Thränenfreude*, the pleasure of tears. To Goethe it demonstrated how a narrative can evolve on the basis of a character's gradual self-disclosure.

The Sorrows of Young Werther has attracted many distinguished translators. As with all works from the past, the translator of Goethe faces the question of how the language of the translation should relate to the language of the original. For instance, should a twenty-first-century translation into English of a novel from the 1770s read like a twenty-first-century English novel or like an English novel from the era of the original?

Werther – the 1774 version – was first translated into English in 1779. The translation is usually attributed to Daniel Malthus, father of the economist Thomas Malthus, though there are grounds to doubt this. By today's standards Malthus's *Werther* is an unacceptable piece of work: not only has it been translated at second hand, through an intermediate French *Passions du jeune Werther*, but passages have been omitted, perhaps because Malthus thought they would offend his public. Nevertheless, Malthus's version affords us a window into how *Werther* was read in the England of Goethe's time. I cite one telling instance.

In his very first letter Werther mentions a former woman friend, and – in the words of a recent English translation – asks rhetorically: 'Could I help it that . . . a real passion was forming in poor Leonore's heart?' Malthus in 1779 rendered Goethe's words as: 'Am I to be blamed for the tenderness which took possession of her heart . . . ?'[15]

We are in the sphere of the tender passions, and the word at issue is *eine Leidenschaft*. *Leidenschaft* is, in every sense of the word, 'passion'; but what is 'passion'? Why does Malthus mute 'passion' to 'tenderness' (or why does his French intermediary mute it to *tendresse*)? We can only surmise that to Malthus the obscure feeling that invades the heart of the young woman in question, given how little we know of her (this is her sole mention in the book), is more likely (or more appropriately) a yielding feeling than a fiery one, more likely (or more appropriately) constant than erratic, and is therefore best rendered as *tenderness*.

Our first impulse may be to say that Malthus mistranslates *Leidenschaft*; yet his choice of 'tenderness' cannot but be deliberate. It may be fairer to say that he here performs an act of cultural translation, translation informed by his embeddedness in the cultural norms of his society, including its norms of feeling (what one feels in one's heart in given circumstances) and its norms of polite discourse (what one says or does not say in given circumstances).

This, then, is what it comes down to: where we, observing the tender passions at work, see passion predominating, an educated Englishman of the 1770s saw tenderness. A translation of *Werther* that is true to our twenty-first-century understanding of Goethe, yet in which readers from the 1770s would have felt at home, is an unattainable ideal.

6. Translating Hölderlin

In the depths of the Second World War, in a London battered by German bombs, a young man named Michael Hamburger, who with his family had fled his native Germany to escape the Nazis, penned a lament in the voice of the poet Friedrich Hölderlin:

> Diotima is dead, and silent
> The island's singing bird.
> The temple I raised from ruin
> Fallen again.
> Where is the flame I stoked . . . ?
> Where are the heroes
> And my pulsing song?
> Nothing stirs on the lakes of time.[1]

In German classrooms children were chanting Hölderlin too:

> O take me, take me up into the ranks,
> so that I do not one day die a common death!
> I do not want to die in vain, what
> I want is to fall on the sacrificial mound

For the Fatherland, to pour out the heart's blood
For the Fatherland.[2]

Who was Hölderlin, who could be made to speak for both a lost past and a National Socialist future?

Friedrich Hölderlin was born in 1770 in the tiny independent duchy of Württemberg in south-western Germany. His father – who died when the boy was two – was an ecclesiastical employee; his mother, the daughter of a clergyman, intended him for the church. He was sent to church schools and then to the prestigious theological seminary in Tübingen.

Württemberg was unusual among German statelets of the late eighteenth century: whereas most were ruled by absolute princes, in Württemberg the powers of the duke were constitutionally constrained by an assembly of non-noble families, the *Ehrbarkeit*, to which the Hölderlins belonged. The *Ehrbarkeit* ran the cultural and intellectual life of the duchy.

Young men who passed the seminary's stiff entrance examination were given a free education on condition they would thereafter serve in Württemberg parishes. Hölderlin was a reluctant seminarian: without success, he tried to persuade his mother to let him study law instead. His mother controlled his not inconsiderable inheritance: he remained dependent, until her death in 1828, on the meagre allowances she doled out.

Though the seminary offered a first-class training in classical languages, theology, and divinity, there was also a stress on obedience to church and state that students found irksome. Hölderlin spent five restless years (1788–93) there, dreaming of an alternative career as a man of letters. Intellectual stimulus came not from his teachers – whom he looked down on for their obsequiousness to authority – but from fellow students, who in his cohort included G. F. W. Hegel and Friedrich Schelling. He himself stood out: 'It was as if Apollo was striding through the hall,' a classmate recalled.[3]

In the seminary Hölderlin wrote enthusiastic, rather strident poems of a pantheistic bent celebrating the universe as a living whole infused with divinity. Their immediate model was Friedrich Schiller, but their philosophical underpinning was ultimately Neoplatonic. As his motto Hölderlin adopted the Greek phrase *en kai pan*, one and all: life constitutes a harmonious unity, our goal must be to merge with the All.

Then burst the bomb of the French Revolution. At the two centres of learning in the duchy, the university and the seminary, revolutionary societies were founded, French newspapers pored over, revolutionary songs sung. Students joyfully endorsed the Declaration of the Rights of Man. When in 1792 the European autocracies launched attacks on France, it was the French armies for which they cheered. The Duke of Württemberg condemned their enthusiasm for 'anarchy and regicide'.[4] What the young philosophical radicals in fact hoped for was the birth of a republic of Württemberg, or of a wider Swabia, under the protection of French arms; they were dismayed when the Terror gathered momentum in France.

There is no doubting Hölderlin's revolutionary sympathies – 'Pray for the French, the champions of human rights,' he instructed his younger sister – but his poems say nothing direct about politics.[5] To a degree this was because he had no models for political poetry; but it was also because of a strong tradition among Germany's intellectual class of not involving itself in politics.

The writer with the strongest following among young idealists was Schiller, and Schiller's political line after 1793 was that the consciousness of the people needed to evolve before true political change could take effect. In his *Letters on the Aesthetic Education of Mankind* of 1794–5 Schiller argued that the human spirit could best be enlightened and liberated by participating in aesthetic play. For proof, one need look no further than ancient Athens, a democratic society that prized the life of the mind.

Hölderlin approved the leading role that Schiller gave the artist, but was disappointed by Schiller's anti-revolutionary stance, as he was dissatisfied with the sceptical divide between politics and ethics maintained by Immanuel Kant: political reform might be desirable, said Kant, but only as an aid to the more important goal of individual moral growth. For a while Hölderlin found in Johann Fichte a guide more to his liking; but in the end even Fichte was not strongly enough committed to a utopian future.

The issue was human freedom and what freedom consisted in. The idealism of Hölderlin, Hegel, and Schelling in their revolutionary phase rested on a conviction that ideas could change the world, that the inner freedom envisaged by Kant, Schiller, and Fichte could be extended, that there could again emerge such a thing as a free society along Athenian lines. If Schiller, following on from Johann Winckelmann, represented a second generation of German philhellenism, Hölderlin, Hegel and Schelling formed a third wave: young men who saw in Greece a model to be emulated and even surpassed, not just in art and philosophy but in democratic practice too.

Similarly with the French Revolution in its glory days. The revolution, said Hölderlin, gave an intimation of how the gap could be bridged between idea and practice, between the realm of the divine and the world. *En kai pan*: what had once been whole and good, and had then fallen apart, could be put together again. To search out traces of lost unity in the chaos of appearance we have the aesthetic sense to rely on; to philosophy and poetry falls the task of healing what was broken.

Nevertheless, the self-betrayal and defeat of the revolution left its mark on Hölderlin as on many other disappointed young Europeans of his generation. 'It would make terrible reading,' wrote his younger contemporary Achim von Arnim in 1815, the year when the autocracies of Europe reasserted their sway, 'to count off all the beautiful German souls who surrendered to madness or suicide or to careers they detested'.[6]

Graduating from the seminary with the degree of magister, fighting against pressure from his mother to look for a parish, Hölderlin established a toehold in literary Jena. An extract from his novel in progress, *Hyperion*, was published in a magazine Schiller edited; with Schiller himself Hölderlin established a quasi-filial relationship. At first Schiller accepted the role genially enough, giving Hölderlin advice about his verse-writing – notably to avoid large philosophical subjects – which Hölderlin ignored. What Hölderlin was really after was a more complicated and indeed Oedipal relationship than the older man cared for – 'I am at times in a secret struggle with your genius, to protect my freedom against it,' Hölderlin confided – and in the end Schiller stopped answering his letters.[7]

In need of an income, Hölderlin took on the first of a series of appointments as resident tutor in the homes of well-to-do families. None of these lasted long – Hölderlin had no particular rapport with children – but the second, with a prominent

Frankfurt family, affected his life decisively. He fell in love with his employer's wife, Susette Gontard, and she with him. Forced to resign, he for a while continued to meet Susette clandestinely. But in 1802, at the age of thirty-four, she contracted tuberculosis and died.

Love affairs between ambitious but penniless young intellectuals and the neglected wives of businessmen are a staple of nineteenth-century romantic fiction. Hölderlin's first biographer, Wilhelm Waiblinger, did his best to assimilate Hölderlin and Susette to the genre: Susette, 'a young woman . . . of enthusiastic soul and fiery, vivacious disposition', was 'inflamed to the highest degree' by Hölderlin's 'gallant, distinguished person, his fine eyes, his youth, his uncommon understanding and eminent talent', as well as his skill in music-making and conversation.[8] The reality transcended the clichés of fiction. Susette's letters to Hölderlin have survived, along with a few of his to her. As one reads them, writes David Constantine in his 1988 biography, 'one's sympathy is continually moved towards that peculiar sadness and outrage which comes when one witnesses an irremediable harm being done'. 'The thwarted relation of Hölderlin and Susette Gontard can properly be called a tragedy'.[9]

To a large degree Susette made Hölderlin as a poet. She gave him back the confidence that Schiller had undermined. She guided him to earlier German poets, Klopstock in particular, as models. But above all she incarnated in his eyes the union of earthly beauty with pure mind to which his more mystical, pantheistic intuitions had pointed him – *en kai pan* – but in which he had lost confidence as he read Kant and Fichte. Susette appears in the two-volume *Hyperion* (1797, 1799) as Diotima, a sage and beautiful woman who guides the steps of Hyperion, a philhellene who has voyaged from his soulless German homeland – where, as he bitterly remarks, poets live like strangers in their own house – to help the Greeks in their struggle against the Ottomans.[10]

Fichte had taught that consciousness is not part of nature but stands outside nature observing it. To Hölderlin the evolution of consciousness had seemed to foster only a dispiriting sense of alienation. Diotima-Susette brings Hyperion-Hölderlin to realize that consciousness can be an agency of spiritual growth, that it is possible to share at a fully conscious level in the divinity of the All. Specifically, the experience of beauty leads to the divine. Thus in his late twenties Hölderlin began to develop a philosophy with Platonic undertones and a strongly aesthetic orientation, coupled with a perspective on history in which the modern world is continually measured against the standard of the ancient.

Hölderlin worked up the Greece of *Hyperion* out of travel books, thereby joining a line of distinguished German philhellenes who never visited Greece, a line that included Goethe and Winckelmann, author of the little book, *Thoughts on the Imitation of Greek Works in Painting and Sculpture* (1755), that had sparked off the philhellenic craze. In *Hyperion* and in poems from the same period Hölderlin adopted Winckelmann's Greece of 'noble simplicity and quiet greatness' as the theatre in which he would thenceforth play out his ideas. If in bygone times men had been free to pursue personal excellence and the life of the mind, then they might be able to do so again in some liberated Germany of the future.

After the Gontards, Hölderlin took on two further tutoring jobs, and was dismissed from each for erratic behaviour. He tried to win a lectureship in Greek at the University of Jena, without success. A friend created for him a position as librarian at the court of Hessen-Homburg, a position that the friend secretly funded. But this happy solution to the problem of how the philosopher-poet might devote himself to what, in a letter to his mother, he called 'the higher and purer activities for which God in his excellence has intended me' came to an abrupt end when the friend was arrested on charges of treason.[11] For a while it seemed that Hölderlin himself might be charged as a co-conspirator; but after a medical examination he was declared of unsound mind (his speech was 'half German, half Greek, half Latin', said the doctor) and allowed to go home to his mother.[12]

To these last years of precarious sanity belongs much of Hölderlin's greatest work: the late hymns, the Sophocles and Pindar translations, the play *The Death of Empedocles* in its final version. He had hoped to use his time in Homburg to write an exposition of his philosophy of poetry, which had hitherto found only fragmentary expression in essays and letters; but, perhaps because he was losing the capacity for extended thought, the job was never done.

One of Hölderlin's biographers has argued that Hölderlin was only pretending to be mad to escape the law. But the weight of evidence suggests otherwise. Hölderlin had been dismissed from his last tutorships because fits of rage made him unfit to teach young children. His attention wandered; he alternated between bursts of activity and withdrawal; he was morbidly suspicious.

In 1806, after his condition had deteriorated further, he was conveyed, kicking and struggling, to a clinic in Tübingen from which he was in due course discharged as harmless but incurable. A cabinetmaker with literary interests took him in and housed him in a tower attached to his home. Hölderlin's mother paid for his upkeep out of his inheritance, assisted by a state annuity. He spent much of his time in his host's garden, walking about alone, gesticulating and talking to himself.

There was a trickle of visitors, who would usually be welcomed with courtly formality. A caller left a record of such a visit. From the elderly poet he requested a few lines 'as a souvenir'. 'Shall they be verses on Greece, Spring, or the Spirit of the Age?' he was asked. The Spirit of the Age, replied the visitor. Hölderlin took out a folio sheet and penned six lines of doggerel, signing them 'Obediently, Sardanelli. 24 May 1748 [sic]'.[13] Under the name Sardanelli and other aliases, Hölderlin continued to write occasional verse until his death in 1843 at the age of seventy-three.

The poet in the tower was not forgotten by the reading public. Editions of his poems appeared in 1826 and 1846. During his lifetime Hölderlin was sentimentalized by romantics as a fragile soul driven to madness by his daimon. Later he fell into neglect, remembered only as an eccentric nostalgist for ancient Greece. Nietzsche had a deeper appreciation of him; but it was not until the first decade of the twentieth century, when he was taken up and promoted by the poet Stefan George, that Hölderlin's star began to rise again. With George commences the reading of Hölderlin as a specifically German prophet-poet that would later bedevil his image. 'The great visionary for his people,' George called him in 1919: 'The cornerstone of the approaching German future and the herald of the New God'.[14]

On the centenary of Hölderlin's death a project was launched to publish all of his writings, a task that would take scholars forty years to complete. For this so-called Stuttgart Edition the principles of classical philology were applied to divide the surviving manuscript material into a core of texts and a secondary corpus of variants. This distinction between text and variant came to prove so contentious among Hölderlin scholars that in 1975 a rival and yet to be completed edition, the so-called Frankfurt Edition, was inaugurated on the principle that there can be no core Hölderlinian text, that we must learn to read the manuscripts as palimpsests of versions overlaying and underlying other versions. For the foreseeable future the notion of a definitive text of Hölderlin is thus in suspension.

One reason for this contest of editions is that, in the ninety-two-page notebook that lies at the heart of the problem, Hölderlin went back and forth between new and old manuscript poems, using different pens and inks in an unsystematic way, dating nothing, allowing what one might at first glance call different versions of the same poem to stand side by side. A deeper reason is that in his last productive years Hölderlin seems to have abandoned the notion of the definitive, to have regarded each seemingly completed poem as merely a stopping place, a base from which to conduct further raids into the unsaid. Hence his habit of breaking open a perfectly good poem, not in order to improve it but to rebuild it from the ground up. In such a case, which is the definitive text, which the variant, particularly when the rebuilding is broken off and not resumed? Are apparently unfinished reworkings to be regarded as abandoned projects, or might Hölderlin have been feeling his way toward a new aesthetics of the fragmentary, and an accompanying poetic epistemology of the flashing insight or vision?

In Germany the Hölderlin centenary of 1943 was celebrated

on a grand scale. Ceremonies took place across the country; hundreds of thousands of Hölderlin readers were printed and distributed to German soldiers. Why this philosopher-poet, elegist of the Greek past and foe of autocracy, should have been adopted as a mascot of the Third Reich is not immediately obvious. Initially the line followed by the Nazi cultural office was that Hölderlin was a prophet of the newly arisen German giant. After the tide of the war turned at Stalingrad, that line was amended: Hölderlin now spoke for European values being defended by Germany against the advancing Asiatic, Bolshevist hordes.

All of this rested on a handful of patriotic poems interpreted in a slanted way, plus some tinkering with the text. Conveniently forgotten was the fact that when Hölderlin wrote of a *Vaterland* he as often as not meant Swabia rather than a wider *Deutschland*: in 1800 *Deutschland* was a cultural term, not a political one. The Nazis certainly did not absorb his warning, in the poem 'Voice of the People', against the 'mysterious yearning toward the chasm' that can overtake whole nations.[15]

The fortunes of Hölderlin under the Nazis are intricately interwoven with his fortunes in the hands of his most influential interpreter, Martin Heidegger. Heidegger's meditations on the place of Germany in history are carried out largely in the form of commentaries on Hölderlin. In the 1930s Heidegger saw Hölderlin as the prophet of a new dawn; when the Reich collapsed he saw him as the consoling poet for dark times when the gods withdraw. While in rough outline this account squares with the Nazi version, it does an injustice to the seriousness with which Heidegger reflects on each line of Hölderlin. To Heidegger in the 'completely destitute time' of the present (he was writing in 1946), when the relevance of poetry is everywhere in doubt, Hölderlin is the one who articulates most clearly the essential calling of the poet, namely to speak the words that bring a new world into being.[16] We read Hölderlin's dark poetry, says Heidegger, not so much to understand him as to keep in contact with him until that future arrives when he will at last be understandable. He quotes Hölderlin: 'The bold spirit, like an eagle / Before the tempests, flies prophesying / In the path of his advancing gods'.[17]

Among the liberal intelligentsia of Hölderlin's Germany there prevailed not just an admiration for Athens as a model society where men devoted themselves to the quest for truth, beauty, and justice, but also a somewhat starry-eyed vision of a past when the divine was a living force in the world. 'Where the gods were more like human beings / Human beings were more godlike,' wrote Schiller in 'The Gods of Greece' (1788). This picture of Greece was based largely on a reading of Greek poetry, to a lesser extent on second-hand accounts of Greek sculpture. An elective affinity was claimed between Germany and Greece, between the German language and the Greek language. A new theory of literature was developed, based on Plato rather than Aristotle, in which key elements of modernist aesthetics are pre-figured: the autonomy of the art object, organic form, the imagination as a demiurgic power.

Out of an idealized vision of Greece grew a movement whose agenda, as formulated by Kant, was to allow 'the germs implanted by nature' in humankind to develop fully, so that 'man's destiny can be fulfilled here on earth'.[18] Beginning with the reforms to the Prussian education system effected by Wilhelm von

Humboldt, reforms that made the study of Greek language and literature the core of the curriculum, philhellenic humanism rapidly came to dominate the education of the German middle classes.

The project of remodelling Germany along Athenian lines was to an extent the brainchild of young men with little social capital save a schooling in the classics (Winckelmann was the son of a shoemaker, Schiller the son of a soldier) but with ambitions to wrest control of cultural life from the Frenchified German courts and to give a new, nationalist meaning to German identity. Within a generation, however, the tincture of revolutionary idealism had been purged from the education system, as the career men and professionals took over. Though it continued to be associated with a lofty if vague liberalism, philhellenism in the academy had by the 1870s become part of a conservative establishment. The new radicals were the archaeologists and textual scholars, Nietzsche among them, to whom the neohumanist version of Greece – Winckelmann's 'noble simplicity and quiet greatness', Humboldt's 'purity, totality and harmony' – ignored too much of Greek reality, the violence and irrationalism of Greek religion, for instance.[19]

At first glance, Hölderlin may seem a typical neohumanist of his generation: a déclassé intellectual alienated from church and state, aspiring toward a utopia in which poets and philosophers would be accorded their rightful due; more specifically, a poet constitutionally trapped in a backward-looking posture, mourning the passing of an age when gods mixed with men ('My friend, we have come too late. Though the gods are living, / Over our heads they live, up in a different world. / . . . Little they seem to care whether we live or do not').[20]

But such a reading underestimates the complexity of Hölder-lin's attitude toward Greece. To him the Greeks were not to be copied but confronted: 'If one is not to be crushed by the accepted . . . there seems little choice but with violent arrogance to pit oneself as a living force against everything learned, given'.[21]

Ramifications of this stance are explored in a letter of 1801. To the Greeks, says Hölderlin, 'holy pathos' and the Apollonian 'fire from heaven' came naturally. Intrinsic to Western thought, on the other hand, are 'Junonian sobriety' and 'clarity of representation'. 'Nothing is more difficult for us to learn than free use of our national traits . . . This sounds like paradox. But I repeat . . . in the advancement of culture [*Bildung*] the intrinsically national will always prove to be of lesser benefit'. The most striking achievement of Greek art was to master sobriety and clarity. Out of admiration for the Greeks, the Western poet may try to recreate Greek pathos and fire; but the profounder task is to master what comes naturally to him. This is why the Greeks are 'indispensable' to us: we study them not in order to imitate them but to understand how unlike them we are.[22]

Not only does this letter belie the picture of Hölderlin as a dreamer lost in the past, it also underlines the originality and rigour of his thinking about art. What the modern poet most clearly lacks, he writes, is technical training (in his own case, long apprenticeship to Greek masters fitted him to domesticate Greek metres more fluently than any of his European contemporaries). We arrive at poetic truth not by giving utterance to our personal feelings but by carrying our individual sensibility (*Gemüth*) and individual experience across into 'analogical material of a different [*fremd*] kind'.

The most intensely inward feeling becomes vulnerable to passing away to the extent that it is not prepared to disown its actual [*wahren*] temporal and sensory connections . . . Precisely for this reason the tragic poet, because he expresses the deepest inward intensity, wholly disowns his own person, his subjectivity, as well as the object present to him, and carries them over [instead] into alien [*fremde*] personality, into alien objectivity.[23]

The great subject of Hölderlin's poetry is the retreat of God or the gods, and the role of the poet in the benighted or destitute times that follow their retreat. As he writes – with palpable diffidence – in the late hymn 'The Rhine':

> Since
> The most Blessed in themselves feel nothing
> Another, if to say such a thing is
> Permitted, must, I suppose,
> Vicariously feel in the name of the gods,
> And him they need.[24]

But what can it be that the gods in their remoteness look to us to feel? We do not know; all we can do is put in words our most intense yearning for their return, and hope that, touched perchance by fire from heaven, our words may to some extent incarnate the Word and thus transform yearning into epiphany. (In his fitful faith in a Word that will use human agency to express itself Hölderlin comes closest to his friend Hegel's historical idealism.)

The Greeks, observed Goethe, did not pine for the infinite

but felt at home in the world. A hankering for a lost 'classic' wholeness is the trademark of the Romantic. Hölderlin's Romantic longing to be reunited with the divine comes to him not just from his early Neoplatonism but also from his Christian roots. In the overarching mythological-historical scheme he constructed, Christ counts as simply the last of the gods to tread the earth before night closes in; but the late hymns suggest the beginnings of a rapprochement, a new intimacy with Christ if not with the Christian religion:

> And yet, and yet,
> You ancient gods and all
> You valiant sons of the gods,
> One other I look for whom
> Within your ranks I love . . .
> My Master and Lord!
> O you, my teacher!
> Why did you keep
> Away?[25]

Where Hölderlin's explorations would have taken him had the light not gone out in his thirty-sixth year is anyone's guess. There is one text from his afterlife in the tower that may suggest the direction of his thought. In 1823 his friend and biographer Waiblinger published a 700-word fragment of poetic prose that he claimed to have extracted from the poet's papers. If we accept its authenticity, it suggests that, in times more destitute than he could ever have foreseen, Hölderlin's fundamental hopefulness remained undimmed – his faith that our creative, meaning-making faculty will see us through. I quote from Richard Sieburth's translation:

> Is God unknown?
> Is he manifest as the sky? This I tend
> To believe. Such is man's measure.
> Well deserving, yet poetically
> Man dwells on this earth. But the shadow
> Of the starry night is not more pure, if I may say so,
> Than man, said to be in the image of God.[26]

★

Michael Hamburger (1924–2007) was born in Germany. In 1933 the Hamburger family emigrated to Britain, where they integrated smoothly into the upper-middle-class intelligentsia. Hamburger was a precocious student, winning a scholarship to Oxford at the age of seventeen to study French and German. His first book of translations, *Hölderlin: Poems and Fragments*, appeared from a small press in 1943.

These early versions he later more or less disowned. In 1952 a new, expanded set of Hölderlin translations appeared, followed in 1966 by what was intended to be a 'definitive selection and rendering'. Though in 1990 some poems were added, the bulk of the augmented edition of 2004 dates from the 1960s.

By this time Hamburger was very much the doyen of translators of modern German poetry. Yet in his memoirs he admits to some exasperation at being best known as a translator. As a young man he clearly had creative ambitions, and for a while poems of his were to be found in anthologies of modern British verse. Read as a whole, his *Collected Poems* tells a story of a writer of some gifts who never quite found his true subject and who, sometime in early middle age, gave up the quest and settled for occasional verse.

There is a passage in one of Hölderlin's letters that Hamburger quotes with clear reference to himself: 'For this is tragic among us, that we leave the realm of the living quite calmly, packed into a container, not that devoured by flames we atone for the flame which we could not master'.[27] For Hamburger the sacred flame he could not master went out early; the life of atonement as translator and scholar he regarded as a sad second best. (There is some irony here in the fact that Hölderlin himself reached audacious poetic heights as a translator.)

In a succession of prefaces and essays Hamburger spelled out his aims as a translator. What he did wrong in 1943, he says, was to privilege literal accuracy over Hölderlin's 'beautifully singular' way of writing: 'No translation of Hölderlin's odes and elegies can be close to the originals without rendering their metres or at least their cadences, and conveying something of their peculiar dynamism, their peculiar stillness, brought about by the tension between a strict form and an impulse beating against it'. He strove therefore for 'the best possible translation of a certain kind', in which word-for-word accuracy is weighed against the need to reproduce Hölderlin's music. He dismissed the kind of free translation practised by Ezra Pound and fashionable in the 1960s under the name of 'imitation': 'occupational therapy for poets partly or temporarily disabled', he called it.[28]

We get an idea of Hamburger's 'best possible' in his version of the ode 'The Poet's Courage', composed around 1800, substantially rewritten a year or two later, and then even more radically reworked under the title 'Timidness'. Hamburger selects the first version.

> For, as quiet near shores, or in the silvery
> Flood resounding afar, or over silent deep
> Water travels the flimsy
> Swimmer, likewise we love to be

> Where around us there breathe, teem those alive, our kin,
> We, their poets; and glad, friendly to every man,
> Trusting all. And how else for
> Each of them could we sing his god?

> Though the wave will at times, flattering, drag below
> One such brave man where, true, trusting he makes his way,
> And the voice of that singer
> Now falls mute as the hall turns blue;

> Glad he died there, and still lonely his groves lament
> Him whom most they had loved, lost, though with
> joy he drowned;
> Often a virgin will bear his
> Kindly song in the distant boughs.

The metre is asclepiadic, an intricate pattern of iambs and dactyls broken by caesurae in the longer first two lines of each four-line strophe. Hamburger renders Hölderlin's versification faithfully, and although one might quibble with certain word choices ('flimsy' might be replaced with 'light-bodied', for instance, and 'grows dim' would be better than 'turns blue'), the musical effect he achieves in English is ravishing, capturing exactly the tone of hope, tentative yet vibrant, with which Hölderlin confronts defeat, a tone that characterizes both his grasp of his vocation and his vision of history.

'If I had not . . . found it necessary to imitate Hölderlin's metres . . . then many of my translations would have become smoother and more acceptable to English ears,' writes Hamburger.[29] He is scathing about what he sees as the unadventurousness of English prosody – its prejudice against classical metres and its unthinking preference for the iamb. At the risk of seeming 'pedestrian and pedantic' he takes it upon himself 'to reproduce even those peculiarities of [Hölderlin's] diction, form and way of thinking which are alien both to myself and to English conventions obtaining either in his time or in ours'. His method works, he believes, as long as the English reader is prepared to approach his renderings 'as poems necessarily different from any written in [the reader's] own language, in his own time'.[30]

The peculiarities of diction and form that Hamburger alludes to are not just Hölderlin's use of Greek metres but his practice of varying poetic diction in accord with a system of 'tonal modulation' that he developed out of hints in Schiller and outlined in a cryptic essay entitled 'Wechsel der Töne'. Hamburger is one of only two translators of Hölderlin who, to my knowledge, have taken the system to heart seriously enough to embody it in their own versions (Cyrus Hamlin is the other).

The sternest test comes in Hölderlin's late poems, where the music becomes more impetuous and the poetic logic – hinging on conjunctions (*denn, aber, nemlich*) used as if they were Greek rather than German – more enigmatic, and where lines of verse are interspersed with what read like memos from the poet to himself ('This river seems / to travel backwards and / I think it must come from the East,' he writes of the Danube. 'Much could / Be said about this'). (p. 583) Here Hamburger's determination to avoid building his own interpretation into the poem issues sometimes in a lifeless literalism. Compare the following two translations of a passage from Hölderlin's poem on the Danube. The first is by Hamburger, the second by Richard Sieburth.

> But here we wish to build.
> For rivers make arable
> The land. For when herbs are growing
> And to the same in summer
> The animals go to drink,
> There too will human kind go.

> This one, however, is called the Ister.
> Beautifully he dwells. The pillars' foliage burns,
> And stirs. Wildly they stand
> Supporting one another; above,
> A second measure, juts out
> The roof of rocks. (p. 581)

> ★

> Let us settle here.
> For the rivers make the land
> Arable. If there be vegetation
> And animals come to water
> At the banks in summer,
> Here men will also go.

And they call this the Ister,
Beautiful his dwelling. Leaves on columns
Burn and quiver. They stand in the wild,
Rising among each other; above which
Surges a second mass,
The roofing of rock.[31]

The words 'build', 'herbs', 'dwells' in Hamburger's version literally translate the wording of the original. 'Beautifully he dwells' sounds as odd in German as in English (it is in fact a Graecism). Sieburth, on the other hand, sees no harm in nudging words until they sit more comfortably in English or clarify the logic of the passage. Thus 'herbs' becomes 'foliage', 'build' becomes 'settle'.

The divergence of approach between the two translators becomes more pointed in the image with which the passage closes. The last three lines clearly refer to rocky crags above the tree level of the valley floor. Sieburth feels free to write 'a second mass / The roofing of rock', even though Hölderlin's word *Maß* ('*Ein zweites Maß* . . . / *Von Felsen das Dach*') means 'measure' rather than 'mass'. Hamburger, perhaps because *Maß* is such a key term in Hölderlin (not only the measure of verse but the Greeks as a measure of ourselves), cautiously retains the sense of measure, plane, dimension, and thus comes up with a less vivid rendering.

It is an open question whether Hamburger's lifelong project was wisely planned – the project of translating into English a body of work whose textual foundation would grow less and less steady over the years, reproducing as far as possible its metrical patterning and play of levels of language. Hamburger seems not to have doubted himself, though the prefaces to succeeding editions betray an increasing defensiveness. There are signs that he does not welcome criticism: errors identified by Paul de Man in his versions of 'Bread and Wine' and 'The Rhine' were left untouched. Perhaps with the Nazi appropriation of Hölderlin at the back of his mind, he tends to treat words like *Vaterland* and *Volk* more gingerly than is necessary, in places translating *Volk* as 'kin' and *Vaterland* as 'my country' or 'our country'. (pp. 261, 333)

Hamburger's achievement is nevertheless considerable. The 2004 edition of *Friedrich Hölderlin: Poems and Fragments* contains about 170 poems, some in alternative versions, plus *The Death of Empedocles* in its second and third drafts, plus the so-called Pindar fragments – in other words, the bulk of Hölderlin's surviving verse, including all the major poems of the years 1800–6. *Empedocles* is particularly well rendered; as for the poems, though Hamburger's versions prove only intermittently to be touched with divine fire, they are a reliable guide to Hölderlin's German and give an echo of his outlandish music.

7. Heinrich von Kleist: Two Stories

Towards the middle of the sixteenth century, there lived on the banks of the Havel a horse dealer by the name of Michael Kohlhaas, the son of a schoolmaster, one of the most fair-minded and at the same time one of the most terrible men of his day . . . The world . . . would have had every reason to bless his memory, if he had not carried one virtue to excess. But his sense of justice turned him into a brigand and a murderer.[1]

Thus opens Heinrich von Kleist's story 'Michael Kohlhaas'. First drafted in 1804, it was given its final form in 1810; in one of many revisions Kleist changes the words describing Kohlhaas from 'extraordinary and fearsome' (*ausserordentlich, fürchterlich*) to 'fair-minded [fair in his dealings] and at the same time terrible' (*rechtschaffen, entsetzlich*). And indeed, the whole story turns on this paradox. The inborn sense which tells Kohlhaas what is just and what is unjust *at the same time* fortifies him against self-doubt and thus makes him a ruthless avenger of the wrong that has been done to him.

The story opens with the fatal event that will turn Kohlhaas from a man of peace into an insurrectionist. A baron, Junker

Wentzel von Tronka, sets up an unauthorized toll gate on the road into Saxony and extorts a pair of horses from the trader. Tronka's men proceed to work the horses almost to death; when Kohlhaas's groom tries to intervene he is mercilessly beaten.

In his quest for redress for the lost horses Kohlhaas scrupulously follows legal channels until he has to face the fact that the administration of the law is in thrall to political forces beyond his influence. Kohlhaas is not a political animal; nor, as a member of the merchant class, is he in a position to assert himself against the big landowners. He is more at home in the sphere of pure justice, where his inner voice can guide his actions. This inner voice tells him to take up arms. As he explains to his wife, and later to Martin Luther, if he has no legal rights then he is in effect an outlaw, outside society and free to declare war on it.

Kohlhaas takes to an extreme the Protestant notion that the individual conscience provides direct access to God. Since God is not a presence in Kleist's fictional universe, we are left, in the case of Kohlhaas, to follow the ways in which an uninterrogated sense of rightness works itself out in the human sphere. Kohlhaas assembles a band of malcontents and, in the cause of getting redress for his grievance, terrorizes the Saxon countryside, setting fire to the cities of Wittenberg and Dresden. From the seat of the 'provisional world government' that he sets up in a captured castle he begins to issue decrees. At first the authorities treat his activities as mere brigandry, but as he attracts more and more supporters they recognize that he threatens to set off a popular uprising.

In the end, effective justice in the earthly sense arrives in the person of the Elector of Brandenburg, who rules that Kohlhaas shall have his horses restored to him in their original condition and that the Junker who took them shall be punished. But he also rules that for his rebellion Kohlhaas must pay the ultimate price. It is a ruling that Kohlhaas, servant of justice, accepts without demur, baring his neck to the executioner's blow.

'Michael Kohlhaas' was one of eight pieces of fiction that Kleist published in the course of his lifetime. He called it an *Erzählung*, a story, but nowadays we would call it a novella, that is to say, a work of medium length with a single action and a single main character, focused on a single topic. It is not hard to imagine 'Michael Kohlhaas' expanded to double its present length, with the circle of personages around the horse dealer more fully characterized and more space being given to the social matrix out of which Kohlhaas emerges as well as to the detail of his depredations – in other words, to imagine 'Michael Kohlhaas' as a novel, more expansive in its style than the highly condensed novella Kleist wrote.

But expansiveness is not a Kleistian virtue. For his fiction Kleist developed a prose style that is uniquely his own, succinct and fast-moving. In Thomas Mann's words, his prose is 'hard as steel yet impetuous, totally matter-of-fact yet contorted, twisted, surcharged with matter'.[2] The forward drive never relents; there is no time for physical description (thus we have little idea of what the personages in his stories look like) or for scene-setting; the focus is always on *what happens.*

This condensed mode of narration derives in part from Kleist's experience writing for newspapers, in part from his theatrical practice. A story by Kleist reads like a taut synopsis of an action that has recently taken place under the storyteller's gaze. The final effect is of intense immediacy. In an essay entitled 'On the Gradual Formulation of Thoughts while Speaking' Kleist questions the notion that the sentences we speak are encodings in words of thoughts we have formulated in our minds. Rather, he suggests, thought takes form in a continuous back-and-forth process as the word-stream unrolls itself. The essay helps us to pin down a paradoxical quality of Kleist's narrative prose: the scene is captured in language of steely precision, yet at the same time it seems to be constructing itself before our eyes.[3]

Kleist was born in 1777 and died on 21 November 1811, aged thirty-four, by his own hand. Although unhappy relations with his family, penuriousness, despair at the course of national affairs, and loss of confidence in his art all played a role, his suicide was ultimately a philosophical act: an expression of the autonomy of the self.

The facts of Kleist's brief life are as follows. He was born into a distinguished military family and designated for a military career. At the age of fourteen he was taken up as an ensign into a Prussian army regiment. After seven years he quit, sick and tired of the brutality of army life. To his family he explained that he needed to study. While nominally preparing for a career in the civil service, he travelled widely before abandoning his studies for an uncertain career as a writer. Along the way the foundations of his world view, inherited from the Enlightenment, were shaken by his encounter with the new sceptical philosophy of Hume and Kant.

He went on to write plays, some of which were staged; he edited an ambitious review of the arts, which collapsed after twelve issues; he edited and wrote for a newspaper, which also failed; he published stories. In all these pursuits he depended on the generosity of his family and of the Prussian state (he himself had no head for money). His family – even his half-sister, to whom he was close – grew more and more reluctant to deal with him. After his scandalous end – which they regarded as a blot on the family name – they destroyed all letters from him that reflected unfavourably on them.

As for his intimate life, Kleist had a lengthy engagement to a young woman from his family circle. His letters (hers have not survived) provide no evidence of any passionate feeling between the two; indeed we have no record of any passionate relations at all in his life, though he had many women friends and though he put an end to himself in a suicide pact with a woman suffering from terminal cancer.

Kleist lived his whole adult life in the shadow of Napoleon Bonaparte's grand plan to redraw the map of Europe and impose French models of administration on its peoples. He conceived a passionate hatred for Napoleon, looking forward to the day when someone would put a bullet through his head.

At the time of Kleist's suicide Prussia was in effect a vassal state of France. The military defeat at Jena in 1806, when Prussian troops turned and fled from the French advance, had caused him deep shame. His pride suffered a further blow when the newspaper he edited in Berlin was emasculated by Prussian censors fearful of antagonizing their new French masters. He flirted with anti-French resistance groups and wrote a fiercely nationalistic play, *Die Herrmannsschlacht*, in which he proposed that Prussians should follow the example of the ancient Germani and take up arms against the invader (the play was not staged in his lifetime). He floated the idea of a patriotic pan-German paper, *Germania*, to be published out of Vienna (the scheme never came to fruition).

Although Kleist's stories are today regarded at least as highly as his plays, he himself thought prose fiction an inferior art. He took up fiction-writing only to fill the pages of the journal he was editing; according to friends, he felt humiliated by the step down. Nonetheless, his stories are carefully crafted and, in their structure, anything but simple. As a general rule, the narration is carried out by a more or less invisible or buried narrator whose interpretation of the action he relays is not necessarily to be taken as final. Thus – to give a simple example – the narrator of 'Michael Kohlhaas' at one point condemns Kohlhaas for the 'diseased and deluded fanaticism' of his manifestoes, forgetting that, as he has elsewhere observed, fanaticism is merely the obverse of a passion for justice. (p. 143) In truth, there is no solid ground in Kleist's stories, no ultimate place where we as readers can take a stand and be sure of ourselves.

The early Kleist, as we get to know him from his letters, was a singularly complacent young man. From his reading of Rousseau and the *philosophes* he got the idea of drawing up a life-plan (*Lebensplan*) to cover not only his own education (*Bildung*) but the education, under his tutelage, of his fiancée Wilhelmine von Zenge. Guided by such a plan, he told her, they could live lives of ideal consistency and coherence.

If Kleist had succeeded in his aim – in planning and then executing a life-project dedicated to the pursuit of virtue by the light of reason – he would not be the writer we know. What happened to derail the well-planned life he envisaged was that he had to confront face to face the epistemological revolution wrought by Immanuel Kant, namely that final knowledge, not only of the world outside oneself but of oneself, is unattainable since what is knowable is constrained and conditioned by inbuilt faculties of the mind.

Yet the so-called 'Kant crisis' of 1801, which undermined the very idea of a rational *Lebensplan*, is only a shorthand way of speaking about a much more complex change of course in Kleist's life, whose causes are only partially visible to us but whose effect was to liberate him from the unpromising persona into which he was busy locking himself and to turn him into one of the great questioning spirits of the age, a writer who used his art as a crucible in which to test the model of Man proposed by the Enlightenment.

The people we encounter in Kleist's mature work are torn between competing forces and impulses. The same is true of Kleist himself. Thus it has proved difficult to pin down his politics. In the 1930s he was embraced by the Nazis as an enemy of liberalism and a Prussian patriot. In our day, by contrast, he has been read as a radical critic of the aristocracy. The truth is that the mature Kleist is sceptical of all systems, indeed of the systematizing spirit that underlies the *Lebensplan* project; yet at the same time he does not wholly lose touch with his youthful enthusiasm for reason, clarity, and order. It is thus not surprising that he has proved too elusive (or too inconsistent) to be stuffed into any particular ideological box.

Where Kleist got his story of the woman who gets pregnant without remembering how it happened is not known for sure: perhaps from Montaigne, perhaps from a Berlin newspaper. More important is what he did to his source, namely to translate it from its original low social context, in which it could be read as no more than a risqué comic anecdote, to a more elevated social context, a step that made its reception much more problematic. 'Even to summarize the plot is to ostracize oneself from polite society,' wrote a disapproving reviewer.[4]

The scandalous plot concerns a widowed noblewoman of spotless reputation, the Marquise of O-, who finds herself inexplicably pregnant. Thrown out of the family home by her parents, she puts an advertisement in a newspaper asking the father of her child to come forward, promising him her hand. On the appointed day a man appears: a Russian count who happened to have an opportunity to rape her while she was in a dead faint, and who has subsequently fallen in love with her. With an unwilling heart, but faithful to her promise, she marries him.

Holes begin to appear in this retelling of the story as soon as we ask: Did the count really rape the marquise? Furthermore, what does 'really' mean when whatever did or did not happen occurred offstage, during a clearly demarcated gap in the narration; and when one of the putative participants claims not to know what did or did not happen because she was unconscious; and when the other has an extraneous motive for asserting that it did happen? Yet further complications arise when we ask: Is it possible not to know whether one has had sexual intercourse? (This last question is particularly pointed because the medico-legal orthodoxy of the Germany of Kleist's day was that a woman could not become pregnant if not sexually aroused.)

Already in 1807 Kleist had written a play, *Amphitryon*, that raised analogous questions. During a night of unutterable sensual bliss the virtuous Alcmene is impregnated by someone she thinks is her husband but later turns out to have been the god Jupiter assuming her husband's form. If not only Alcmene's physical senses but her innermost heart failed to tell her who was with her in bed, can she be sure of anything? Can she even be sure she is herself?

The narrator who tells the story of the marquise suggests obliquely that the author of the lady's pregnancy may be supernatural (the origin of the child, 'precisely because it was more mysterious, seemed all the more godly than that of other people' – words added when Kleist revised the story in 1810), and thus that beneath the banal mystery of who did the deed may lie a more profound mystery.[5] Having hinted at these depths, Kleist veers away. But behind the happy solution proposed by the story to the riddle of the child's paternity, the marquise's obscure air of disquiet suggests that the comic genre in which she finds herself may not be where she truly belongs.

Kleist came to maturity when German literature, dominated by the figures of Schiller and Goethe, was at its apogee. Though Goethe and Kleist never met, they did have an unfortunate clash. Goethe, in his role as theatre director, put on a production of one of the younger writer's plays which was hissed off the stage. The fault was Goethe's – the production was poorly done – but Kleist's quickness to take umbrage (it was said that he had to be restrained from challenging Goethe to a duel) lost him Goethe's support.

There were also political reasons for bad feeling between the two. Goethe was unsympathetic to Prussian nationalism and ambivalent about Napoleon: it was no bad idea, in his eyes, that Germans should continue to live in a loose confederation of culturally autonomous states. But the ultimate root of the hostility between the two playwrights was Kleist's vaulting Oedipal ambition to supplant Goethe.

Hostility to Kleist did not prevent Goethe from having a shrewd insight into the way his plays were constructed, an insight that can be applied to his fiction too. Kleist had a tendency to locate important events offstage, said Goethe, then to base his dramatic action on the repercussions of those events. He criticized the result as 'invisible theatre'.[6]

The theatre of 'The Marquise von O-' is indeed invisible: whatever it is that gives rise to the marquise's pregnancy, and thus to the action of the story, takes place not only offstage (that is, outside the narrative) but (it would seem) unbeknown to the marquise herself. Kleist's originality lies in creating a vehicle in which the invisibility and indeed inscrutability of the originating action becomes the engine of the narrative, as the characters onstage struggle to work out what has truly happened.

8. Robert Walser, *The Assistant*

In 1905 Robert Walser moved from his native Switzerland to Berlin. He was twenty-seven years old; with a book already behind him, his ambition was to build a literary career. Before long his work began to appear in prestigious magazines; he was welcomed in serious artistic circles. In faraway Prague he was read and admired by the young Franz Kafka; indeed, on the basis of his early stories and sketches Kafka was taken to be a Walser epigone.

But the role of metropolitan intellectual was not one that came easily to Walser. After a few drinks he tended to become rude and aggressively provincial. Gradually he withdrew from society to a solitary, frugal life in bedsitters. In these surroundings he wrote his first four novels, of which three have survived: *Der Geschwister Tanner* (*The Tanner Children*, 1906), *Der Gehülfe* (*The Assistant*, 1908), and *Jakob von Gunten* (1909), all of which draw for their material on his own experience.

In 1913 he gave up on Berlin and returned to Switzerland, 'a ridiculed and unsuccessful author' (his own self-disparaging words), where he made a precarious living contributing to the literary supplements.[1] In the collections of his poetry and short prose that continued to appear he turned more and more to the

Swiss social and natural landscape. He wrote two further novels. The manuscript of one, *Theodor*, was lost by his publishers; the other, *Tobold*, was destroyed by Walser himself.

After the First World War, taste waned for his kind of writing, easily dismissed as whimsical and belletristic. Though he prided himself on his frugality, he had to close down what he called his 'little prose-piece workshop'.[2] His precarious mental balance began to waver. He felt more and more oppressed by the censorious gaze of neighbours, by their demand for respectability. He moved from lodgings to lodgings. He drank heavily, heard voices, had anxiety attacks. He attempted suicide. Since his siblings would not take him in, he allowed himself to be committed to a sanatorium. 'Markedly depressed and severely inhibited,' ran the initial medical report. 'Responded evasively to questions about being sick of life'.[3]

Institutional routine gave him some stability. He declined opportunities to leave the asylum, preferring to pass his time in chores like gluing paper bags or sorting beans. He remained in full possession of his faculties; he continued to read newspapers and magazines; but, after 1932, he did not write. 'I'm not here to write, I'm here to be mad,' he told a visitor.[4] On Christmas Day, 1956, children stumbled upon him in a snowy field, frozen to death.

Handwriting was one of the sites where Walser's psychic disturbance had first manifested itself. During his thirties he began to suffer from psychosomatic cramps of the right hand. Attributing the cramps to unconscious animosity toward the pen as a tool, he abandoned the pen in favour of the pencil.

Writing with a pencil was important enough for Walser to dub it his 'pencil system' or 'pencil method'.[5] The pencil method meant not only the use of a pencil but also a radical change in his script. At his death he left behind some five hundred sheets of paper covered from edge to edge in delicate, minute, pencilled calligraphic signs, a script so difficult to read that his executor at first mistook it for a secret code. All of his later works, including his last novel *Der Räuber* (*The Robber*, 1925) (twenty-four sheets of microscript, some 150 pages in print), have come down to us via the pencil method.

Although a project to bring together Walser's writings was initiated before his death, it was only after the first volumes of a more scholarly Collected Works began to appear in 1966, and after he began to be read in England and France, that he gained widespread attention in Germany. Today Walser is best known for his four novels, even though these constitute only a fraction of his literary output, and even though the genre of the novel was not what he felt to be his forte. His own uneventful yet, in its way, harrowing life was his only true subject. All of his prose pieces, he suggested in retrospect, might be read as chapters in 'a long, plotless, realistic story', a 'cut up or disjoined book of the self [*Ich-Buch*]'.[6]

The Assistant has been overshadowed by its successor, the more wildly inventive and radically subversive *Jakob von Gunten*, with which it shares a basic plot: a young man enters the household of a couple who are going through a crisis, takes what he wants from them, then moves on.

Jakob von Gunten is set in a big city, in the Benjamenta Institute, a school for butlers, where the teaching is done by Fräulein Lisa Benjamenta, sister of the principal. The Benjamentas are a forbidding pair, but the young hero Jakob soon penetrates their mystery, then sets about imposing his will on them. Lisa Benjamenta conceives a passion for him. When he thwarts her, she pines away and dies. Herr Benjamenta closes down his school, pleads with the boy to be his friend and come wandering the world with him. The tale thus ends in the triumph of the malice-driven provincial upstart, with his delight in nasty pranks, his cynicism about civilization and about values in general, his contempt for the life of the mind, his simplistic beliefs about how the world really works (it is run by big business to exploit the little man), and his elevation of obedience to the highest of virtues.

Walser's emotional involvement with the class from which he came, the class of shopkeepers and clerks and schoolteachers, ran deep. Berlin had offered him a chance to escape his social origins, to defect to the déclassé cosmopolitan intelligentsia. Having tried that route and failed, he returned to the embrace of provincial Switzerland. Yet he never lost sight of – indeed, was not allowed to lose sight of – the illiberal, conformist tendencies of his class, its intolerance of people like himself, dreamers and vagabonds.

In *The Assistant*, the young hero, Joseph Marti, is hired as clerk and general factotum by the inventor Herr Carl Tobler. During the year that he holds the position, Joseph is in a good position to chronicle the slow decline of Tobler's enterprise and the loss of his splendid home.

Walser is not interested in the tragic aspect of these events – the bourgeois tragedy of the fall of the house of Tobler. Nor is he interested in turning Tobler into that figure of comedy, the hare-brained inventor. Tobler's inventions – the Advertising Clock, the Bullet-Vending Machine, the Invalid Chair, the

Deep-Drilling Machine — are no more absurd than real-life devices that caught the fancy of the public of the time and made fortunes for their inventors: the safety bicycle, the air rifle. Nor, finally, is Walser concerned to chart the moment in history when the inventor as man of ideas gives way to the inventor-entrepreneur, who in turn will give way to the inventor as salaried employee of big capital. Joseph's role in the Tobler establishment may be secondary, but it is Joseph, not Tobler, who is the hero of the book, and the overcoming of the Toblers by Joseph that is Walser's theme.

Though Joseph's salary never gets paid, he does receive, as part of the deal, a comfortable room and all his meals chez Tobler. Thus, unavoidably, he comes into close contact with Frau Tobler.

A vigorous, unattached young man thrown into the company of an attractive, dissatisfied older woman is a situation rich in narrative possibilities: the young man can be made to suffer the pangs of unassuaged love, for instance; or alternatively can have a guilty affair with his mistress. But although Joseph is without a doubt sensible of Frau Tobler's charms, and although Frau Tobler seems at times to be leading him on, when the moment arrives for Joseph to reveal his feelings, it is not love that he expresses but disapproval: disapproval of Frau Tobler's cold-hearted treatment of her little daughter Silvi.

Joseph is too much of a child himself to have parental feelings. Of the four Tobler children it is not the boys with whom he indentifies, nor with vain, golden-haired Dora, but with Silvi, a disturbed child who regularly wets her bed and is then harshly punished by the housemaid, with the mother's approval. It would be wrong to say that Joseph is fond of Silvi: as Frau Tobler pleads in her own defence, it is hard to be fond of so unattractive and indeed animal-like a child. Rather, what disturbs Joseph is that for failing to meet the Toblers' expectations Silvi has in effect been expelled from the bosom of the family and turned over to the merciless regime of the servant class. In Silvi's fate Joseph fears he may see his own.

Toward the Tobler couple Joseph's feelings are profoundly ambivalent. On the one hand he can barely believe his good luck in landing in such a comfortable situation, which for its duration lifts him out of the class into which he was born and provides him with the home he has never had. On the other he resents his subordinate position and the indignities to which he is continually exposed. For although the Toblers have rescued him from manual labour they have not raised him to their own social level. Their household turns out to be little different from the Benjamenta Institute, preparing its graduates for membership of the ill-defined interclass of butlers and scriveners and governesses, a rung or two higher on the social ladder than labouring folk or domestic servants, meagrely paid yet expected to observe middle-class norms of dress and deportment. Like Jakob von Gunten, Joseph Marti is full of inchoate, ill-concealed resentment toward the people who give him orders and whose manners he imitates.

Joseph's ambivalence expresses itself in various ways: in the alternating fits of diligence and indifference with which he carries out his duties; in his behaviour toward Tobler, sometimes obsequious, sometimes insubordinate. None of this is calculated. Joseph is a creature of moods and impulses. He may speak in well-formed periods, but what he says is barely under his control. In the course of a single address to Tobler he reproaches his employer for daring to remind him of the comforts of his situation, then retreats and apologizes for his insubordinate tone, then withdraws his apology and defends his insubordination as vital to his own self-respect. Tobler replies by bursting into laughter and issuing a summary command. Transformed at once into his timid everyday self, Joseph obeys.

The currents of feeling between Joseph and Frau Tobler are equally volatile. Frau Tobler's behaviour veers between seductiveness and haughtiness; Joseph is sometimes captivated by her, sometimes coldly critical.

The Toblers, under incessant stress from creditors, staring ruin and social humiliation in the face, are as unstable as Joseph in their moods. Living with the Toblers is like being onstage in an Italian opera. There is enough of the Swiss–German in Joseph to make the experience uncomfortable for him. Yet the Toblers provide him with a more satisfying experience of family life than anything he has known (his own family has only the most shadowy presence in the book: a psychologically afflicted mother, a father a slave to routine). The Tobler's villa, with its expensive copper roof, has become not just his residence but his home. It is thus a huge step he takes at the end of the novel, when – asserting his return to his social origins – he demands his unpaid wages, bids farewell to the site of order and passion, of comfort and tumult, where he has spent the past year, and goes out to face the future.

During his year with the Toblers Joseph evolves and matures in one important sense: he learns to be part of a family, a less than perfect family, it must be admitted, in which he is required to give rather more love than he receives, and in which his place is always precarious. But in another sense he remains constant.

The constant part of his character is what is deepest and most mysterious about him, making the ignoble side of him – his blindness, his vanity, his self-satisfaction – irrelevant. That constant part emerges in his relations with the natural world, and in particular with the Swiss landscape during the cycle of the seasons. Joseph is not religious in any normal sense, nor does he have interesting thoughts (his diary is banal), but he is capable of a profound, almost animal immersion in nature, and through him Walser is able to express what lies at the heart of this book: a celebration of the wonder of being alive.

What days these were, wet and stormy, and yet there was still something magical about them . . . The yellow and red leaves burned and gleamed feverishly through the foggy gray of the landscape. The red of the cherry tree's leaves had something incandescent and aching and raw about it, but at the same time it was beautiful and brought peace and cheer to those who saw it. Often the entire countryside of meadows and trees appeared to be wrapped in veils and damp cloths, above and below and in the distance and close at hand everything was gray and wet. You strode through all of this as if through a gloomy dream. And yet even this weather and this particular sort of world expressed a secret gaiety. You could smell the trees you were walking beneath, and hear ripe fruit dropping in the meadows and on the path. Everything seemed to have become doubly and triply quiet. All the sounds seemed to be sleeping, or afraid to ring out. Early in the morning and late in the evening, the slow exhalations of foghorns could be heard across the lake, exchanging warning signals off in the distance and announcing the presence of boats. They sounded like the plaintive cries of helpless animals. Yes, fog was present in abundance. And then, now and again, there would be yet another beautiful day. And there were days, truly autumnal days, neither beautiful nor desolate, neither particularly agreeable nor particularly gloomy, days that were neither sunny nor dark but rather remained consistently light and dark from morning to dusk, so that four in the afternoon presented just the same vision of the world as eleven in the morning, everything was quiet and pale gold and faintly mournful, the colors withdrew into themselves as if dreaming worried dreams. How Joseph adored days like this. Everything appeared to him beautiful, light and familiar. This slight sadness on the part of nature banished all his cares, even his thoughts . . . The world looked so peaceful, so calm and good and pensive. You could go anywhere you liked, it was always the same pale, full image, the same face, and this face was gazing at you earnestly and with tenderness.[7]

Walser wrote a lot of poetry in the course of his lifetime – it occupies hundreds of pages in the collected edition – but no single poem can have the resonance of a passage like this one, embedded as it is in the history of the experiencing subject. We see and smell what Joseph sees and smells; but we also know what the seasons mean in Joseph's life, and what cares and anxieties they so strongly counterbalance. Rapt, celebratory prose like this allows us into the mind of a man to whom the landscape of Switzerland, in its changing moods, is an ever-present benign presence, yet who can feel an equal gratitude for the comfort of a warm bed.

9. Gustave Flaubert, *Madame Bovary*

Madame Bovary is the story of an unimportant little woman from the French provinces, who, bored with marriage to a bumbling rural physician, embarks on a pair of extramarital liaisons, neither of which goes well. To indulge her taste for fancy goods she gets hopelessly into debt, then in desperation takes rat poison and kills herself.

In its day the novel was read as a document of the new school of Realism: both anti-romantic (a cold-eyed exposé of the sentimental myths by which its heroine lives) and anti-bourgeois (an attack on the philistinism and censoriousness of a society that allows no breathing space to romantic souls). A contemporary caricature showed the author of the book, Gustave Flaubert, clad in a surgeon's apron, holding aloft on a scalpel Emma's bleeding heart. This image of Flaubert as a clinical writer – with all the overtones that the word 'clinical' has come to carry – was reinforced by the leading critic of the day, Charles Augustin Sainte-Beuve, who reminded his readers that Flaubert came from a medical family (his father was a respected surgeon) and hailed him as a leading light of a new wave in literature, 'scientific, experimental, adult, powerful, a little harsh'.[1]

In fact Flaubert's attitude toward 'scientific' realism was

highly ambivalent. He certainly believed that the novelist should adopt an objective stance toward his characters, allowing their destiny to follow its logical course, in the same way that the scientist does not intrude himself into his experiments. He also practised and perfected a French prose of 'clinical' precision. Yet by temperament and inclination he felt himself to be a Romantic, a hangover from the past in the France of Napoleon III. He had no ties with artists of the realist avant-garde, of whom Gustave Courbet was the most notorious. Indeed, once he had completed *Madame Bovary* he plunged into *Salammbô*, a story of passionate love set in ancient Carthage, with lavish battle scenes and lurid descriptions of torture and human sacrifice.

Madame Bovary came out in 1857, when Flaubert was in his mid-thirties. It was his first published novel, and was conceived at a strange crossroads in his life. Haunted by Bruegel's painting *The Temptation of St Anthony*, which he had seen during his travels in 1845, he had spent eighteen months in a state of absorption writing the story of the hermit saint in voluptuous prose. But the pair of close friends to whom he read the completed work, 500 pages long, reacted with dismay and persuaded him to abandon it as unpublishable. As a corrective, as a way of disciplining his imagination and stripping his prose of its metaphoric excesses, he undertook, on their advice, to tackle a subject that would permit of no lyrical flights: adultery in a humdrum French provincial town.

What makes Flaubert a novelist's novelist is his ability to formulate larger issues (for instance, should the erotic adventures and subsequent suicide of a provincial nobody count for as much as the passion and death of Cleopatra?) as problems of composition – in this case, what would be the best language and narrative technique for Emma, a language and technique that should neither diminish her nor inflate her importance, that would allow her to express her case (or allow her case to express itself) without making her into a puppet voicing her author's opinions?

Flaubert's intuition was that a novel of the kind he envisaged, focused on the anatomy of a single character, without much overt action, need not lack dramatic interest, that in the right hands psychological analysis could have the same swiftness, clarity, and forward drive as narrative. It was all a matter of style, of giving to prose composition the same close attention that one gave to verse.

While he was working on *Madame Bovary*, Flaubert wrote a series of midnight letters to his then mistress, the writer Louise Colet. These letters became in effect a record of his progress with the novel and an exploration of the challenges it threw up. Some penned in states of exaltation, others in fits of despondency, they have become justly famous, and form an inseparable pendant to the *Bovary* project.

The irony of his situation, he confesses to Louise, is that he has committed himself heart and soul to an undertaking for which he has no natural talent:

> The books I am most eager to write are precisely those for which I am least endowed. *Bovary*, in this respect, will have been an unprecedented tour de force . . . its subject, characters, effects, etc. – are all alien to me . . . I am like a man playing the piano with lead balls attached to his knuckles.[2]

Despite the frustrations he describes in his letters – principally the frustration of working on a miniature canvas – Flaubert never slackens or compromises. Isolated in his country retreat with only his mother and his young niece for company, he plunges deeper and deeper into the imagined life of his Emma. *'Madame Bovary, c'est moi,'* he said or is claimed to have said years later. What did he mean – or rather, since it is undocumented, what does this gnomic utterance mean, an utterance that has acquired legendary status? Perhaps no more than that he had put his all into bringing Emma off, that in the white heat of creation the individual self of the artist is consumed and absorbed into his creative self. But Charles Baudelaire, who of all Flaubert's contemporaries saw most clearly how radically he had redrawn the map of fiction, seized on this point: that in order to write Emma, Flaubert must have inhabited her so thoroughly that in some sense he must have become her, become a woman; but also, correspondingly, that in his hands Emma had become somewhat 'bizarre and androgynous', a being of female form driven by an essentially masculine mode of desiring, imperious, dominating, and intent on physical satisfaction.[3]

In this respect it is instructive to compare Emma with the other great adulteress of nineteenth-century fiction, Anna Karenina. In one of the most sobering scenes of Tolstoy's novel, the curtain opens on Anna and Vronsky just after they have first had intercourse. Far from being happy, Anna is devoured with guilt and in despair because she can think of no one from whom to ask pardon. As for Vronsky, gazing on Anna's body he feels like a murderer contemplating the corpse of his victim.

Emma feels no such burden of guilt. Her lovemaking with Rodolphe in the woods outside Yonville has opened up to her a whole a new world of sensation, which Flaubert captures in vivid synaesthetic metaphors:

Silence was everywhere; something sweet seemed to come forth from the trees. She felt her heartbeat return, and her blood coursing through her flesh like a river of milk. Then, far away . . . she heard a vague, prolonged cry, a voice which lingered; and in silence she heard it mingling like music with the last pulsations of her throbbing nerves. (p. 116)

That evening, gazing in a mirror, she sees herself mysteriously transfigured. 'I have a lover!' she whispers joyously. It is as if a legion of adulterous women, sister heroines in the romances she has been consuming, raise their voices around her in enchanting song. (p. 117)

It would be false to say Emma lacks any moral sense; but to her morality means maintaining standards of propriety and obeying the teachings of religion; and, ever since her childhood, religion has been bound up with and indeed corrupted by the more spectacular, sensuous aspects of Catholic ritual. Her yearnings, volatile and inchoate, have the power to lead her indifferently on the path of vice or the path of virtue; while the kind of spiritual guidance she needs is beyond the capacities of the Yonville parish priest.

As his affair with Emma progresses, Rodolphe treats the doctor's young wife more and more casually. Emma learns a lesson from the experience, and by the time she commences her second affair, with Léon, she has acquired a new steeliness. Now it is the young man who is the novice, the erotic plaything, the one to be used and depraved.

He never questioned her ideas; he accepted all her tastes; he was becoming her mistress rather than she his. She had tender words and kisses that thrilled his soul. Where could she have learned this corruption so deep and well masked as to be almost unseizable? (p. 201)

The ferocity of Emma's passion grows to frighten her lover, but he lacks the courage to break off the affair.

Both Rodolphe and Léon, in their different ways, sense that Emma is engaging not with them as they are but with stereotypes she is projecting onto them from her romantic reading. It is only her husband whom Emma sees as he is, unillusioned, and for being nothing but what he is she despises him. Sainte-Beuve reproves Emma for failing to grasp that if one cannot tolerate some degree of ennui, life will be unbearable. But if there is one feature that sets Emma apart from the other wives of Yonville, it is her inability, her outright refusal to tolerate ennui in the form of a husband who bores her and a child for whom she has no tenderness.

The subtitle of *Madame Bovary* is *Moeurs de province*: the way people live in the provinces. Petty adulteries have always been part of that way of life. The project on which Flaubert's writer friends persuaded him to embark was to anatomize the life of a petty provincial adulteress. But under the writer's pen that adulteress turned into something greater as, in effect, she took over her author, became him.

The letters to Louise Colet record that process. In December 1853, immediately after composing the scene in which Emma and Rodolphe make love for the first time in the forest, Flaubert writes to Louise in a state of rapture:

Today . . . man and woman, lover and beloved, I rode in the forest on an autumn afternoon under the yellow leaves, and I was the horses too, the leaves, the wind, the words my people spoke, even the red sun that made them half-shut their love-drowned eyes.[4]

At times of such intensity, writing is no longer a matter of finding the words to represent a given, pre-existing world. On the contrary, writing brings a world into being. 'Everything one invents is true . . . My poor Bovary, without a doubt, is suffering and weeping at this very instant in twenty villages in France.'[5]

This radical idealism, which Flaubert elsewhere calls 'aesthetic mysticism', is in his eyes the very contrary of materialism. Unlike the realist novelist, he does not hold up a mirror to the misery of real life as a first step toward combating the material causes of misery. 'Nothing will extirpate suffering, nothing will eliminate it,' he writes to Louise. 'Our purpose [as writers] is not to dry it up, but to create outlets for it.'[6]

In her quest for ever more intense erotic sensation, in her love of beautiful clothes and fabrics, Emma is an aesthete too, if of a superficial kind. What had been conceived at the beginning as a mocking case-study of provincial manners has grown in Flaubert's hands into a concentrated project in bringing to the fore the heroic strain in Emma's petty adventures. Despite the resemblance between the arcs of their lives, Emma is no sister to Anna Karenina. On the contrary, she is a distant granddaughter of Alonso Quixano, the hero of Cervantes' epic of provincial life. There may be no end to the sufferings of Emma's sisters in villages all across France, but at least, reading the story of her adventures, they can dream of themselves as famous heroines too.

For Baudelaire was right: whatever reservations we might have about Emma, she has 'real greatness'. There is an element of the heroic in the tenacity with which she asserts her right to desire in the face of the pious disapproval of society; an element of the heroic too in her choice of death over humiliation.

Madame Bovary came out in instalments in a review run by friends of Flaubert's. Alerted by irate readers, Napoleon III's censors instituted proceedings against the publishers and the author on the grounds that the novel was an outrage against public morals and religion. But the censors had underestimated their opponent. Through family connections Flaubert marshalled influential supporters. A prominent trial lawyer was engaged; the public's curiosity was aroused; interest in Flaubert's work spread. In the end the prosecution lost its case. However, the judges did not allow the occasion to pass without expressing their distaste for the book and reprimanding the author for choosing to depict vice without comment.

In the same year Baudelaire was prosecuted for breaching public morals in *Les Fleurs du mal*. He was found guilty and fined.

The judges misunderstood Flaubert. The real target of his scorn in *Madame Bovary* was not public morals or religion but *bêtise*, stupidity, the unquestioning, complacent endorsement of *bien-pensant* opinion, exemplified by all the main characters, not excluding Emma herself, but represented best by Monsieur Homais, the town pharmacist, who in due course will be welcomed into the Légion d'Honneur.

Flaubert treats stupidity as a kind of spiritual malaise; but the intensity of his scorn for it can also justly be seen as a reaction to the stagnation of political life in the France of his day, where, after the failure of the revolution of 1848 and the seizure of power by Napoleon III, the feeling had spread widely among the younger generation that there was no role for them in the life of the nation. His most concentrated attack on stupidity is his *Dictionary of Received Ideas*, not published during his lifetime. The *Dictionary* embodies the deadpan humour of direct quotation that is the basis of his last novel, *Bouvard and Pécuchet*; but the approach is also characteristic of *Madame Bovary*, where characters continually reveal themselves in the fatuous commonplaces they express. It was fundamental to Flaubert's practice as an artist that, as long as an event can be presented with accurate observation and in the right words, it will speak for itself. 'An author in his book must be like God in the universe, present everywhere and visible nowhere.'[7]

10. Irène Némirovsky, Jewish Writer

The reputation of Irène Némirovsky, in the English-speaking world as in her adopted France, rests on *Suite Française*, an unfinished multipart novel that appeared in print only in 2004, some sixty years after its author's death. During her lifetime Némirovsky was best known for an early work, the novel *David Golder* (1929). Astutely promoted by its publisher and swiftly adapted for stage and screen, *David Golder* was a runaway commercial success.

Némirovsky never struck it quite as rich in the rest of her short career (she died at the age of thirty-nine, a victim of the Final Solution). She wrote a great deal, her books sold well, but in an age when experimental modernism held the high ground her work was too conventional in form to gain serious critical attention. After the war she slid into obscurity. When in 1978 Germaine Brée published her authoritative survey of French literature of the half-century 1920–70, Némirovsky did not figure among her top 173 writers (nor, however, did Colette). Even feminist critics ignored her.

All of that changed when *Suite Française* – the manuscript of which had by amazing good luck survived the war – was published. Against all precedent, Némirovsky was awarded the Prix

Renaudot posthumously. *Suite Française* became both a critical success and a bestseller. Hastily her publishers began reprinting her *oeuvre*, most of which is now also available in English translation from the hand of Sandra Smith.

With its large cast of characters and wide social range, *Suite Française* was more ambitious than anything Némirovsky had earlier attempted. In it she takes a hard look at France during the blitzkrieg and the subsequent occupation. She saw herself as following in the line of Chekhov, who had addressed the 'mediocrity' of his own times 'without anger and without disgust, but with the pity it deserved'. In preparation for her task she reread *War and Peace*, studying Tolstoy's method of rendering history indirectly, through the eyes of his characters.[1]

Of the four or five novels of the planned *Suite*, only the first two were actually written. At the centre of the second is a young woman, Lucile Angellier, whose husband is a prisoner of war and who has to share her home with a Wehrmacht officer billeted on her. The officer, Lieutenant Valk, falls deeply and respectfully in love with her, and she is tempted to respond. Can she and he, nominal enemies, not transcend their political and national differences and, in the name of love, make a separate peace; or must she, in the name of patriotism, deny herself to him?

Today it may seem puzzling that a writer confronting the crisis for the French conscience precipitated by defeat and occupation should have framed that crisis in such romantic terms. For the war in which France was involved was not just a matter of political differences spilling over onto the battlefield: it was also a war of conquest and extermination whose goal it was to wipe certain despised peoples from the face of the earth and enslave others.

Genocide is of course not the enterprise Valk signed up for. Lucile has even less of an inkling of Hitler's larger plan. But that is hardly the point. Had Némirovsky appreciated how monstrous the new war was, how different in essence it was from the Franco-German hostilities of 1870 and 1914, she would surely, one thinks, have given herself a different plot to work with, one that would pivot on the question not of whether a separate peace was attainable between individuals but rather – for instance – of whether honourable German soldiers should not disobey the orders of their political masters, or of whether French civilians like Lucile should not be prepared to risk everything to save the Jews amongst them.

(Interestingly, Lucile does risk her life to save a fugitive, but that fugitive is not a Jew – there is no significant Jewish presence in *Suite Française*. As for Valk, Némirovsky's design was for him to die fighting for the Reich on the Eastern Front.)

Unlike *War and Peace*, which, as Némirovsky reminds herself in her diary, was written half a century after the event, *Suite Française* is written from 'on the burning lava'.[2] It was planned to cover the occupation from its beginning to its hypothetical end. The first two parts take us until mid-1941. What would happen next – in the novel as in the real world – Némirovsky could not of course foresee: in her diary she called it 'God's secret'.[3] In relation to herself, God's secret was that, in July 1942, she would be picked up at her home by the French police and delivered to the German authorities for deportation. Weeks later she would be dead of typhus in Auschwitz. In all, some 75,000 Jews would be shipped from France to the death camps, a third of them full French citizens.

Why did the Némirovskys (Irène, her husband Michel

Epstein, and their two daughters) not flee France while there was time? Refugees from tsarist Russia, Michel and Irène were, technically speaking, stateless persons residing in France, and therefore unusually vulnerable. Yet even when, in the mid-1930s, popular opinion began to harden against foreigners, and the anti-Semites on the French right, emboldened by events in Germany, began to beat their drums, the two did nothing to regularize their status. Only in 1938 did they exert themselves to obtain papers of naturalization (which, for whatever reason, were not issued), and go through the motions of renouncing the Judaic faith in favour of the Catholic.

After the capitulation of French forces in mid-1940 they had an opportunity to relocate from Paris to Hendaye, a stone's throw from the Spanish border. Instead they chose the village of Issy-l'Évêque in Burgundy, inside the German-administered zone. In Issy, as anti-Jewish measures began to bite (bank accounts of Jews were frozen, Jews were forbidden to publish, Jews had to wear the yellow star), the truth may have begun to dawn on them, though not the full truth (it was only in the winter of 1941–2 that word began to filter down to the administrators of the conquered territories that the solution of the so-called Jewish Question was to take the form of genocidal extermination). As late as the end of 1941, Némirovsky seems to have believed that whatever might befall the Jew in the street would not befall her. In a letter addressed to Marshal Pétain, head of the Vichy puppet government, she pleads that as an *honorable* (respectable) foreigner she deserves to be left in peace.[4]

There are two broad reasons why Irène Némirovsky should have considered herself a special case. The first is that for most of her life it had been her heart's desire to be French; and, in a country with a long history of harbouring political refugees but notably unreceptive to notions of cultural pluralism, being fully French meant being neither a Russian émigré who wrote in French nor a French-speaking Jew. At its most juvenile (see her partly autobiographical novel *Le Vin de solitude*), her wish took the form of a fantasy of being reborn as a 'real' Frenchwoman with a name like Jeanne Fournier. (Némirovsky's youthful heroines are typically spurned by their mothers but cherished by more-than-motherly French governesses.)

The problem for Némirovsky as a budding writer in the 1920s was that, aside from her facility in the French language, the capital she commanded on the French literary market consisted in a body of experience that branded her as foreign: daily life in old Russia, pogroms and Cossack raids, the revolution and the civil war, plus to a lesser extent the shady world of international finance. In the course of her career she would thus alternate, according to her sense of the temper of the times, between two authorial selves, one *pur sang* French – 'Jeanne Fournier' – the other exotic. As a French authoress she would compose books about 'real' French families expressing an irreproachably French sensibility, books with no whiff of foreignness about them. After 1940 this French self took over entirely, as publishers became more and more nervous about the presence of Jewish writers on their lists.

As for the exotic self, exploiting it required a careful balancing act. To avoid being labelled a Russian who wrote in French, she would keep her distance from Russian émigré society. To avoid being cast as a Jew, she would be ready to mock and caricature Jews. On the other hand, unlike such Russian-born contemporaries as Nathalie Sarraute (née Cherniak) and Henri

Troyat (né Tarassov), she published under her Russian name in its French form, until the wartime ban on Jewish writers led her to resort to a pseudonym.

The second broad reason why Némirovsky should have thought she would escape the fate of the Jews is that she had cultivated influential friends on the right, even the far right. In the months between her arrest and his own, these friends were the first people her husband contacted with pleas to intercede. To bolster her case he even scoured her books for useable anti-Semitic quotes. All of these friends let her down, mainly because they were powerless. They were powerless because, as it began to become clear, when the Nazis said all Jews they meant all Jews with no exceptions.

For her compromises with the anti-Semites – who, as the Dreyfus affair had made plain a half-century before, were fully as influential in France, at all levels of society, as in Germany – Némirovsky has had to undergo the most searching interrogation, notably by Jonathan Weiss in his biography of her.[5] I do not propose to extend that interrogation here. Némirovsky made some serious mistakes and did not live long enough to correct them. Misreading the signs, she believed, until it was too late, that she could evade the express train of history bearing down on her. Of the large body of work she left behind, some can safely be forgotten, but a surprising amount is still of interest, not only for what it tells us about the evolution of a writer now in the process of being absorbed into the French canon but as the record of an engagement with the France of her day that is never less than intelligent and is sometimes damning.

Irène Némirovsky was born in Kiev in 1903. Her father was a

banker with government connections. An only child, she had French governesses and spent summer vacations on the Côte d'Azur. When the Bolsheviks took power the Némirovskys transferred their base to Paris, where Irène enrolled at the Sorbonne and dawdled for five years over a degree in literature, preferring partying to studying. In her free time she wrote stories. Interestingly, though Paris was the hub of international modernism, the magazines to which she sent her work were conservative in their literary and political outlook. In 1926 she married Epstein, a man from the same milieu (Russian Jewry, banking) as herself.

For her first foray into the novel form Némirovsky drew heavily on her family background. David Golder is a financier and speculator with a special interest in Russian oil. He owns an apartment in Paris and a villa in Biarritz. He is growing old, he has a heart problem, he would like to begin winding down. Behind him, however, flogging him on like a galley slave, are two women: a wife who despises him and flaunts her infidelity, and a daughter with expensive tastes in cars and men. When he has his first heart attack, his wife bribes the doctor to tell him it is not serious; when swings in the market bankrupt him, his daughter uses sexual wiles to get him to stagger out one last time to do battle in the boardrooms.

David Golder (1929) is a novel of stock characters and extravagant emotions, with a heavy debt to Balzac's *Le Père Goriot*. Golder himself is a stereotypically unscrupulous man of business. His wife is obsessed with her looks; his daughter is so locked into her round of pleasures that she barely sees her parents as human. But these crude materials undergo some development and modulation. Between Golder's wife and her lover of many years – a parasitic minor aristocrat who may well be the daughter's natural father – there are moments of near domestic affection. The daughter is allowed a chapter of lyrical sex and gastronomy in Spain to persuade us of her claim that pleasure is a good in itself. And beneath the lineaments of the titan financier we get to see first the mortal man frightened of death, then the little boy from the shtetl.

The last pages of the book are as affecting as anything Némirovsky wrote. Sick and dying, Golder boards a tramp steamer at a Black Sea port. In his last hours he is tended by a young Jew with his own dreams of getting to America and making his fortune. In his company, Golder drops the masks of the French and Russian languages and returns to the Yiddish of his childhood; in his last vision he hears a voice calling him home.

There is plenty of anti-Semitic caricature in *David Golder*. Even the ending can be accommodated to the world view of the anti-Semite: beneath a veneer of cosmopolitanism Golder's deepest loyalties turn out after all to be Jewish. In an interview given in 1935 Némirovsky conceded that if Hitler had been in power when she was writing the book she would have 'written it differently'. Yet considering its sympathy for the lonely and unloved Golder, battling on three fronts with ruthless competitors, predatory women, and a failing body, it is hard to see the book as at core anti-Semitic. Némirovsky seems to have felt so too: in the interview she goes on to say that to have purged the text *at the time* – that is, without an adequate political motive – would have been wrong, 'a weakness unworthy of a true writer'.[6]

On the back of the success of *David Golder* in its various incarnations Némirovsky built a prosperous career as woman of letters. At her peak she was bringing in considerably more money than her husband, who was a bank executive. The couple kept a spacious apartment in Paris with domestic staff (maid, cook, governess); they took vacations at fashionable resorts. Their lifestyle would become unsustainable once measures against Jews participating in the economy came into effect. By the time they were deported in 1942, the Némirovskys were in dire financial straits.

Le Bal (1930) is a slighter affair. M. and Mme Alfred Kampf, petit-bourgeois arrivistes who have made a fortune on the stock market, plan a grand ball to mark their coming out in Paris high society. To their unloved daughter Antoinette falls the task of mailing invitations to the selected two hundred fashionable guests. Full of resentment against her mother, Antoinette secretly destroys the invitations. The great night comes and no guests arrive. With grim pleasure Antoinette watches as her parents, humiliated in front of the servants, go to pieces. In the last scene she pretends to console her weeping mother, while inwardly revelling in her victory.

The inimical mother-daughter couple recurs often in Némirovsky's fiction, the mother determined to repress the daughter who, by emerging into womanhood, threatens to overshadow and supersede her, the daughter fighting back with whatever weapons are at her disposal. It is perhaps Némirovsky's most telling weakness as a writer that she is unable to do anything with this material beyond reproducing it again and again.

Les Mouches d'automne (1931), translated into English as *Snow in Autumn* and not to be confused with the later novel *Les Feux de l'automne*, follows the declining years of Tatiana, faithful nanny to the Karines, exiles who, on the basis of the considerable fortune they have smuggled out of Russia, have adapted with ease to life in France. It is Tatiana, yearning for the country estate where she grew up and unable to make sense of her new environment, who emerges as the principal victim of the revolution. Neglected by the Karines, her mind wandering, she leaves the apartment one foggy morning and is drowned, or drowns herself, in the Seine.

The novella owes a general debt to Chekhov and a specific debt to 'Un Coeur simple', Flaubert's coolly factual story of a similarly faithful retainer. Aside from the arbitrary ending – Némirovsky's endings tend to be cursory, perhaps a consequence of her habit of starting a new project before the old one was properly finished – it is an accomplished piece of work, opposing old-fashioned fidelities to the new, casual sexual mores that the younger Karines find so attractive.

L'Affaire Courilof (1933) assumes the form of a memoir written by a member of a terrorist cell, telling of how, shortly before the failed 1905 revolution, he infiltrated the staff of Count Courilof, the Tsar's Minister of Education, with the object of carrying out a spectacular assassination. Posing as a Swiss doctor, he becomes the intimate observer of Courilof's dual struggle with cancer and political rivals who are using his marriage to a woman with a dubious past to engineer his downfall.

Slowly the would-be assassin begins to appreciate the better qualities of his victim: his stoicism, his refusal to distance himself from the wife he loves. When the time comes to hurl the bomb, he cannot do it: a comrade has to take his place. Arrested and sentenced to death, he escapes across the border, returning later to enjoy a career in the Soviet secret police during which he tortures and executes enemies of the state without compunction, before being purged and exiled to France, where he pens his memoir.

Redolent of the Conrad of *Under Western Eyes*, *The Courilof Affair* is Némirovsky's most overtly political novel. (Conrad, the anglicized Pole, impressed Némirovsky as a model of successful acculturation.) The central plot device – a foreigner with fake medical papers becomes the confidant of one of the most powerful men in Russia – may be implausible, but it pays off handsomely. The gradual humanization of an assassin brought up in the most blinkered of revolutionary circles is masterfully done: Némirovsky allows herself all the space she needs to trace his erratic moral evolution. Courilof emerges as something like a hero, a complex man, severe but incorruptible, touchingly vain, devoted to the service of a sovereign whom he personally despises. For all his weaknesses, he stands for values that this ultimately elegiac book endorses: a cautious liberalism, the culture of the West.

Of Némirovsky's novels of the period 1939–41, when she was trying to prove herself an unambiguously French author, the most notable are *Les Biens de ce monde* (published posthumously in 1947), which follows the fortunes of a family of paper manufacturers in the years before and after the First World War, and *Les Feux de l'automne* (published 1957), which has at its centre a woman coping with a wayward husband in the Paris of the interwar years. In both cases the milieu is impeccably French: no foreigners, no Jews.

Both novels offer a diagnosis of the state of France. They blame the nation's decline, culminating in the defeat of 1940, on political corruption, lax morals, and slavish imitation of American business practices. The rot set in, they suggest, when servicemen coming home from the trenches in 1919, instead of being entruswith with the task of reconstructing the nation, were fobbed off with easy sex and the lure of speculative riches. The virtues the books endorse are much the same as those promoted by the Vichy government: patriotism, fidelity, hard work, piety.

As works of art the novels are unremarkable – part of Némirovsky's aim in writing them was to show how well she could operate in the staid genre of the family-fortunes saga as practised by Roger Martin du Gard and Georges Duhamel. Their strengths lie elsewhere. They reveal how intimately Némirovsky knew ordinary petit-bourgeois Parisians – their domestic arrangements, their amusements, their little economies and extravagances, above all their placid satisfaction with the *bonheur* of their lives. Némirovsky was remote from the experiments in the novel form going on around her: of her American contemporaries, those she seems to appreciate most are Pearl Buck, James S. Cain, and Louis Bromfield, whose *Monsoon* she took as a model for the first part of *Suite Française*.

As chronicles of the impact of wider forces on individual destinies, these most 'French' of Némirovsky's novels tend to be rather dutifully naturalistic. The writing comes most to life when her interest in the psychology of moral compromise is engaged, as when the heroine of *Les Feux de l'automne* begins to have doubts about the celibate path she has been following. Are her women friends right after all? Is chastity *démodé*? Is she going to be left on the shelf?

In these two novels Némirovsky shows herself ready to take on traditionally masculine forms like battle narratives, where she acquits herself more than adequately. She also composes lengthy set pieces about the evacuation of cities – clogged roads, cars piled high with household goods, etc.– that in effect rehearse the powerful chapters opening *Suite Française*, in which defeated soldiers and panic-stricken city-dwellers flee the German advance. About the selfishness and cowardice of the civilian population in the face of danger she is scathing.

Both novels extend chronologically into the present of the Second World War and thus into the territory of *Suite Française*. Némirovsky clearly saw a role for herself as chronicler and commentator on unfolding events, even without knowing how the war would turn out. If we can extrapolate to the author from her characters, she would seem to stand behind Agnès, the most rock-solid figure in *Les Biens de ce monde*: 'We will rebuild. We will fix things. We will live'.[7] Wars come and go but France endures. Vis-à-vis the German occupiers her approach is, understandably, ultra-cautious: they barely figure on her pages. Released after a year in a prisoner-of-war camp, a French serviceman breathes not a word against his captors.

The notebooks of Némirovsky's last year disclose a far less sanguine view of the Germans, together with a hardening of her attitude toward the French. We may conclude that the manuscript of the *Suite* that has come down to us embodies a degree of prudent self-censorship. The diaries also reveal a foreboding that she will be read only posthumously.

Constructing herself as an unhyphenated French novelist was only half of Némirovsky's life-project. While she was shoring up her French credentials she was also delving into her Russian Jewish past. Published in 1940, just before restrictions on Jewish authors came into effect, *Les Chiens et les loups* has as its heroine Ada Stiller, a Jewish girl who grows up in the Ukraine but moves to Paris, where she lives from hand to mouth painting scenes of the world she has left behind, scenes too

'Dostoevskian' in tone for French tastes.[8] Complicated plotting involving wealthy relatives and financial skulduggery results in Ada being deported from France; the book ends with her facing a precarious future as an unwed mother somewhere in the Balkans.

At the heart of Les Chiens is the question of assimilation. Ada is torn between two men: Harry, the scion of a wealthy Russian-Jewish family, married to a French Gentile but drawn mystically to Ada; and Ben, a macher from the same shtetl as Ada, who believes she and he inherit a strain of 'madness' that sets them apart from the 'Cartesian' French.[9] Which of them should she follow? To which side does her heart incline: to the side of dogs like Harry, tame, assimilated, or of wolves like Ben?

Sexual desire plays no part in Ada's decision-making. The inner voice that will tell her which future to choose, as dog or as wolf, will be the voice of her ancestors, the same voice heard by the dying David Golder. It will warn her that people like Harry, caught between two races (sic), Jewish and French, have no future. (Similarly, at a climactic moment in Suite Française, Lucile will feel 'secret movements of [the] blood' that will tell her she cannot belong to a German.)[10] Despite himself, Harry must concur: his assimilated self is not real but a mask. Yet he cannot rid himself of the mask without tearing his flesh.

We should bear in mind how matters stood in France at the time when Némirovsky was composing Les Chiens, among her novels the one most directly concerned with the nature of Jewish identity. On the eve of the war France's Jewish population numbered some 330,000, most of them recent arrivals, foreign-born. At first they had been welcomed – France had suffered huge losses of manpower in the First World War – but after 1930, with the economy in decline and unemployment high, that welcome began to sour. The influx of a half-million refugees after Franco's victory in Spain only hardened anti-immigrant sentiment.

French anti-Semitism extended across the social spectrum and had several strands. One was the traditional anti-Judaism of the Catholic right. Another relied on the burgeoning pseudo-science of race. A third, hostility to 'Jewish' plutocracy, became the province of the socialist left. Thus when popular resentment began to fester against refugees, Jewish refugees in particular, there was no substantial political grouping prepared to stand up in their defence.

France's established population of secularized Jews, too, viewed with unease the flood of poor cousins pouring in from the East, cousins who adhered to their own language, dress, and cuisine, followed their own rites, were riven by their own political factions. Spokesmen for French Jewry tried to warn the new arrivals that their unwillingness to fit in would give fresh impetus to the anti-Semites, but got nowhere. 'The nightmare of old assimilated French Jewry had come true: what was perceived as an uncontrollable flood of exotic oriental Jews has compromised the position of them all,' write Michael Marrus and Robert Paxton.[11]

The Judaic slant of *Les Chiens et les loups* – a more substantial, more ambitious, and less equivocal work than *David Golder* – thus comes as somewhat of a surprise, considering Némirovsky's own assimilationist record and her comfortable place in French society. Partly as a result of happenstance but mainly because her innermost soul tells her so, Némirovsky's Ada Stiller opts not for the tame dogs of the fashionable daytime suburbs but for the wolves from the Eastern darknesses – the wolves from whom most dogs prefer to distance themselves, not wishing to be reminded of their origins.

Set mainly in Russia around the time of the revolution, published in 1935 but probably written years earlier, *Le Vin de solitude* is a study in mother–daughter relations for which Némirovsky draws freely on her own life-history. Hélène Karol is a gifted, precocious adolescent. Her father is a war profiteer, selling obsolete weaponry to the Russian government. Her mother, Bella, is a beautiful but depraved society hostess ('To hold in her arms a man whose name she did not know, or where he came from, a man who would never see her again – that alone gave her the intense frisson she craved').[12] Antagonistic to her daughter, Bella does all she can to undermine and humiliate her (a rerun of *Le Bal*). To revenge herself, Hélène sets out to steal her mother's current lover. In doing so she strays into murkier and murkier moral territory. Lying in the man's arms, she glances into a mirror and sees her own face, 'voluptuous, triumphant, reminding her . . . of her mother's features when she was young'.[13] Troubled by this transformation, she dismisses him:

> You are the enemy of all my childhood . . . Never will I be able to live happily with you. The man I want to live side by side with would never have known my mother, or my home, not even my language or my native country; he would take me far away, it doesn't matter where.[14]

Le Vin de solitude is part novel, part autobiographical fantasy, but mainly an indictment of a mother who casts her daughter in the role of sexual rival, thereby robbing her of her childhood and precipitating her too early into a world of adult passions. *Jézabel* (1936) is an even more lurid attack on the mother figure. Here a narcissistic socialite of a certain age, obsessed with her public image, purposely lets her nineteen-year-old daughter bleed to death in childbirth rather than have it emerge that she herself has become a grandmother (years later the spurned grandchild will return to blackmail her). Books like *Jézabel*, dashed off in a hurry, offering sensationalistic glimpses into the lives of the fast set, make it easier to understand why Némirovsky was not taken seriously by the literary world of her day.

Némirovsky's real-life mother was, by all accounts, an unsympathetic person. When in 1945 her orphaned granddaughters, aged sixteen and eight, turned up on her doorstep, she refused them shelter ('There are sanatoriums for poor children,' she is reputed to have said).[15] Nonetheless, it is a pity we will never hear her side of the story.

11. Juan Ramón Jiménez, *Platero and I*

Platero and I is usually thought of as a children's book. In the book trade it is certainly marketed as such. Yet in this set of vignettes held together by the figure of the donkey Platero there is much that an impressionable child will find hard to bear, and in addition much that is beyond the range of interest of children. I therefore find it better to conceive of *Platero and I* as impressions of the life of a town, Juan Ramón Jiménez's home town of Moguer in Andalusia, recollected by an adult who has not lost touch with the immediacy of childhood experience. These impressions are recorded with the delicacy and restraint that is proper when side by side with the adult reader is an audience of children.

Besides the ever-present gaze of the child, there is a second and more obvious gaze in the book: the gaze of Platero himself. Donkeys are, to human beings, not particularly beautiful creatures – not as beautiful as (to speak only of herbivores) gazelles or even horses – but they do have the advantage of possessing beautiful eyes: large, dark, liquid – *soulful*, we sometimes call them – and long-lashed. (We find the smaller, redder eyes of pigs less beautiful. Is this the reason why we do not find it easy to love or befriend these intelligent, friendly, humorous beasts?

As for insects, their organs of sight are so alien to us that it is not easy to find a place in our affections for them.)

There is a terrible scene in Dostoevsky's novel *Crime and Punishment* in which a drunken peasant beats an exhausted mare to death. First he beats her with an iron bar, then he beats her over the eyes with a club, as if above all he wants to extinguish the image of himself in her eyes. In *Platero and I* we read of an old blind mare who is chased away by her owners but insists on returning, angering them so much that with sticks and stones they kill her. Platero and his owner (this is the term our language provides for us – it is certainly not the word Jiménez uses) come upon the mare lying dead by the roadside; her sightless eyes seem at last to see.

When you die, Platero's master promises his little donkey, I will not abandon you by the roadside but bury you by the foot of the great pine that you love.

It is the mutual gaze, between the eyes of this man – a man whom the gypsy children mock as crazy, and who tells the story of *Platero and I* rather than of *I and Platero* – and the eyes of 'his' donkey that establishes the deep bond between them, in much the same way that a bond is established between mother and infant at the moment when their gazes first lock. Again and again the mutual bond between man and beast is reinforced. 'From time to time Platero stops eating to look at me. I from time to time stop reading to look at Platero'.[1]

Platero comes into existence as an individual – as a character, in fact – with a life and a world of experience of his own at the moment when the man whom I call his owner, the crazy man, sees that Platero sees him, and in the act of seeing acknowledges him as an equal. At this moment 'Platero' ceases to be just a label and becomes the donkey's identity, his true name, all that he possesses in the world.

Jiménez does not humanize Platero. To humanize him would be to betray his asinine essence. By its asinine nature, Platero's experience is closed off and impenetrable to human beings. Nevertheless, this barrier is now and again breached when for an instant the poet's vision, like a ray of light, penetrates and illuminates Platero's world; or, to make the same claim in a different form, when the senses that we human beings possess in common with the beasts, infused with our heart's love, permit us, through the agency of Jiménez the poet, to intuit that experience. 'Platero, his dark eyes scarlet from the sunset, walks off gently to the pool of crimson and rose and violet waters; he dips his mouth gently into the mirrors which seem to turn liquid at his touch; and through his great throat flows the heavy stream of shadowy, bloodlike water'. (p. 37)

'I treat Platero as if he were a child . . . I kiss him, tease him, infuriate him; he understands very well that I love him and he bears me no spite. He is so like me that I have come to believe that he dreams my very dreams'. (p. 58) Here we tremble on the edge of the moment so urgently longed for in the fantasy lives of children, when the great divide between species crumbles away and we and the creatures who have so long been exiled from us come together in a greater unity. (How long exiled? In the Judaeo-Christian myth, the exile dates from our expulsion from Paradise, and the end of exile is yearned for as the day when the lion shall lie down with the lamb.)

At this moment we see the crazy man, the poet, behaving toward Platero as joyfully and affectionately as small children behave toward puppies and kittens; and Platero responds as young animals do to small children, with equal joy and affection, as if they know, as well as the child knows (and the sober, prosaic adult does not), that we are finally all brothers and sisters in this world; also that no matter how humble we are we must have someone to love or we will dry up and perish.

In the end Platero dies. He dies because he has swallowed poison, but also because the lifespan of a donkey is not as long as that of a man. Unless we choose to befriend elephants or turtles, we will mourn the deaths of our animal friends more often than they will mourn ours: this is one of the hard lessons that *Platero and I* does not shirk. But in another sense Platero does not die: always this 'silly little donkey' will be coming back to us, braying, surrounded by laughing children, wreathed in yellow flowers. (p. 45)

12. Antonio Di Benedetto, *Zama*

The year is 1790, the place an unnamed outpost on the Paraguay River ruled from faraway Buenos Aires. Don Diego de Zama has been here for fourteen months, serving in the administration, separated from his wife and sons.

Nostalgically Zama looks back to the days when he was a *corregidor* with a district of his own to run: 'Doctor Don Diego de Zama! . . . The forceful executive, the pacifier of Indians, the warrior who rendered justice without recourse to the sword . . . who put down the native rebellion without wasting a drop of Spanish blood.'[1]

Now, under a new, centralized system of government meant to tighten Spain's control over its colonies, chief administrators have to be Spanish-born. Zama serves as second-in-command to a Spanish *gobernador*: as a creole, an *americano* born in the New World, he can aspire no higher. He is in his mid-thirties, his career is stagnating. He has applied for a transfer; he dreams of the letter from the viceroy that will whisk him away to Buenos Aires, but it does not come.

Strolling around the docks, he notices a corpse floating in the water, the corpse of a monkey who had dared to quit the jungle and dive into the flux. Yet even in death the monkey is trapped amid the piles of the wharf, unable to escape downriver. Is it an omen?

Besides his dream of being returned to civilization, Zama dreams of a woman, not his wife, much as he loves her, but someone young and beautiful and of European birth, who will save him not only from his present state of sexual deprivation and social isolation but also from a harder to pin down existential condition of yearning for he knows not what. He tries to project this dream upon various young women glimpsed in the streets, with negligible success.

In his erotic fantasies his mistress will have a delicate way of making love such as he has never tasted before, a uniquely European way. How so? Because in Europe, where it is not so fiendishly hot, women are clean and never sweat. Alas, here he is, womanless, 'in a country whose name a whole infinity of French and Russian ladies – an infinity of people across the world – [have] never heard'. To such people, Europeans, *real* people, America is not real. Even to him America lacks reality. It is a flatland without feature in whose vastness he is lost. (p. 34)

Male colleagues invite him to join them in a visit to a brothel. He declines. He has intercourse with women only if they are white and Spanish, he primly explains.

From the small pool of white and Spanish women at hand he selects as a potential mistress the wife of a prominent landowner. Luciana is no beauty – her face puts him in mind of a horse – but she has an attractive figure (he has spied on her, bathing naked). He calls upon her in a spirit of 'foreboding, pleasure, and tremendous irresolution', unsure how one goes about seducing a married lady. And indeed, Luciana proves to be no pushover. In his campaign to wear her down, she is always a move ahead of him. (p. 43)

As an alternative to Luciana there is Rita, the Spanish-born daughter of his landlord. But before he can get anywhere with her, her current lover, a vicious bully, humiliates her grossly in public. She pleads with Zama to avenge her. Although the role of avenger attracts him, he finds reasons not to confront his formidable rival. (Di Benedetto provides Zama with a neatly Freudian dream to explain his fear of potent males.)

Unsuccessful with Spanish women, Zama has to resort to women of the town. Generally he steers clear of mulattas 'so as not to dream of them and render myself susceptible and bring about my downfall'. The downfall to which he refers is certainly masturbation, but more significantly involves a step down the social ladder, confirming the metropolitan cliché that creoles and mixed breeds belong together. (p. 10)

A mulatta gives him an inviting look. He follows her into the dingier quarter of the town, where he is attacked by a pack of dogs. He dispatches the dogs with his rapier, then, 'swaggering and dominant' (his language), takes the woman. Once they are finished, she offers in a businesslike way to become his kept mistress. He is offended. 'The episode was an affront to my right to lose myself in love. In any love born of passion, some element of idyllic charm is required.' Later, reflecting on the fact that dogs are as yet the only creatures whose blood his sword has spilled, he dubs himself 'dogslayer'. (pp. 57, 58, 66)

Zama is a prickly character. He holds a degree in letters and does not like it when the locals are not properly respectful. He is under the impression that people mock him behind his back, that plots are being cooked up to humiliate him. His relations with women – which occupy most of the novel – are character-ized by crudity on the one hand and timidity on the other. He is vain, maladroit, narcissistic, and morbidly suspicious; he is prone to accesses of lust and fits of violence, and endowed with an endless capacity for self-deception.

He is also the author of himself, in a double sense. First, eve-rything we hear about him comes from his own mouth, including such derogatory epithets as 'swaggering' and 'dogslayer', which suggest a certain ironic self-awareness. Second, his day-to-day actions are dictated by the promptings of his unconscious, or at least his inner self, over which he makes no effort to assert con-scious control. His narcissistic pleasure in himself includes the pleasure of never knowing what he will get up to next, and thus of being free to invent himself as he goes along. On the other hand – as he intermittently recognizes – his indifference to his deeper motives may be generating his many failures: 'something greater, I knew not what, a kind of potent negation, invisible to the eye . . . superior to any strength I might muster or rebellion I might wage' may be dictating his destiny. (p. 97)

It is his self-cultivated lack of inhibition that leads him to launch an unprovoked knife attack on the only colleague who is well disposed toward him, then to sit back while the young man takes the blame and loses his job.

Zama's incurious and indeed amoral attitude toward his own violent impulses led some of his first readers to compare him with the Meursault of Albert Camus' novel *L'Étranger* (existen-tialism was in vogue in the Argentina of the 1950s, when *Zama* first appeared). But the comparison is not helpful. Though he carries a rapier, Zama's weapon of choice is the knife. The knife betrays him as an *americano*, as does his lack of polish as a seducer, and (Di Benedetto will later imply) his moral immaturity. Zama is a child of the Americas. He is also a child of his times, the heady 1790s, justifying his promiscuity by invoking the rights of man – specifically the right to have sex (or, as he prefers to put it, to 'lose himself in love'). The configuration, cultural and historical, is Latin American, not French (or Algerian).

More important than Camus as an influence was Jorge Luis Borges, Di Benedetto's elder contemporary and the dominant figure in the Argentine intellectual landscape of his day. In 1951 Borges had delivered an influential lecture, 'The Argentine Writer and Tradition', in which, responding to the question of whether Argentina should be developing a literary tradition of its own, he poured scorn on literary nationalism: 'What is our Argentine tradition?... Our tradition is all of Western culture. . . Our patrimony is the universe.'[2]

Friction between Buenos Aires and the provinces has been a constant of Argentine history, dating back to colonial times, with Buenos Aires, gateway to the wider world, standing for cosmopolitanism, while the provinces adhered to older, nativist values. Borges was quintessentially a man of Buenos Aires, whereas Di Benedetto's sympathies lay with the provinces: he chose to live and work in Mendoza, the city of his birth in the far west of the country.

Though his regional sympathies ran deep, Di Benedetto as a young man was impatient with the stuffiness of those in charge of the cultural institutions of the provinces, the so-called generation of 1925. He immersed himself in the modern masters – Freud, Joyce, Faulkner, the French existentialists – and involved himself professionally in cinema, as a critic and writer of screenplays (Mendoza of the post-war years was a considerable centre of film culture). His first two books, *Mundo animal* (1953) and *El pentágono* (1955), are resolutely modernist, with no regional colouring. His debt to Kafka is particularly clear in *Mundo animal*, where he blurs the distinction between human and animal along the lines of Kafka's 'Report to an Academy' or 'Investigations of a Dog'.

Zama takes up directly the matter of Argentine tradition and the Argentine character: what they are, what they should be. It thematizes the cleavage between coast and interior, between European and American values. Naively and somewhat pathetically, its hero hankers after an unattainable Europe. Yet Di Benedetto does not use his hero's comical Hispanophilism to push the case for regional values and the literary vehicle associated with regionalism, the old-fashioned realist novel. The river port where *Zama* is set is barely described; we have little idea how its people dress or occupy themselves; the language of the book sometimes evokes, to the point of parody, the eighteenth-century novel of sentiment, but more often calls up the twentieth-century theatre of the absurd (Di Benedetto was an admirer of Eugène Ionesco and of Luigi Pirandello before him). To the extent that *Zama* satirizes cosmopolitan aspirations, it does so in a thoroughly cosmopolitan, modernist way.

But Di Benedetto's engagement with Borges was more extensive and complex than mere critique of his universalism and suspicion of his patrician politics (Borges called himself a Spencerian anarchist, meaning that he disdained the state in all its manifestations, while Di Benedetto thought of himself as a socialist). For his part, Borges clearly recognized Di Benedetto's talent and indeed, after the publication of *Zama*, invited him to the capital to give a lecture at the National Library, of which he was director.

In 1940, along with two writer colleagues associated with the magazine *Sur*, Borges had edited an *Antología de la literatura fantástica*, a work that had a far-reaching effect on Latin American literature. In their prologue the editors argued that, far from being a debased subgenre, fantasy embodied an ancient, preliterate way of seeing the world. Not only was fantasy intellectually respectable, it also had a precursor tradition among Latin American writers which was itself a branch of a greater world tradition. Borges' own fiction would appear under the sign of the fantastic; the fantastic, deployed upon the characteristic themes of regional literature, with the narrative innovations of William Faulkner superadded, would give birth to the magic realism of Gabriel García Márquez.

The revaluation of the fantastic advocated by Borges and the writers around *Sur* was indispensable to Di Benedetto's growth. As he testified in an interview shortly before his death, fantasy, coupled with the tools provided by psychoanalysis, opened the way for him as a writer to explore new realities. In the second part of *Zama*, the fantastic comes to the fore.

The story resumes in 1794. The colony has a new governor. Zama has acquired a woman, a penniless Spanish widow, to satisfy his physical needs, though he does not live with her. She has borne him a son, a sickly child who spends his days playing in the dirt. Her relations with Zama are entirely without tenderness. She 'allows him in' only when he brings money. (p. 102)

A clerk in the administration named Manuel Fernández is discovered to be writing a book during office hours. The governor takes a dislike to Fernández and demands that Zama find a pretext for dismissing him. Zama reacts with irritation, directed not at the governor but at this hapless young idealist, this 'book-writing homunculus' lost in the outer reaches of empire. (p. 107)

To Zama, Fernández innocently confides that he writes because it gives him a sense of freedom. Since the censor is unlikely to permit publication, he will bury his manuscript in a box for his grandchildren's grandchildren to dig up. 'Things will be different then.' (p. 106)

Zama has run up debts that he cannot settle. Out of kindness, Fernández offers to support Zama's irregular family – indeed, to marry the unloved widow and give the child his name. Zama responds with characteristic suspiciousness: what if it is all a scheme to make him feel indebted?

Short of money, Zama becomes a boarder in the home of a man named Soledo. Included in Soledo's household is a woman, seen only fleetingly, who is at one point claimed (by the servants) to be Soledo's daughter and at another to be his wife. There is another mystery woman too, a neighbour who sits at her window staring pointedly at Zama whenever he passes. Most of Part 2 is concerned with Zama's attempts to solve the riddle of the women: Are there two women in the household or just one, who performs rapid changes of costume? Who is the woman at the window? Is the whole charade being orchestrated by Soledo to make fun of him? How can he get sexual access to the women?

At first, Zama takes on the riddle as a challenge to his ingenuity. There are pages where, with a nudge from his translator, he sounds like one of Samuel Beckett's heroes of pure intellect, spinning one far-fetched hypothesis after another to explain why the world is as it is. By degrees, however, Zama's quest grows more urgent and indeed fevered. The woman at the window reveals herself: she is physically unattractive and no longer young. Half drunk, Zama feels free to throw her to the ground and '[take] her with vehemence', that is, rape her, then, when he is finished, demand money. He is back on familiar psychic terrain: on the one hand he has a woman whom he can despise but who is sexually available, on the other a woman (or perhaps two women) who in all her/their 'fearsome charm', can continue to be the unattainable (and perhaps inexistent) object of his desire. (pp. 149, 150)

Zama took a long time to gestate but was written in a hurry. The haste of its composition shows most clearly in Part 2, where the dreamlike topography of Soledo's residence will be as confusing to the reader as it is to Zama, drifting from room to darkened room trying to grasp what it is that he is after. Confusing yet fascinating: Di Benedetto lets go of the reins of narrative logic and allows the spirit to take his hero where it will.

There is a rap at the door. It is a ragged, barefoot boy, a mysterious messenger who has appeared in Zama's life before and will appear again. Behind the boy, as if in tableau, a trio of runaway horses are engaged in trampling a small girl to death.

I returned to my quarters as if harvesting the darkness, and with a new faculty – or so it seemed – of perceiving myself from without. I could see myself gradually transformed into a figure of mourning, the shadows, soft as bat's down, adhering to me as I passed . . . I was going to confront something, someone, and I understood that I was to choose it or choose for it to die. (p. 152)

A feminine presence wafts past. Zama raises a candle to the being's face. It is *she*! But who is she? His senses reel. A fog seems to invade the room. He staggers into bed, wakes up to find the woman from the window watching over him, 'compassionate affection, an amorous and self-abnegating pity in her eyes. . . [a woman] without mystery'. Bitterly she observes how in thrall he is to the enchantments of 'that other glimpsed figure', and delivers a homily on the perils of fantasy. (pp. 153, 154)

Rising at last from his sickbed, Zama decides that the entire episode of 'harvesting the darkness' is to be explained – and explained away – as the product of a fever. He backtracks from the obscurer regions into which hallucination has been leading him, falters in his hesitant self-exploration, reinstates the dichotomy of fantasy (fever) and reality that he was in the process of breaking down.

To grasp what is at stake at this moment, we need to hark back to Kafka, the writer who did the most to shape Di Benedetto's art, both directly and through the mediation of Borges. As part of his project of rehabilitating the fantastic as a literary genre, Borges had in the mid-1930s published a series of articles on Kafka in which, crucially, he distinguished between dreams, which characteristically lay themselves open to interpretation, and the nightmares of Kafka (the long nightmare of Josef K. in *The Trial* is the best example), which come to us as if in an undecipherable language. The unique horror of the Kafkan nightmare, says Borges, is that we know (in some sense of the word *know*) that what we are undergoing is not real, but, in the grip of the hallucinatory *proceso* (process, trial), are unable to escape.

At the end of Part 2, Zama, a character in what amounts to an historical fantasy, dismisses as insignificant because unreal the hallucinatory fantasy he has just undergone. His prejudice in favour of the real continues to hold him back from self-knowledge.

After a gap of five years, the story resumes. Zama's efforts to secure a transfer have failed; his amours seem to be a thing of the past.

A contingent of soldiers is being sent out to scour the wilds for Vicuña Porto, a bandit of mythical status – no one is even sure what he looks like – on whom all the colony's woes are blamed.

From the time he spent as *corregidor*, Zama recalls a Vicuña Porto who fomented rebellion among the Indians. Though the troops are to be led by the incompetent, pig-headed Capitán Parrilla, Zama joins them, hoping that a spectacular success will advance his cause.

One dark night on the trail a nondescript soldier takes Zama aside. It is Vicuña Porto himself, masquerading as one of Parrilla's men and thus in effect hunting himself. He confides that he wishes to quit banditry and rejoin society.

Should Zama betray Porto's confidence? The code of honour says no; but the freedom to obey no code, to follow impulse, to be perverse, says yes. So Zama denounces Porto to Parrilla and at once feels 'clean in every fibre of [his] being'.

Without compunction Parrilla arrests both Zama and Porto. Hands bound, face swollen with fly-bites, Zama contemplates being paraded back in the town: 'Vicuña Porto, the bandit, would be no more defeated, repugnant, and wretched than Zama, his accessory.' (p. 187)

But the bandit turns the tables. Murdering Parrilla in cold blood, he invites Zama to join his band. Zama refuses, whereupon Porto hacks off his fingers and abandons him, muti-lated, in the wilds.

At this desperate juncture salvation appears in the form of the barefoot boy who has haunted Zama for the past decade. 'He was me, myself from before . . . Smiling, like a father, I said, "You haven't grown . . ." With irreducible sadness he replied, "Neither have you."' (p. 198)

Thus ends the third and last part of *Zama*. In the somewhat too facile lesson that its hero-narrator invites us to draw, searching for oneself, as Vicuña Porto has been pretending to do, is much like the search for freedom, 'which is not *out there* but within *each one*'. What we most truly seek lies within: our self as we were before we lost our natural innocence. (p. 180)

Having seen in Parts 1 and 2 a bad Zama, a Zama misled by vain dreams and confused by lust, we find in Part 3 that a good Zama is still recoverable. Zama's last act before losing his fingers is to write a letter to his infinitely patient wife, seal it in a bottle, and consign it to the river: 'Marta, I haven't gone under.' 'The message was not destined for Marta or anyone out there,' he confides. 'I had written it for myself.' (p. 196)

The dream of recovering Eden, of making a new start, ani-mated European conquest of the New World from the time of Columbus. Into the independent nation of Argentina, born in 1816, poured wave after wave of immigrants in quest of a utopia that turned out not to exist. It is not surprising that frustrated hope is one of the great, subterranean themes of Argentine lit-erature. Like Zama in his river-port in the wilds, the immigrant finds himself dumped in an anything but Edenic site from which there is no obvious escape. *Zama* the book is dedicated to 'the victims of expectation'.

Zama's adventures in wild Indian territory are related in the rapid, clipped style Di Benedetto learned by writing for the cinema. Part 3 of the novel has been given great weight by some of Di Benedetto's critics. In the light of Part 3, *Zama* is read as the story of how an *americano* comes to cast off the myths of the Old World and commit himself not to an imaginary Eden but to the New World in all its amazing reality. This reading is supported by the rich textual embedding that Di Benedetto supplies: exotic flora and fauna, fabulous mineral deposits, strange foodstuffs, savage tribes and their customs. It is as though for the first time in his life Zama is opening his eyes to the plenitude of the continent. That all this lore came to Di Benedetto not from personal experience – he had not set foot in Paraguay – but from old books, among them a biography of one Miguel Gregorio de Zamalloa, born 1753, *corregidor* during the rebellion of Túpac Amaru, last of the Inca monarchs, is an irony that need not trouble us.

Antonio Di Benedetto was born in 1922 into a middle-class family. In 1945 he abandoned his legal studies to join *Los Andes*, the most prestigious newspaper in Mendoza. In due course he would become, in all but name, editor-in-chief. The owners of the newspaper dictated a conservative line, which he felt as a constraint. Until his arrest in 1976 – for violating that constraint – he thought of himself as a professional journalist who wrote fiction in his spare time.

Zama (1956) was his first full-length novel. It received appropriate critical attention. Not unnaturally in a country that saw itself as a cultural outlier of Europe, attempts were made to supply it with a European parentage. Its author was identified first as a Latin American existentialist, then a Latin American *nouveau romancier*. During the 1960s the novel was translated into a number of European languages, English not included. In Argentina *Zama* has remained a cult classic.

Di Benedetto's own contribution to this debate on paternity was to point out that if his fiction, particularly his short fiction, might sometimes seem blank, lacking in commentary, as if recorded by a camera eye, that might be not because he was imitating the practice of Alain Robbe-Grillet but because both of them were actively involved in cinema.

Zama was followed by two further novels and several collections of short fiction. The most interesting of these works is *El silenciero* (*The Silencer*), the story of a man (never named) who is trying to write a book but cannot hear himself think in the noise of the city. His obsession with noise consumes him, eventually driving him mad.

First published in 1964, the novel was substantially revised in 1975 so as to give its reflections on noise greater philosophical depth (Schopenhauer comes to figure prominently) and to forestall any simple, sociological reading of it. In the revised edition noise acquires a metaphysical dimension: the protagonist is caught up in a hopeless quest for the primordial silence preceding the divine *logos* that brought the world into being.

El silenciero goes further than *Zama* in its use of the associative logic of dream and fantasy to propel its narrative. As a novel of ideas that includes ideas about how a novel can be put together, as well as in its mystical streak, *El silenciero* very likely pointed the direction Di Benedetto would have followed as a writer, had history not intervened.

★

On 24 March 1976, the military seized power in Argentina, with the collusion of the civilian government and to the relief of a large segment of the population, sick and tired of political violence and social chaos. The generals at once put into effect their master plan or 'Process for National Reorganization'. General Ibérico Saint-Jean, installed as governor of Buenos Aires, spelled out what *El Proceso* would entail: 'First we will kill all the subversives, then we will kill their collaborators, then their sympathizers, then those who remained indifferent, and finally we will kill the timid.'[3]

Among the many so-called subversives detained on the first day of the coup was Di Benedetto. Later he would (like Josef K.) claim not to know why he was arrested, but it is plain that it was in retaliation for his activities as editor of *Los Andes*, where he had authorized the publication of reports on the activities of right-wing death squads. (After his arrest, the proprietors of the newspaper wasted no time in washing their hands of him.)

Detention routinely began with a bout of 'tactical interrogation', the euphemism for torture, intended to extract information but also to make it plain to the detainee that he or she had entered a new world with new rules. In many cases, writes Eduardo Duhalde, the trauma of the first torture, reinforced by having to watch or listen to the torture of other prisoners, marked the prisoner for the rest of his/her life. The favoured instrument of torture was the electric prod, which induced acute convulsions. After-effects of the prod ranged from intense muscular pain and paralysis to neurological damage manifested in dysrhythmia, chronic headaches, and memory loss.[4]

Di Benedetto spent eighteen months in prison, mostly in the notorious Unit 9 of the Penitentiary Services of La Plata. His release came after appeals to the regime by Heinrich Böll, Ernesto Sabato, and Jorge Luis Borges, backed by PEN International. Soon afterwards he went into exile.

A friend who saw him after his release was distressed by how he had aged: his hair had turned white, his hands trembled, his voice faltered, he walked with a shuffle. Although Di Benedetto never wrote directly about his prison experience – he preferred to practise what he called the therapy of forgetting – press interviews allude to vicious blows to the head ('Since that day my capacity to think has been affected'); to a session with the cattle prod (the shock was so intense that it felt as if his inner organs were collapsing); and to a mock execution before a firing squad when the one thought in his mind was: What if they shoot me in the face?[5]

Fellow inmates, most of them younger than he, recalled that he seemed bewildered by the brutal prison regime, trying to make sense of the random assaults he suffered from guards when the essence of these assaults was that they should be unpredictable and – like a Kafkan nightmare – make no sense.

Exile took Di Benedetto to France, to Germany, and eventually to Spain, where he joined tens of thousands of other refugees from Latin America. Though he had a contract for a weekly column in a Buenos Aires newspaper, and enjoyed a residency at the MacDowell Colony in New Hampshire, he recalled his exile as a time when he lived like a beggar, stricken with shame whenever he saw himself in the mirror.

In 1984, after civilian rule had been reinstalled, Di Benedetto returned to an Argentina ready to see in him an embodiment of the nation's desire to purge itself of its recent past and make a fresh start. But it was a role he was too aged, too beaten down, too bitter to fulfil. The creative energy that prison and exile had taken away from him was irrecoverable. 'He began dying. . . on the day of his arrest,' remarked a Spanish friend. 'He continued to die here in Spain. . . and when he decided to return to his own country it was only in search of a more or less decent ending.' His last years were marred by recriminations. Having first been welcomed back, he said, he had then been abandoned to even greater poverty than in Spain. He died in 1986 at the age of sixty-three.[6]

During his exile in Spain Di Benedetto published two collections of short fiction, *Absurdos* (1978) and *Cuentos de exilio* (1983). Some of the pieces in *Absurdos* had been written in prison and smuggled out. The recurring theme of these late stories is guilt and punishment, usually self-punishment, often for a transgression one cannot remember. The best known, a masterpiece in its own right, is 'Aballay', made into a film in 2011, about a gaucho who decides to pay for his sins in the manner of the Christian saint Simeon Stylites. Since the pampas has no marble columns, Aballay is reduced to doing penitence on horseback, never dismounting.

These sad, often heartbreaking late stories, some no more than a page in length – images, broken memories – make it clear that Di Benedetto experienced exile not just as an enforced absence from his homeland but as a profoundly internalized sentence that had somehow been pronounced upon him, an expulsion from the real world into a shadowy afterlife.

Sombras, nada mas... (1985), his last work, can most charitably be looked on as the trace of an experiment not carried all the way through. Finding one's way through *Sombras* is no easy task. Narrators and characters merge one into another, as do dream and represented reality; the work as a whole tries doggedly but fails to locate its own *raison d'être*. A mark of its failure is that Di Benedetto felt compelled to provide a key explaining how the book was put together and offering guidance on how to read it.

Zama ends with its hero mutilated, unable to write, waiting in effect for the coming of the man who a century and a half later will tell his story. Like Manuel Fernández burying his manuscript, Di Benedetto – in a brief testament penned shortly before his death – affirmed that his books were written for future generations. How prophetic this modest boast will be, only time will tell.

13. Leo Tolstoy, *The Death of Ivan Ilyich*

In 1884, at the height of his fame as a novelist, Leo Tolstoy produced a strange autobiographical document which, because of its controversial comments on religion, had to be published abroad. Entitled *Confession*, it told of a spiritual crisis that he had undergone in 1877 during which his life had ceased to have any meaning and he had come within a hair's breadth of committing suicide.

Even before 1877, he further confessed, he had begun to lose faith in the value of artistic endeavour and the importance of his own writing. This set him apart from his contemporaries, who seemed to believe that, religion having lost its relevance to the modern world, the artist should take over from the priest as moral and spiritual guide. Art should be the new religion, they said, great works of art the new scriptures. He could not agree. How could artists, who in his experience were usually bad and immoral people, act as moral guides to humankind?

Nevertheless, despite his doubts about his vocation, he had gone on writing and publishing, receiving acclamation and monetary reward for work that he privately considered to be worthless.

We should think twice before conceding to Tolstoy the right

he claims in *Confession* to dismiss his earlier literary works. 1877, the year of his spiritual crisis, was also the year in which *Anna Karenina* was completed. It is inconceivable that the man who wrote that novel was not committed, heart and soul, to its writing, that on the contrary he secretly believed the pages issuing from his hand were worthless. *Confession* is a powerful piece of writing with an air of urgent sincerity that sweeps the reader along. No less than in the case of *Anna Karenina*, one must believe that the man who wrote *Confession* was committed, heart and soul, to its writing. But the fact that in *Confession* Tolstoy in effect calls the author of *Anna Karenina* an impostor, writing in bad faith, does not mean that the author of *Anna Karenina* was truly an impostor. *Confession* has no right to claim that, by its nature as autobiography, it speaks a more authoritative truth than a mere novel can speak. Indeed, for anyone who takes seriously the religious pretensions of art, which would include the belief that beauty and truth are one and the same thing, *Anna Karenina* must speak a higher truth than *Confession*, since it is by far the more ambitious of the two works, by far the more beautiful aesthetic construct. But one does not have to elevate art to the status of a religion to know that *Anna Karenina* is not false at its core. *Anna Karenina* is true through and through. The only point of contention is what kind of truth it tells.

What does *Anna Karenina* say to its readers? What, crudely speaking, is the message of the novel? Ever since Tolstoy's day this has been a live issue. To the vast majority of readers today, *Anna Karenina* is the story of a beautiful woman who abandons a joyless marriage for the sake of love, but then has to suffer the punishment of being driven out of society, and in despair commits suicide. In other words, the novel speaks uncritically on Anna's side. An extreme variant of this uncritical reading sees Anna (like her spiritual sister Emma Bovary) as a rebel against an oppressive patriarchal order who is ultimately punished by her male author by being killed off. In the reading of the story that Tolstoy himself handed down, however, Anna forsakes her husband and child to follow the selfish path of personal fulfilment and ends her life, predictably, in a moral wilderness. Readers should take Anna as an example not of how to live but of how not to live.

The crisis of 1877, insofar as it concerned Tolstoy the writer as distinct from Tolstoy the man, resolved itself into a single ethical question: How shall I use my gifts to do good to my fellow man? For two decades Tolstoy wrestled with this question, testing a range of answers of which the clearest and simplest (though not necessarily the truest) was that it was his duty to bring to the modern world the essential teachings of Jesus, in a language that the simplest peasant could understand. Accordingly, almost all of Tolstoy's post-1877 writing is Christian in inspiration and suspicious of aesthetic artifice.

The first work embodying this newly formulated attitude toward art and the artistic vocation was the story 'Master and Man' (1881), which tells of a prosperous merchant named Brekhunov who undertakes a risky cross-country journey by horse-sled in the dead of winter in order to settle a deal that will bring in big profits. Despite many warnings Brekhunov persists in his foolish enterprise, and ends up freezing to death.

The 'man' (*rabotnik*, worker) whom Brekhunov takes along on his journey, a peasant named Nikita, sees the calamity into which his master's greed – as well as his incompetence as a navigator – is leading them, yet follows him and obeys his commands. The fact that Nikita alone survives the night in the open is not the consequence of any action on his part. In a deep sense, Nikita does not care what happens to him, but puts himself in the hands of God. 'Besides masters like Vassily Andreich [Brekhunov] whom he had served here, he always felt himself dependent in this life on the chief master . . . and . . . that master would not mistreat him'.[1]

Brekhunov is a bad person, self-centred, dishonest, avaricious, reckless, and domineering. He treats Nikita as a member of a lower species, on a par with the horse that draws their sled, a creature to whom life is not as important as it is to him, Brekhunov, who is involved in so many important business deals. At the height of the snowstorm, in an effort to save himself, he rides off on the horse, leaving Nikita behind, though he knows that Nikita, who is wearing only a threadbare caftan and boots with holes, will probably freeze to death. Justifying himself, he reflects: 'As for him [Nikita] . . . it's all the same if he dies. What kind of life has he got! He won't feel sorry for his life, but for me, thank God, there's something to live for'. (p. 243)

The horse, the third actor in the drama, conveys Brekhunov not to safety and warmth but in a circle back to the freezing peasant. Then there occurs something totally unpredictable. Brekhunov opens his double fur coat and lies down on top of Nikita, warming him with his own body. He lies there until morning comes, the storm abates, and rescuers arrive. By that time the master who had everything to live for is dead, while the man of no importance survives.

The Christian message of the story is crystal clear: he who loses himself shall save himself; the workings of divine mercy are inscrutable. What makes 'Master and Man' a triumph of art is less obvious because it is so paradoxical. Tolstoy is usually thought of as a realist; *War and Peace* and *Anna Karenina* are admired as masterpieces of realism. One of the tenets of realism is that acts have causes, from which it follows that the novelist has a duty to supply plausible psychological motives for the actions of his characters. But Brekhunov sacrifices his life for no reason at all. His sacrifice is, in the words of the English idiom, 'out of character', implausible, even unbelievable. Yet it is implausible or unbelievable only to the secular mind. The believer understands that Brekhunov acts out of character because God has spoken to him, because the divine has intervened in his life. In bringing God as an actor into his story, Tolstoy has issued a challenge to the rational, secular basis of fictional realism.

The novella *The Death of Ivan Ilyich* (1886) is the best known and most admired of Tolstoy's late works. When he read it for the first time, the composer Peter Ilyich Tchaikovsky was overwhelmed. In his diary he wrote: 'More than ever I am convinced that the greatest author-painter who has ever lived is Leo Tolstoy . . . Patriotism has no part in my belief in Tolstoy's immense, almost divine importance.'[2]

Ivan Ilyich evokes this kind of reaction because of the impression it gives, via the remorseless pace of its narrative and the stripped-down texture of its prose, that its author is impatient with the fictions with which we customarily clothe life in order to make it bearable – the fiction, for example, that as we near death we can count on the loving care of our family, or the fiction that either medical science or divine mercy or both will ensure that our last days do not become an unrelieved storm of agony and terror.

Ivan Ilyich Golovin is an unremarkable man, a legal bureaucrat who makes up for an unhappy marriage by burying himself in his work. Fortunately his career flourishes; at home he is able to achieve some sort of truce with his sour wife. Then suddenly, for no good reason and far too early in life, he is struck down by a seemingly undiagnosable illness. His doctors cannot help him – in his eyes, they do not even try. Abandoned by his family, who disapprove of his unseemly suffering as a breach of social decorum, he is left to face his death supported only by the young manservant Gerasim, who cleans up his excrement and takes the edge off the pain by sitting for hours on end with Ivan Ilyich's legs hoisted on his shoulders. When Ivan Ilyich tries to thank him, Gerasim brushes the thanks aside. What he is doing for Ivan Ilyich someone will do for him, he says, when his time comes.

At last Ivan's sufferings come to an end. As his wife reports after his death, with characteristic selfishness: 'For three whole days he screamed incessantly. It was unbearable. I can't understand how I endured it . . . Ah, what I've endured!'[3]

'The past history of Ivan Ilyich's life was most simple and ordinary and most terrible,' we read at the beginning of the story. (p. 47) The words 'most simple and ordinary' belong to Ivan Ilyich. The words 'most terrible' come from Tolstoy himself, and constitute an indictment of an unenlightened life, a life wasted in futile, meaningless pursuits.

Yet, when it comes, Ivan's death, which has threatened to be as meaningless as his life, turns out to be not entirely unenlightened. On the third day of his screaming he is 'suddenly' struck as if by a physical force, and realizes that the end is near. His son, a timorous boy who spends his days locked up in his room masturbating, approaches the deathbed, presses his lips to Ivan's hand, and weeps. At that instant a revelation comes to Ivan: that he has not lived a good life, but also that there is still time to put it right. He opens his eyes, sees his son as if for the first time, and feels sorry for him. He looks at his wife and feels sorry for her too. He tries to say the word 'Forgive', but cannot pronounce it. Nonetheless, all is 'suddenly' resolved. The pain is gone. The terror of death is gone. The physical death-agony, the contortions of the expiring body, will continue for hours; but release from the world has already come. (p. 90)

The key word, here as in 'Master and Man', is 'suddenly'. Whatever it is that 'suddenly' happens to Brekhunov or to Ivan Ilyich is unforeseeable and at the same time inescapable. The grace of God manifests itself, and suddenly, all at once, the world is new. In both of these stories Tolstoy pits his powerful rhetoric of salvation against the commonsense scepticism of the consumer of fiction, who like Ivan Ilyich in his heyday looks to works of literature for civilized entertainment and no more.

14. On Zbigniew Herbert

Zbigniew Herbert lived most of his life (1924–98) under regimes that were inimical to what we can loosely call freedom of expression. His writing bears evidence of his historical situation as a man trying to live out a poetic and intellectual vocation in a hostile environment. The traces can sometimes be overt – for example, in his satiric counter-attacks on the regime – but are more usually concealed by ironic masks or Aesopian language.

Herbert was not a poet-martyr as, say, Osip Mandelstam was. Nevertheless, the record shows a lifetime of principled opposition first to the Nazis, then to the Communists. Until well into his thirties he led a fringe existence, with none of the rewards that someone of his education and talents might have expected. After the 1956 thaw, his growing reputation opened up opportunities for travel outside Poland and eventually led to residencies, fellowships and visiting professorships in the West. But unlike his contemporary Czesław Miłosz he chose against exile.

The unspectacular, unheroic species of integrity and stubbornness that characterizes Herbert's life weaves its thread through his poetry too. For the sake of brevity (a Herbertian virtue) I will call this theme *the faithful life*, picking up the word *faithful* from the last line of 'The Envoy of Mr Cogito', a poem to which I will return (the line reads simply 'Be faithful Go').[1] The faithful life is not the same as the life of faith: the difference between the two (namely that you do not need to have faith to be faithful) might be called central to Herbert's ethic, were it not for the fact that privileging the faithful life over the life of faith and erecting it into a credo, an article of faith, would at once qualify it for sceptical interrogation of the Herbertian variety.

In Herbert's *oeuvre* there is a steady stream of poems that turn on an opposition between purity (purity of theory, purity of doctrine), which he aligns with the divine or angelic, and the impure, the messy, the human. The best known of these is 'Apollo and Marsyas' (1961). Apollo, who is a god and therefore inhuman and therefore without human feelings, flays alive the satyr Marsyas, reacting to Marsyas' prolonged howl of agony with nothing but a fastidious shudder. Apollo has won the musical contest (Marsyas is undergoing the fate of the loser), but Marsyas' howl, rudimentary though it may be as music, expresses every atom of his exposed (skinned) human (ungodlike) being with a petrifying intensity that the god cannot equal.

This is only one of a number of poems that put the case for the human in its unequal contest with the divine. The world that God has created, and that carries the imprint of divine reason, may be perfect in theory but is hard to bear in reality ('In the Studio'). Even the next world turns out to be pretty unendurable by human standards. As new arrivals discover at the heavenly gates, not the tiniest memento of their old life will be allowed to accompany them; even babes are to be removed from their mothers' arms 'since as it turns out / we shall be saved each one alone'. God's Heaven turns out to have an uncanny resemblance to Auschwitz ('At the Gate of the Valley').

What is wrong with systems, to Herbert, is that they are systems. What is wrong with laws is that they are laws. Beware of angels and other executives of perfection. The only angel even tentatively to be counted on the side of humanity is the seventh one, Shemkel, who is kept in the squad only out of respect for the sacred number seven. 'Black nervous / in his old threadbare nimbus', Shemkel has been fined many times for illegal importation of sinners ('The Seventh Angel').

Marxism, one need barely point out, is deeply coloured by Christian eschatology. The world of achieved communism in which each will receive according to his need and the state (earthly power) will have withered away, is, literally, heaven on earth. Herbert's satirical reports on heaven are inevitably also reports on life in the workers' state. In heaven, because the materials to hand are human and therefore imperfect, certain compromises have to be made. Forgone are the luminous circles, the choirs of angels, etc.; what we end up with is an afterlife not too different from life in People's Poland ('Report from Paradise').

The most interesting of Herbert's afterlife poems comes from the 1983 collection *Report from a Besieged City*, arguably the strongest of the nine collections he published. In a poem called 'Mr Cogito's Eschatological Premonitions', his persona Mr Cogito reflects on life after death and on what kind of resistance he will be capable of mounting when he has at last to confront the heartless, bloodless angels and their demand that he give up his humanity. Smell, taste, even hearing – these he will be prepared to relinquish. But to hold on to the senses of sight and touch he will be prepared to suffer torture:

to the end he will defend
the splendid sensation of pain
and a couple of faded images
in the pit of a burned-out eye.

Who knows, thinks Mr Cogito to himself, maybe the angelic
interrogators will at last give up, declare him 'unfit / for heavenly / service', and let him return

along an overgrown path
on the shore of a white sea
to the cave of the beginning.

The image of Mr Cogito under torture at the hands of the angels
repeats the image of Marsyas tortured by Apollo. The gods
believe they are omniscient as well as omnipotent; but in fact
suffering as animal beings suffer, unable to escape the body in
pain, is beyond their ken. Being powerless is beyond the powers
of the gods.

(It will not escape the reader's attention that in the greater
pantheon there is a god who responds to the charge of being
above and beyond suffering by committing himself to suffering
in a human way, without relief, unto death. This god, the Christian Jesus, has no presence in Herbert's poetic universe.)

In 'Mr Cogito's Eschatological Premonitions', the ironic treatment of heaven – and by implication of all doctrines of salvation
or perfectibility – has not been left behind, and the knife-turn of
paradox is still central to its argument on behalf of the human
right to feel pain. But in this late poem Herbert goes beyond the
neat irony and lapidary perfection of such earlier pieces as 'Report

from Paradise': in its last lines it opens out to a world (the path, the sea, the cave) as strange and beautiful and mysterious as the world we mortals live in, a world we cannot forget and cannot bear to leave (but must leave and must forget, for ever).

There are several dozen Mr Cogito poems. As a personage Mr Cogito makes his first appearance in the collection *Mr Cogito* (1974), and he remains a strong presence in *Report from a Besieged City*. He starts his life as a self-deprecating mask (persona) for the poet, not too different in spirit and style from the wry but hapless little-man cartoon characters who flourished in Polish and Czech cinema of the Cold War years. A poem like 'Mr Cogito's Abyss', about the abyss ('not the abyss of Pascal / . . . not the abyss of Dostoevsky / . . . an abyss / to Mr Cogito's size') that follows Mr Cogito around like a pet dog, might be a fitting script for one of these cartoons.

The risk a poet runs in investing too heavily in a persona of the stature of Mr Cogito was, I suspect, clear to Herbert from the beginning. 'From Mythology', a prose poem in the early collection *Study of the Object* (1961), spells out the danger. It presents itself as a potted history of religion, ironical in its dismissive brevity. Stage one: savages dancing around idols. Stage two: the Olympians (thunderbolts, creaking beds). Stage three: the age of irony; people carry around in their pockets votive statues of the god of irony, made of salt. 'Then came the barbarians. They too valued highly the little god of irony. They would crush it under their heels and add it to their dishes.'

The god of irony, believed by his devotees to be all-powerful, able to wither his foes with his knowing smile, turns out to be powerless against the barbarians. Worse than that: they relish him, or at least use him as relish. To translate the allegory baldly:

the ironist can find himself participating in a morally degrading game with the powers that be in which, as long as he pretends not to be confronting them, they will pretend to take no notice of him. So much for irony, not only as a political strategy but as an ethical refuge, a way of life.

If Mr Cogito is not to be crushed under the heel of the barbarian and used as a condiment, if the Mr Cogito poems are not to suffer the fate of being bought by high-ups in the regime as birthday presents for their wives, or even of finding themselves on the school syllabus, then Mr Cogito cannot just be Mr Zbigniew Herbert, *homme moyen sensuel*, rhymester and Polish citizen, viewed in the shrinking and distorting glass of irony. He must be more.

In an important respect, Mr Cogito is like Don Quixote (with whom he is explicitly associated in the very first of the Cogito poems, 'On Mr Cogito's Two Legs'): he is a creature whose creator only gradually comes to realize how large a poetic weight he can bear. The Quixote of the first chapters of Book One of his adventures is a foolish old buffer. The Quixote of Book Two is larger than the pygmies who surround him, larger even than the knights of old who are his constant companions. 'Mr Cogito Bemoans the Pettiness of Dreams', near the beginning of the Cogito series, is a poem based on a common and rather petty trick: using the absence of material (the loss of inspiration) as the material of a poem. 'The Envoy of Mr Cogito', with which the series concludes, is one of the great poems of the twentieth century.

The not entirely transparent title of 'The Envoy' invites one to read it as an envoi addressed (*Go*) both to the collection of poems *Mr Cogito* and to the self who appears in it, at last unmasked. It can be read by itself, and even by itself its force is undeniable; but for its proper effect it needs to be read as the last of the *Mr Cogito* collection, looking back on its avatars and unmasking them in the cause of telling the truth. Reading it in this way, as a demand – indeed a command – to the self to persist in the faithful life even in the absence any credible faith, one must be struck by its rhetorical grandeur and moral ferocity, not qualities one usually associates with Herbert, but potentialities that the reader may well have sensed from the beginning, behind the ironic masks.

There is one strain notably absent from Herbert's poetic *oeuvre*: the erotic. Of course poets are not obliged to write love poems. But all the evidence of Herbert's essays on art and travel suggest a sensibility open to experience and acutely responsive to beauty. 'Prayer of the Traveller Mr Cogito', from the 1983 collection, though not a great poem in itself, is a heartfelt and palpably sincere prayer of thanks for the gift of life: 'I thank you O Lord for creating the world beautiful and various and if this is Your seduction I am seduced for good and past all forgiveness'.

But after the 1950s the erotic fades out of Herbert's work, save in one late poem, 'Oath' (1992), which looks back with regret to beautiful women glimpsed and then lost, in particular a woman in a newsagent's in the Antilles:

> for a moment I thought that – if I went with you –
> we would change the world
> I will never forget you –
> a startled flutter of lids
> matchless tilt of a head
> the bird's nest of a palm.

Regret at a life not fully lived, and doubt that his achieved work has compensated for that, become a gnawing theme in Herbert's late poetry. Of course one might say that the Soviet empire made it hard for any of its subjects to live a full life – in other words, that history was more to blame than the man himself. But to so nagging and lucid a self-doubter as Herbert, shifting the blame is not an acceptable strategy. The hero of his poem 'Why the Classics' (1969) is Thucydides, who makes no excuses for his failure as a general during the Peloponnesian War: he faces his judges, reports the facts, and accepts his punishment. Herbert's verdict on himself comes in a pair of poems, 'Mr Cogito and the Imagination' and 'To Ryszard Krynicki – A Letter' (both 1983) in which, crucially, he identifies his greatest virtue as a moral being – namely, his steady, undeceived vision of the world – as his principal limitation as a poet:

> he adored tautologies
> explanations
> *idem per idem*
>
> a bird is a bird
> slavery slavery
> a knife a knife
> death is death

'Mr Cogito's imagination / moves like a pendulum / it runs with great precision / from suffering to suffering'. For this Mr Cogito 'will be counted / among the species *minores*'.

'So little joy – sister of the gods – in our poems Ryszard,' he writes to his friend Krynicki, 'too few glimmering twilights mirrors wreaths ecstasies'. Or, as he puts it in an even more searingly personal poem, 'memory too large / and a heart too small' ('A Small Heart').

Of course there is irony at work here. Poetry may tell a higher truth, but that does not mean it is exempted from having to tell elementary truths too, truths that stare us in the face. The poem that mocks Mr Cogito for confining himself to tautologies also implicitly invites us to ask, *Yet who besides Mr Cogito was saying in 1956 that slavery is slavery?*

But irony can come wrapped in irony. The decision to become an ironist for life can, ironically, backfire; or, to recall the extended figure that Herbert uses in 'A Small Heart', the bullet that you fired decades ago can go all the way around the globe and hit you in the back. The infallible but rudimentary moral sense that you pretended to disparage but really affirmed when you wrote the poem 'The Knocker' in the 1950s ('my imagination / is a piece of board . . . I thump on the board / and it prompts me / with the moralist's dry poem / yes – yes / no – no') begins to sound very tired by the 1980s. Worse than that: what has been the point of a life spent thumping the same old board?

This is the pessimistic question that Herbert asks in poem after poem as he looks back over his life. But is it the right question? There is an alternative way of understanding why it is that, looking back from the 1980s, a poet like Herbert should feel exhausted and defeated. As long as slavery was slavery – under Stalin, under Gomulka – Mr Cogito knew his way (and knew his vocation). But when slavery modulated into subtler forms of servitude, as in the reform era presided over by Gierek, when shops were suddenly stocked with imported goods bought with borrowed money, or even more markedly when Poland made its entry into the world of globalized consumerism in 1989, Mr Cogito's power to do justice to a new reality failed him. (This is hardly a damning charge: who among the world's poets has measured up to the challenge of late capitalism?)

> Mr Cogito's monster
> lacks all dimensions
>
> it's hard to describe
> it eludes definitions
> it's like a vast depression
> hanging over the country
>
> it can't be pierced
> by a pen
> an argument
> a spear.['Mr Cogito's Monster']

There is one further quality of his hard-to-describe monster that Mr Cogito might have mentioned: that it has somehow managed to transcend, or at least get beyond, good and evil, and is thus out of reach of the dry moralist's *yes/no*. To the monster all things are good in the sense that all things are consumable, including the ironist's little salt artefacts.

15. The Young Samuel Beckett

In 1923 Samuel Barclay Beckett, aged seventeen, was admitted to Trinity College, Dublin, to study Romance languages. He proved an exceptional student, and was taken under the wing of Thomas Rudmose-Brown, Professor of Romance Languages, who did all he could to advance the young man's career, securing for him on graduation first a visiting lectureship at the prestigious Ecole Normale Supérieure in Paris, then a position back at Trinity College.

After a year and a half at Trinity, performing what he called the 'grotesque comedy of lecturing', Beckett resigned and fled back to Paris.[1] Yet even after this let-down, Rudmose-Brown did not give up on his protégé. As late as 1937 he was still trying to nudge Beckett back into the academy, persuading him to apply for a lectureship in Italian at the University of Cape Town. 'I may say without exaggeration,' he wrote in a supporting letter, 'that as well as possessing a sound academic knowledge of the Italian, French and German languages, [Mr Beckett] has remarkable creative faculty'. (pp. 524–5)

Beckett felt genuine fondness and respect for Rudmose-Brown, a Racine specialist with an interest in the contemporary French literary scene. Beckett's first book, a monograph on Proust (1931), though commissioned as a general introduction to this challenging new writer, reads more like an essay by a superior graduate student intent on impressing his professor. Beckett himself had severe doubts about the book. Rereading it, he 'wondered what [he] was talking about', as he confided to his friend Thomas McGreevy. It seemed to be 'a distorted steam-rolled equivalent of some aspect or confusion of aspects of myself . . . tied somehow on to Proust . . . Not that I care. I don't want to be a professor'. (p. 72)

What dismayed Beckett most about professorial life was teaching. Day after day this shy, taciturn young man was required to confront in the classroom the sons and daughters of Ireland's Protestant middle class, and persuade them that Ronsard and Stendhal were worthy of their attention. 'He was a very impersonal lecturer,' reminisced one of his better students. 'He said what he had to say and then left the lecture room . . . I believe he considered himself a bad lecturer and that makes me sad because he was so good . . . Many of his students would, unfortunately, agree with him'.[2]

'The thought of teaching again paralyses me,' Beckett wrote to McGreevy from Trinity in 1931 as a new term approached. 'I think I will go to Hamburg as soon as I get my Easter cheque . . . and perhaps hope for the courage to break away'. (p. 62) It took another year before he found that courage. 'Of course I'll probably crawl back with my tail coiled round my ruined poenis [*sic*],' he wrote to McGreevy. 'And maybe I won't'.[3]

The Trinity College lectureship was the last regular job Beckett held. Until the outbreak of war, and to an extent during the war too, he relied on an allowance from the estate of his father, who died in 1933, plus occasional handouts from his mother and elder brother. Where he could find it, he took on translation work and reviewing. The two pieces of fiction he published in the 1930s – the stories *More Pricks Than Kicks* (1934) and the novel *Murphy* (1938) – brought in little in the way of royalties. He was always short of money. His mother's strategy, as he observed to McGreevy, was 'to keep me tight so that I may be goaded into salaried employment. Which reads more bitterly than it is intended'. (p. 312)

Footloose artists like Beckett tended to keep an eye on exchange rates. The cheap franc after the First World War had made France an attractive destination. An influx of foreign artists, including Americans living on dollar remittances, turned Paris of the 1920s into the headquarters of international modernism. When the franc climbed in the early 1930s the transients took flight, leaving only diehard exiles like James Joyce behind.

Migrations of artists are only crudely related to fluctuations in exchange rates. Nevertheless, it is no coincidence that in 1937, after a new devaluation of the franc, Beckett found himself in a position to quit Ireland and return to Paris. Money is a recurrent theme in his letters. His letters from Paris are full of anxious notations about what he can and cannot afford (hotel rooms, meals). Though he never starved, he lived a genteel version of a hand-to-mouth existence. Books and paintings were his sole personal indulgence. In Dublin he borrows £30 to buy a painting by Jack Butler Yeats, brother of W. B. Yeats, that he cannot resist. In Munich he buys the complete works of Kant in eleven volumes.

Among the jobs that Beckett contemplated were: office work (in his father's quantity-surveying firm); language instruction (in a Berlitz school in Switzerland); school teaching (in Bulawayo, Southern Rhodesia); advertising copywriting (in London); piloting commercial aircraft (in the skies); interpreting (between

French and English); and managing a country estate. There are signs that he would have taken the position in Cape Town had it been offered (it was not); through contacts at the then University of Buffalo, in the state of New York, he also drops hints that he might look kindly on an offer from that quarter (it did not come).

The career that he fancied most of all was in cinema. 'How I would like to go to Moscow and work under Eisenstein for a year,' he writes to McGreevy. (p. 305) 'What I would learn under a person like Pudovkin,' he continues a week later, 'is how to handle a camera, the higher *trucs* of the editing bench, & so on, of which I know as little as of quantity surveying'. (p. 311) In 1936 he sends a letter to Sergei Eisenstein:

> I write to you . . . to ask to be considered for admission to the Moscow State School of Cinematography . . . I have no experience of studio work and it is naturally in the scenario and editing end of the subject that I am most interested . . . [I] beg you to consider me a serious cinéaste worthy of admission to your school. I could stay a year at least. (p. 317)

Despite receiving no reply, Beckett informs McGreevy he will 'probably go [to Moscow] soon'. (p. 324)

How is one to regard plans to study screenwriting in the USSR in the depths of the Stalinist night: as breathtaking naivety or as serene indifference to politics? In the age of Stalin and Mussolini and Hitler, of the Great Depression and the Spanish Civil War, references to world affairs in Beckett's letters can be counted on the fingers of one hand.

There is no doubt that, politically speaking, Beckett's heart was in the right place. His contempt for anti-Semites, high and low, comes out clearly in his letters from Germany. 'If there is a war,' he informs McGreevy in 1939, 'I shall place myself at the disposition of this country' – 'this country' being France, Beckett being a citizen of neutral Ireland. (p. 656) But questions about how the world should be run do not seem to interest him much. One searches the letters in vain for thoughts on the role of the writer in society. A dictum he quotes from a favourite philosopher, the second-generation Cartesian Arnold Geulincx (1624–69), suggests his overall stance toward the political: *Ubi nihil vales, ibi nihil velis*, which may be glossed: Don't invest hope or longing in an arena where you have no power.

It is only when the subject of Ireland comes up that Beckett now and again allows himself to vent a political opinion. An essay by McGreevy on J. B. Yeats provokes him to a fit of ire. 'For an essay of such brevity the political and social analyses are rather on the long side,' he writes.

I received almost the impression . . . that your interest was passing from the man himself to the forces that formed him . . . But perhaps that . . . is the fault of . . . my chronic inability to understand as member of any proposition a phrase like 'the Irish people', or to imagine that it ever gave a fart in its corduroys for any form of art whatsoever . . . or that it was ever capable of any thought or act other than the rudimentary thoughts and acts belted into it by the priests and by the demagogues in service of the priests, or that it will ever care . . . that there was once a painter in Ireland called Jack Butler Yeats. (pp. 599–600)

McGreevy was Beckett's closest and most faithful correspondent outside his family. James Knowlson, Beckett's biographer, describes McGreevy as

> a dapper little man with a twinkling sense of humour [who] . . . conveyed an impression of elegance, even when, as was often the case, he was virtually penniless . . . He was as confident, talkative, and gregarious as Beckett was diffident, silent, and solitary.[4]

Beckett and McGreevy had become acquainted in Paris in 1928. Though McGreevy was the older by thirteen years, the two hit it off at once. But their itinerant lifestyles meant that for much of the time they could keep in touch only via the mails. For a decade they exchanged letters on a regular, sometimes weekly, basis. Then, for unexplained reasons, their correspondence tailed off.

McGreevy was a poet and critic, author of an early study of T. S. Eliot. After his *Poems* of 1934 he more or less abandoned poetry, devoting himself to art criticism and later to his work as director of the National Gallery in Dublin. In Ireland there has recently been a revival of interest in him, though less for his attainments as a poet, which are slight, than for his efforts to import the practices of international modernism into the introverted world of Irish poetry. Beckett's own feelings about McGreevy's poems were mixed. He approved of his friend's avant-garde poetics, but was discreetly non-committal about his Catholic and Irish nationalist bent.

Beckett's letters from the 1930s are packed with comments on artworks he has seen, music he has heard, books he has read.

Among the earlier of these, some are just silly, the pronouncements of a cocky tyro – 'Beethoven's Quartets are a waste of time,' for example. (p. 68) Among the writers who have to endure the lash of his youthful scorn are Balzac ('The bathos of style & thought [in *Cousine Bette*] is so enormous that I wonder is he writing seriously or in parody') and Goethe (than whose drama *Tasso* 'anything more disgusting would be hard to devise'). (pp. 245, 319) Apart from forays into the Dublin literary scene, his reading tends to be among the illustrious dead. Of English novelists, Henry Fielding and Jane Austen win his favour, Fielding for the freedom with which he interjects his authorial self into his stories (a practice he himself takes over in *Murphy*). Ariosto, Sainte-Beuve, and Hölderlin also get approving nods.

One of the more unexpected of his literary enthusiasms is for Samuel Johnson. Struck by the 'mad terrified face' in the portrait by James Barry, he comes up in 1936 with the idea of turning the story of Johnson's relationship with Hester Thrale (best known in our day for her voluminous diaries) into a stage play. It is not the great pontificator of Boswell's *Life* who engages him, as the letters make clear, but the man who struggled all his life against indolence and the black dog of depression. In Beckett's version of events, Johnson takes up residence with the much younger Hester and her husband at a time when he is already impotent and therefore doomed to be a 'Platonic gigolo' in the *ménage à trois*. He suffers first the despair of 'the lover with nothing to love with', then heartbreak when the husband dies and Hester goes off with another man. (pp. 352, 397, 489)

'Mere existence is so much better than nothing, that one would rather exist even in pain,' said Dr Johnson.[5] The Hester Thrale of Beckett's projected play will fail to understand that a man can prefer to love hopelessly than to feel nothing at all, and thus fail to recognize the tragic dimension of Johnson's love for her.

In the confident public man who privately struggles against listlessness and depression, who sees no point in living yet cannot face annihilation, Beckett clearly detects a kindred spirit. Yet after an initial flurry of excitement over the Johnson project, his own indolence supervenes. Three years pass before he puts pen to paper; halfway through Act One he abandons the work.[6]

Before he discovered Johnson, the writer whom Beckett had elected to identify with was the famously active and productive James Joyce, Shem the Penman. His own early writing, as he cheerfully admits, 'stinks of Joyce'. (p. 81) But only a handful of letters passed between Beckett and Joyce. The reason is simple: during the times when they were closest (1928–30, 1937–40) – times when Beckett acted as Joyce's occasional secretary and general dogsbody – they were living in the same city, Paris. Between these two periods their relations were strained and they did not communicate. The cause of the strain was Beckett's treatment of Joyce's daughter Lucia, who was infatuated with him. Though alarmed by Lucia's evident instability of mind, Beckett, much to his discredit, allowed the relationship to develop. When he finally broke it off, Nora Joyce was furious, accusing him – with some justice – of exploiting the daughter to maintain access to the father.

It was probably not a bad thing for Beckett to be expelled from this dangerous Oedipal territory. By the time he was re-enlisted, in 1937, to help with the proofreading of *Work in Progress* (later *Finnegans Wake*), his attitude to the master had become less fraught, more charitable. To McGreevy he confides:

Joyce paid me 250 fr. for about 15 hrs. work on his proofs . . . He then supplemented it with an old overcoat and 5 ties! I did not refuse. It is so much simpler to be hurt than to hurt. (p. 574)

And again, two weeks later:

He [Joyce] was sublime last night, deprecating with the utmost conviction his lack of talent. I don't feel the danger of the association any more. He is just a very lovable human being. (p. 581)

The night after he wrote these words Beckett got into a scuffle with a stranger in a Paris street and was stabbed. The knife just missed his lungs; he had to spend two weeks in hospital. The Joyces did everything they could to help their young compatriot, having him moved to a private ward, bringing him custard puddings. Reports of the assault made it into the Irish newspapers; Beckett's mother and brother travelled to Paris to be at his bedside. Among other unexpected visitors was a woman Beckett had met years earlier, Suzanne Deschevaux-Dumesnil, who would in due course become his companion and then his wife.

The aftermath of the assault, reported to McGreevy with some bemusement, seems to have revealed to Beckett that he was not as alone in the world as he liked to believe; even more curiously, it seemed to confirm him in his decision to make Paris his home.

Though Beckett's literary output during the pre-war years is fairly thin – the Proust monograph; an apprentice novel, *Dream of Fair to Middling Women*, disowned and not published during his lifetime; the stories *More Pricks Than Kicks*; *Murphy*; a volume of poems; some book reviews – he is far from inactive. He reads extensively in philosophy from the pre-Socratics to Schopenhauer. On Schopenhauer he reports: 'A pleasure . . . to find a philosopher that can be read like a poet, with an entire indifference to the apriori forms of verification'. (p. 550) He works intensively on Geulincx, reading his *Ethics* in the original Latin: his study notes have recently been unearthed and published as a companion to a new English translation.[7]

A rereading of Thomas à Kempis elicits pages of self-scrutiny. The danger of Thomas's quietism for someone who, like himself, lacks religious faith ('I . . . seem never to have had the least faculty or disposition for the supernatural') is that it can confirm him in an 'isolationism' that is, paradoxically, not Christlike but Luciferian. Yet is it fair to take Thomas as a purely ethical guide, stripping him of any transcendental dimension? In his own case, how can an ethical code save him from the 'sweats & shudders & panics & rages & rigors & heart burstings' that he suffers?

'For years I was unhappy, consciously & deliberately,' he continues to McGreevy in language notable for its directness (gone are the cryptic jokes and faux Gallicisms of the early letters),

> I isolated myself more & more, undertook less & less & lent myself to a crescendo of disparagement of others & myself . . . In all that there was nothing that struck me as morbid. The misery & solitude & apathy & the sneers were the elements of an index of superiority . . . It was not until that way of living, or rather negation of living, developed such terrifying physical symptoms that it could no longer be pursued, that I became aware of anything morbid in myself. (p. 258)

The crisis to which Beckett alludes, the mounting sweats and shudders, had arrived in 1933, when after the death of his father his own health, physical and mental, deteriorated to a point where his family became concerned. He suffered from heart palpitations and had nocturnal panic attacks so severe that his elder brother had to sleep in his bed to calm him. By day he kept to his room, lying with his face to the wall, refusing to speak, refusing to eat.

A doctor friend had suggested psychotherapy, and his mother offered to pay. Beckett consented. Since the practice of psychoanalysis was not yet legal in Ireland, he moved to London, where he became a patient of Wilfred Bion, some ten years his senior and at the time a trainee therapist at the Tavistock Institute. In the course of 1934–5 he met with Bion several hundred times. Though his letters reveal little about the content of their sessions, they make it clear he liked and respected him.

Bion concentrated on his patient's relations with his mother, May Beckett, against whom he was consumed by pent-up rages yet from whom he was unable to cut himself loose. Beckett's own way of putting it was that he had not been properly born. Under Bion's guidance he achieved a regression to what in an interview late in life he called 'intrauterine memories' of 'feeling trapped, of being imprisoned and unable to escape, of crying to be let out but no one could hear, no one was listening'.[8]

The two-year analysis was successful insofar as it freed Beckett of his symptoms, though these threatened to resurface when he visited the family home. A 1937 letter to McGreevy suggests that he had yet to make his peace with his mother. 'I don't wish her anything at all, neither good nor ill,' he writes.

I am what her savage loving has made me, and it is good that one of us should accept that finally . . . I simply don't want to see her or write to her or hear from her . . . If a telegram came now to say she was dead, I would not do the Furies the favour of regarding myself even as indirectly responsible.

Which I suppose all boils down to saying what a bad son I am. Then Amen. (pp. 552–3)

Beckett's novel *Murphy*, completed in 1936, the first work in which this chronically self-doubting author seems to have taken genuine if transient creative pride (before long, however, he would be dismissing it as 'a very dull work, painstaking, creditable & dull'), draws on his experience of the London therapeutic milieu and on his reading in the psychoanalytic literature of the day. (p. 589) Its hero is a young Irishman who, exploring spiritual techniques of withdrawal from the world, achieves his goal when he inadvertently kills himself. Light in tone, the novel is Beckett's response to the therapeutic orthodoxy that the patient should learn to engage with the larger world on the world's terms. In *Murphy*, and even more in Beckett's mature fiction, heart palpitations and panic attacks, fear and trembling or willed oblivion, are entirely appropriate responses to our existential situation.

Wilfred Bion went on to make a considerable mark on psychoanalysis. During the Second World War he pioneered group therapy among soldiers returning from front-line duty (he had himself suffered battle trauma in the First World War: 'I died on August 8th 1918,' he wrote in his memoirs).[9] After the war he underwent analysis with Melanie Klein. Though his most important writings were to be on the epistemology of transactions between analyst and patient, for which he developed an idiosyncratic algebraic notation that he called 'the Grid', he continued to work with psychotic patients experiencing irrational dread, psychic death.

Attention has been given of late, by both literary critics and psychoanalysts, to Beckett and Bion and what influence they might have had on each other. Of what actually passed between them we have no record. Nevertheless, one can venture to say that psychoanalysis of the kind that Beckett underwent with Bion – what one might call proto-Kleinian analysis – was an important passage in his life, not so much because it relieved (or appears to have relieved) his crippling symptoms or because it helped (or appears to have helped) him to break with his mother, but because it confronted him, in the person of an interlocutor or interrogator or antagonist in many ways his intellectual equal, with a new model of thinking and an unfamiliar mode of dialogue.

Specifically, Bion challenged Beckett – whose devotion to the Cartesians shows how much he had invested in the notion of a private, inviolable, non-physical mental realm – to re-evaluate the priority he gave to pure thought. Bion's Grid, which accords phantasy processes their full due in mentation, is in effect an analytic deconstruction of the Cartesian model of thinking. In the psychic menagerie of Bion and Klein, Beckett may also have found hints for the protohuman organisms, the Worms and bodiless heads in pots, that populate his various underworlds.

Bion seems to have empathized with the need felt by creative personalities of Beckett's type to regress to pre-rational darkness and chaos as a preliminary to an act of creation. Bion's major theoretical work, *Attention and Interpretation* (1970), describes a mode of presence of analyst to patient, stripped of all authority and directedness, that is much the same (minus the jokes) as that adopted by the mature Beckett toward the phantom beings who speak through him. Bion writes:

To attain the state of mind essential for the practice of psycho-analysis I avoid any exercise of memory; I make no notes . . . If I find that I am without any clue to what the patient is doing and am tempted to feel that this secret lies hidden in something I have forgotten, I resist any impulse to remember . . .

A similar procedure is followed with regard to desires: I avoid entertaining desires and attempt to dismiss them from my mind . . .

By rendering oneself 'artificially blind' [a phrase that Bion quotes from Freud] through the exclusion of memory and desire, one achieves . . . the piercing shaft of darkness [that] can be directed on the dark features of the analytic situation.[10]

★

While the decade of the 1930s may have felt to Beckett like years of blockage and sterility, we can in retrospect see that they were being used by deeper forces within him to lay the artistic and philosophical – and perhaps even experiential – foundations of the great creative outburst that came in the late 1940s and early 1950s. Despite the idleness for which he continually castigates himself, Beckett did an enormous amount of reading. But his self-education was not just literary. In the course of the 1930s he turned himself into a formidable connoisseur of painting, with a concentration on medieval Germany and the Dutch seventeenth century. The letters from his six-month visit to Germany are overwhelmingly about art – about paintings he has seen in museums and galleries or, in the cases of artists not allowed to exhibit publicly, in their studios. These letters are of unique interest, giving an intimate glimpse into the art world in Germany at the peak of the Nazi offensive against 'degenerate art' and 'Art-Bolshevism'.

The moment of breakthrough in Beckett's aesthetic *Bildung* comes during the German visit, when he realizes he is able to enter into dialogue with paintings on their own terms, unmediated by words. 'I used never to be happy with a picture till it was literature,' he writes to McGreevy in 1936, 'but now that need is gone'. (p. 388)

His guide here is Cézanne, who came to see the natural landscape as 'unapproachably alien', an 'unintelligible arrangement of atoms', and had the wisdom not to intrude himself into its alienness. In Cézanne 'there is no entrance anymore nor any commerce with the forest, its dimensions are its secret & it has no communications to make', Beckett writes. (pp. 223, 222) A week later he pushes the insight further: Cézanne has a sense of his own incommensurability not only with the landscape but – on the evidence of his self-portraits – with 'the life . . . operative in himself'. (p. 227) Herewith the first authentic note of Beckett's mature, post-humanist phase is struck.

It was to some degree a matter of chance that the Irishman Samuel Beckett should have ended his life as one of the masters of modern French letters. As a child he was sent to a bilingual French–English school not because his parents wished to prepare him for a literary career but because of the social prestige of French. He excelled in French because he had a talent for languages, and when he studied them did so diligently. Thus there was no pressing reason why in his twenties he should have learned German, beyond the fact that he had fallen in love with a cousin who lived in Germany; yet he worked up his German to a point where he could not only read the German classics but also write correct if stiff formal German himself. Similarly he learned Spanish well enough to publish a body of Mexican poetry in English translation.

One of the recurring questions about Beckett is why he turned from English to French as his main literary language. On this subject a revealing document is a letter he wrote, in German, to a young man named Axel Kaun whom he had met during his 1936–7 tour of Germany. In the frankness with which it addresses his own literary ambitions, this letter to a comparative stranger comes as a surprise: even to McGreevy he is not so ready to explain himself.

To Kaun he describes language as a veil that the modern writer needs to tear apart if he wants to reach what lies beyond, even if what lies beyond may only be silence and nothingness. In this respect writers have lagged behind painters and musicians (he points to Beethoven and the silences in his scores). Gertrude Stein, with her minimalist verbal style, has the right idea, whereas Joyce is moving in quite the wrong direction, toward 'an apotheosis of the word'. (p. 519)

Though Beckett does not explain to Kaun why French should be a better vehicle than English for the 'literature of the non-word' that he looks forward to, he identifies '*offizielles Englisch*', formal or cultivated English, as the greatest obstacle to his ambitions. (p. 518) A year later he has begun to leave English behind, composing his new poems in French.

16. Samuel Beckett, *Watt*

In June 1940 Paris was occupied by German forces. Although he was a citizen of a neutral country, Beckett offered his services to the French Resistance. In 1942, fearing imminent arrest by the Gestapo, he and his wife fled Paris and found refuge on a farm near Roussillon in Provence.

Although Beckett had already been at work on *Watt* when they left Paris, the bulk of the book was written in Roussillon. In 1945, after the war had ended, he submitted it to a series of British publishers, without success (one described it as too 'wild and unintelligible' to publish). Gradually, as he threw himself into new projects, he lost interest in the fate of *Watt*. In a letter to a friend he dismissed it as 'an unsatisfactory book, written in dribs and drabs, first on the run, then of an evening after the clodhopping [i.e., farm labour], during the occupation'.[1]

In part because the British public had shown so little interest in his work, in part because he had come to feel that what he called 'official' English was frustrating his ambition to write 'a literature of the non-word', but mainly because he had decided that his future lay in France, Beckett began to compose in French. 'I do not think I shall write very much in English in the future,' he confided to the same friend.[2]

Watt was eventually published, in 1953, by an English-language literary review based in Paris, in association with a French publisher of erotic literature (Olympia Press, later to publish Vladimir Nabokov's *Lolita*). Its distribution in Ireland was banned by the authorities.

After he had become famous, and the anglophone world had woken up to his existence, Beckett routinely prepared English translations of his works. *Watt* was an exception: he did not want the book to be translated at all. Under pressure from his publishers, he at last agreed to permit a French edition. However, the job was (in his eyes) so poorly done that he revised the translation himself, making a number of changes to the text in the process. There is thus some question whether the English or the French version should be regarded as definitive.

The ambivalence of Beckett's feelings about the book can to an extent be attributed to the circumstances of its composition, in the remote countryside, in enforced and wearisome isolation. It is hard to believe at any other time in his life Beckett would have had the energy or the interest to list laboriously the eighty different ways in which four items of furniture can be arranged in a room over the course of twenty days, or to describe the twenty individual glances that have to be passed before the five members of a committee can be sure that each has glanced at each of the others. Beckett was right to claim that there is a certain madness in the Cartesian project of methodizing the operations of the human intellect; but there was also a certain madness in the form that his satire of methodized reason took.

Watt, the eponymous hero, is – at first sight – a clownish man with a strange method of walking, which he seems to have learned out of a book, and not even the most rudimentary social graces. We observe him catch a train from the city of Dublin to the suburb of Foxrock, where he makes his way to the home of one Mr Knott, for whom he has been engaged as a manservant. In a lengthy monologue, Arsene, the servant whom he will be replacing, explains the workings of the Knott household: there are always two servants on the premises, he says, of whom only the senior or greater has direct access to the master.

Watt spends a period (a year?) as the lesser servant, then a period as the greater servant, then in turn departs. After an unspecified interval we come upon him again in an asylum for the insane, where he is befriended by a patient named Sam. To Sam he relates in garbled form the story of his time in the Knott household. This Sam in turn relates to us, in the form of a book titled *Watt*.

Watt's years with Mr Knott (as related by Sam) may have been uneventful, yet the experience must have been disturbing enough (we infer) to render him insane. He has lost his mind because, despite his most strenuous efforts, he failed to understand Mr Knott (and his household) – more specifically, failed to know Mr Knott in his fullness. Everything that Mr Knott did, everything that happened in his household, he subjected to exhaustive rational analysis, yet in every instance the analysis failed to reveal with certainty the truth of Mr Knott. At the end of Watt's stay Mr Knott was as much of a mystery as he was on the day when Watt arrived.

To the reader, viewing Mr Knott and his household from the outside, there is nothing mysterious going on, nothing worthy of prolonged investigation. Mr Knott is simply an eccentric old man who lives in a big house in Foxrock which he never leaves. But – though the final words of the book, 'no symbols where none intended', constitute an authorial warning against over-interpretation – the book has no *raison d'être* if we do not (provisionally) accede to Watt's inarticulate and unexpressed vision of the household: that Mr Knott is in some sense the Deity and that he, Watt, has been summoned to serve Him.[3] In this interpretation, Watt's failure to know God results from a failure of the intellect, a failure of human reason, a failure of the method (learned, like walking, out of a book) that he employs in order to arrive at knowledge of the divine.

The method in question derives from René Descartes. It was set down by Descartes in 1637 in his *Discourse on the Method of Rightly Conducting the Reason*, since when it has been the orthodoxy of the scientific enterprise:

1. To accept nothing as true which I do not clearly recognize to be so; that is to say, to accept nothing unless presented to my mind so clearly and distinctly that I can have no occasion to doubt it.
2. To divide up each of the difficulties which I examine into as many parts as possible.
3. To carry on my reflections in due order, commencing with objects that are the most simple and easy to understand, in order to rise little by little . . . to knowledge of the most complex.
4. In all cases to make enumerations so complete and reviews so general that I shall be certain of having omitted nothing.[4]

This is the method that Watt applies to all phenomena that present themselves to his senses, from the visit of the piano tuners to the activities of Mr Knott himself. The sober, unquestioning application of the Cartesian method, the method of science, to events in the Knott household results in the intellectual comedy that makes up the bulk of *Watt*.

Watt is a philosophical satire in the tradition of François Rabelais and (closer to home) of Jonathan Swift and Laurence Sterne. But the impulse behind it is not merely sceptical (sceptical of the arch-advocate of the cultivation of scepticism as a habit of mind, Descartes). If we decode the cryptic, back-to-front utterances of Watt in the asylum, we arrive at a clue as to what that impulse is:

Of nought. To the source. To the teacher. To the temple. To him I brought. This emptied heart. These emptied hands. This mind ignoring. This body homeless. To love him my little reviled. My little rejected to have him. My little to learn him forgot. Abandoned my little to find him. (p. 166)

[Reviled my little to love him; rejected my little to have him; forgot my little to learn him; abandoned my little to find him. To him I brought this emptied heart, these emptied hands, this ignoring mind, this homeless body: to the temple, to the teacher, to the source of nought.]

Watt seeks to know God or 'God', for whom Knott/Not stands as a token. He undertakes his quest in a spirit of humility, without preconceptions; but Knott proves to be unknowable – unknowable not only to the rational intellect but ultimately unknowable too. As St Augustine could have told Watt, we can never know what God is, we can only know what He is not. Indeed, on the very first day of his service Arsene had given him a warning to the same effect: 'What we [servants] know partakes in no small measure of the nature of what has so happily been called the unutterable or ineffable, so that any attempt to utter or eff it is doomed to fail, doomed, doomed to fail'. (p. 62)

Arsene is here evoking a passage from Geulincx's *Ethics* that Beckett had thought important enough to copy into one of his notebooks: 'Ineffabile . . . id est dicitur, non quod cogitare aut effari non possumus (noc enim *nihil* esset: num *nihil* et *non cogitabile* idem sunt)' ['Ineffable . . . is that which we cannot understand and grasp (which is *nothing*: in fact, *nothing* and *not thinkable* are the same thing)'].[5]

It is this deeper layer beneath the surface comedy of Watt's behaviour, his dogged metaphysical quest to know the unknowable, think the unthinkable, express the inexpressible, in the face of failure after failure, that lends him his pathos, makes him more than just a clown of the intellect.

As a piece of writing, *Watt* is uneven in quality. In his early stories, collected in *More Pricks Than Kicks*, Beckett had a tendency to show off his learning in a rather juvenile way, to mix high and low verbal registers and indulge in facile wordplay. The opening pages of *Watt* exhibit some of the same features. It is only when Watt reaches Knott's residence that Beckett begins to achieve the kind of sustained prose he has been searching for, the blend of lyricism and parody unique to *Watt*. Some of the episodes that make up a fundamentally episodic book maintain the quality of a high comic aria from beginning to end (one thinks here not only of Arsene's monologue but of the visit of the Galls, father and son; of Mr Knott's eating arrangements; of the famished dog required to consume the leftovers of his meal, and the Lynch family whose duty it is to maintain the dog). Other episodes lack inspiration: the visits of Mrs Gorman the fish-woman, for instance. The pages-long listings of permutations and combinations of objects are tedious but their tedium is part of the conception of the book, a fable cum treatise that for long stretches manages to be hypnotically fascinating.

17. Samuel Beckett, *Molloy*

Samuel Beckett was an Irishman who during his early career wrote in his native English but for his later and more important work switched to French. The break between the English and French phases of his career was defined by the Second World War. When the war broke out Beckett was resident in Paris. As a citizen of a neutral country he ought to have been able to carry on with his life under the German occupation; but his activities on behalf of the French Resistance forced him to go into hiding in the rural South. It was there that he composed his last substantial work in English, the novel *Watt*.

The great creative period in his life, the period that brought into being the *Trois romans* (published 1951–3), as well as the groundbreaking play *En attendant Godot* (first performed in 1953), came shortly after the war, between 1946 and 1949. The work he wrote thereafter, fiction and theatre, was commanding but did not exceed in its ambitions the work of his great period or take him in new directions. The *Trois romans*, of which *Molloy* was the first, would remain his most enduring achievement in fiction.

Why did Beckett move from writing in English to writing in

French? Part of the answer must be that by 1946 it had become clear to him that France was and would in future be his home. Another part of the answer was that the French language was hospitable to a savage directness of tone that he wanted to cultivate. This capacity of French had been more than adequately demonstrated by Louis-Ferdinand Céline in his novels *Voyage au bout de la nuit* (1932) and *Mort à credit* (1936).

Molloy is a mysterious work, inviting interpretation and resisting it at the same time. Is it a story about two men, Molloy and Moran, or are Molloy and Moran the same person? How does time work in the world where Molloy and Moran (or Molloy/Moran) have their existence: does it move forward linearly or does it come around in a circle? Do the beings who issue commands to Moran belong to this world or to another one?

The task of reducing *Molloy* to order has preoccupied scholars of Beckett's work. One way that has been proposed to make sense of the book is to read the second section as a work of fiction written by Molloy about a character named Moran who sets out on a journey to find his author. Moran's outward journey is then a metaphor for Molloy's journey into himself; Moran eventually 'finds' Molloy, his author, by turning into him. The first objective sign of this metamorphosis is the sudden pain in his knee that ends up paralysing his leg, leaving him in the same quandary as Molloy at the beginning of the book, needing to ride a bicycle with only one good leg.

But we may equally plausibly argue that Moran, not Molloy, is the figure of the author. At the end of his narrative, obeying a voice that tells him to submit a report on his failed quest for Molloy, Moran writes as follows:

Then I went back into the house and wrote, It is midnight.
The rain is beating on the window. It was not midnight. It
was not raining.[1]

If someone writes that the rain is beating on the window when
in fact the rain is not beating on the window, he is lying or,
more grandly, producing a fiction. Do these cryptic final sentences hint that Moran has from the beginning been the author
of the work of fiction we are reading? In that case, is Moran not
just another name for Beckett?

The fact that there is no consensus on how – at this most basic
level – to read the novel suggests that we may need to put aside
the question of how to make it rationally explicable, how to
reduce it to order. Trying to make sense of *Molloy* may not be
the best or most fruitful way to approach the book.

The reader's first impression and most enduring memory of
Molloy is of its prose, which is both gripping and subtle, a vehicle
that Beckett is here in the process of fashioning for his own
powerful and subtle intelligence. In each half of the book, but
particularly in the first, the monologue drives relentlessly forward; yet its forward motion is held in check by doubts and
qualifications, most of them darkly comic. Out of the struggle
between, on the one hand, the inexplicable, quasi-physical drive
to move forward, and on the other the braking power of the
critical intellect, comes the characteristic movement of Beckett's
fictional prose, elegant in the flow of its verbal music yet com-
pulsively turning in upon itself.

Beckett is commonly thought of as an 'intellectual' writer.
He was certainly a man of acute intellect and wide learning. But
from this it does not follow that the intellect was the wellspring

of his writing. More than any other work of his, *Molloy* comes from a source deep within its author, a source perhaps inaccessible to the intellect. With greater and greater confidence, Beckett was able to draw upon the source that had opened itself to him in *Molloy* in a larger creative project that would change the face of contemporary theatre and might have changed the face of contemporary fiction too if his novels had achieved the same wide exposure as his plays.

Molloy is, among other things, a story, or two interlocked stories told by two interlocked narrators: Molloy (no forename) and Moran (forename Jacques).

Should one call Molloy and Moran characters or should one call them voices? Molloy is a tramp or vagabond, decrepit and given to bouts of sudden violence. Moran is a comfortably situated widower (or so one infers – he has a son but there is no mention of a wife), rigid in his habits, malicious in spirit, profoundly self-satisfied. To a degree, then, each has both a place in society, or at least on its fringes, and a set of personal characteristics making up a 'personality'. To a degree, each conforms to the common notion of what a novelistic character should be. Furthermore, with the passage of time one of the two, Moran, can be said to 'develop' in the way that characters in the classic novel do: he becomes less rigid, less sure of himself, even humble. (Molloy does not change: he remains as he is from beginning to end.)

Yet after reading the book the memory that one retains is not of having been in the company of a personage or two personages, but of having listened to, or been inhabited by, a voice or voices. Here is the voice that calls itself 'Molloy':

It is not the kind of place where you go, but where you find yourself, sometimes, not knowing how, and which you cannot leave at will, and where you find yourself without any pleasure, but with more perhaps than in those places you can escape from, by making an effort, places of mystery, full of the familiar mysteries. I listen and the voice is of a world collapsing endlessly, a frozen world, under a faint untroubled sky, enough to see by, yes, and frozen too. And I hear it murmur that all wilts and yields, as if loaded down, but there are no loads, and the ground too, unfit for loads, and the light too, down towards an end it seems can never come. For what possible end to these wastes where true light never was, nor any upright thing, nor any true foundation, but only these leaning things, forever lapsing and crumbling away, beneath a sky without memory of morning or hope of night. These things, what things, come from where, made of what? And it says that here nothing stirs, has never stirred, will never stir, except myself, who do not stir either, when I am there, but see and am seen. Yes, a world at an end, in spite of appearances, its end brought it forth, ending it began, is that clear enough? And I too am at an end, when I am there, my eyes close, my sufferings cease and I end, I wither as the living can not. (p. 40)

This is not the voice of an individual, a 'character' (in this case Molloy), but the communal voice of much of Beckett's fiction from *Molloy* onwards. It is a voice that seems to echo, or take dictation from, another remoter and more mysterious voice (except that in this universe all mysteries are without mystery, or – to say the equivalent – everything is equally mysterious, equally baffling to the intellect), a voice which describes a dreamlike, terminal world where the sun barely gives off heat or light and life barely clings to the surface of the planet.

During the 1930s Beckett underwent analysis with Wilfred Bion, who was later to establish himself as a leader in the British school of psychoanalysis. Beckett's experience with Bion led him to place greater and greater trust in free association and the so-called talking cure, not simply as a therapeutic method but also as a way of getting in touch with a source which it is futile to name as either the Self or the Other and is therefore best left under the name Beckett himself offered: L'Innommable. What he came to trust about the talking cure, in specific, was the onus it placed on the patient to talk and keep talking without reflecting on the meaning of what he was saying and without wondering when or whether he had come to the point or come to the end.

The talking cure is the basis of passages like the one quoted above, but only the basis. The great achievement of *Molloy* is to allow the doubting, interrogatory intellect, frowned upon in psychotherapy, back into the prose, so that – miraculously – the monologue is able to proceed without interruption, without breakdown, without silences, while the formulae and automatisms of the language can nevertheless be isolated and held up for sceptical inspection.

The second half of *Molloy* belongs to Moran and the monologue of Moran. Moran introduces himself as one of the agents of a being named Youdi, who uses a certain Gaber to convey his orders. It is Gaber who instructs Moran that he is to track down Molloy. Molloy, it turns out, is only one of a number of so-called patients whom Moran has in the past hunted. Among others he can name are Murphy, Watt and Mercier. What Moran is to do when he finds Molloy he either forgets or is not told.

Moran's quest is fruitless. At the end of a year, sick and dispirited, deserted by his son (who for a while has played the secondary, 'straight' role in the kind of two-man comedy familiar to Beckett from the music hall and the cinema and frequently employed in his stage plays), he is again visited by Gaber. Gaber reports an oracular pronouncement from the lips of Youdi: that life is 'a thing of beauty . . . and a joy for ever'. (p. 165) Moran can make no sense of the words. Can Youdi possibly mean human life, he wonders?

Although Youdi and Gaber have only a minor presence in the novel, the obvious allusions contained in their names to Yahweh, the God of the Old Testament, and Gabriel, his messenger, may tempt the reader to conclude that there is a religious underpinning to the book, and thus to give Moran's quest for Molloy a religious meaning, in much the same way that the network of agents and messengers in Franz Kafka's novels *The Trial* and *The Castle* has given rise to a range of religious readings of Kafka.

In the case of Beckett, however, one ought to be cautious about giving too much weight to the religious – specifically Christian – element. Beckett was not a believer, nor – brought up in a Protestant home – was he scarred by the intolerant brand of Christianity preached by the Irish Catholic clergy and memorialized by his countryman James Joyce. Christian thought and Christian mythology are pervasive in Beckett's work, but they are not the source of his inspiration. Angels acting as messengers between man and God are a piece of structural machinery that Beckett incorporates into *Molloy* in much the same way that he adapts from Greek literature the machinery of Odysseus's oft-interrupted journey back to his wife Penelope (Molloy meets with women clearly based on Circe and Nausicaa) and uses that machinery to give narrative form to Molloy's journey back to his mother.

Similar caution ought to be exercised about the beings whom we encounter at the beginning of Molloy's own narrative, beings who won't let him die, who somehow compel him to write and then take away the pages he has written for their own obscure purposes. These opening passages are most simply read as a sardonic comment by the author on his own situation. They link Molloy, as a being after whom a book of Beckett's is named, with a series of other Beckett heroes whom Moran will claim to have encountered: Murphy, Watt, Mercier. At the time when *Molloy* was first published, in 1951, the French reading public could hardly have been expected to know who these three personages were, since *Murphy* (1938) had appeared only in England, while *Watt* and *Mercier et Camier* existed only in manuscript. Murphy, Watt and Mercier are avatars of Molloy, as Molloy will turn out to be an avatar of the Malone of *Malone meurt*, and Malone will be an avatar of the Unnamable in *L'Innommable* (the series does not end there).

I hasten to add that I call these fictional personages avatars one of another solely because the term is convenient. There is no system of avatars in Beckett, and having the status of an avatar carries no metaphysical meaning. The question Beckett is touching on here is not what man's place in the universe may be vis-à-vis the angels, but who is writing and why whoever it is that is writing goes on writing, book after book.

In the mainstream novel of nineteenth-century Europe, characters are driven by their individual will to act in their own interest. It is this self-interested, will-driven behaviour that defines them as autonomous individuals and gives rise to the drama of clashing wills on which the novel thrives.

In Beckett, however, not only do people not know who they are or what their interests may be, they know nothing, or, to put it more accurately, have no way of distinguishing between what they know and what is coming into their minds from elsewhere. Instead of acting in their own interest, they obey voices whose origin is mysterious to them. As for the reputed autonomy of the individual, this is the subject of jokes without end in Beckett's *oeuvre*.

In Beckett's writings people hear voices and have visions. These visions, limited in repertoire, often originate in memories that have stuck with Beckett from his childhood. The exploration of such visions or memories can correctly be called fiction because in Beckett there is no hard line – indeed, no line at all – between memory and fiction. Much of Beckett's intellectual comedy consists in trying out one hypothesis after another in an effort to make sense of involuntary visions.

In the orthodox and largely unexamined conception of language that reigns in the classic novel, language is a communication system that people employ in order to control their environment, achieve their goals, and realize their desires. In Beckett, language is a self-enclosed system, a labyrinth without issue, in which human beings are trapped. Subjecthood, the sense of being a subject and having a self, dissolves as one follows the twists and turns of a voice which speaks through one but whose source is unknown (does it come from inside or from outside?).

Why not silence, rather than endless monologue? Molloy has no answer: 'Not to want to say, not to know what you want to say, not to be able to say what you think you want to say, and never to stop saying, or hardly ever, that is the thing to keep in mind, even in the heat of composition.' (p. 28)

18. Eight Ways of Looking at Samuel Beckett

One.

As Hugh Kenner explained to us long ago in his essay 'The Cartesian Centaur', Samuel Beckett is a philosophical dualist.[1] Specifically, Beckett writes as if he believes that we are made up of, that we are, a body plus a mind. Even more specifically, he writes as if he believes that the connection between mind and body is mysterious, or at least unexplained. At the same time Beckett – that is to say, Beckett's mind – finds the dualistic account of the self ludicrous. This split attitude is the source of much of his comedy.

According to this standard account, Beckett believes that our constitution is dual, and that our dual constitution is the *fons et origo* of our unease in the world. He also believes there is nothing we can do to change our constitution, least of all by philosophical introspection. This plight renders us absurd.

But what is it exactly that is absurd: the fact that we are two different kinds of entity, body and mind, linked together; or the belief that we are two different kinds of entity linked together? What is it that gives rise to Beckett's laughter and Beckett's tears, which are sometimes hard to tell apart: the human condition, or philosophical dualism as an account of the human condition?

Beckett the philosophical satirist attacks and destroys the dualist account again and again. Each time the dualist account resurrects itself and re-confronts him. Why does he find it so hard to walk away from the struggle? Why does he persist in his split attitude toward the split self of dualism? Why does he not take refuge in its most appealing alternative, philosophical monism?

Two.

I presume that the answer to the last question, why Beckett is not a monist, is that he is too deeply convinced he is a body plus a mind. I presume that, however much he might like to find relief in monism, his everyday experience is that he is a being that thinks, linked somehow to an insentient carcass that it must carry around with it and be carried around in; and that this experience is not only an everyday, once-a-day experience but an experience experienced at every waking instant of every day. In other words, the unremitting undertone of consciousness is consciousness of non-physical being.

So monism does not offer Beckett salvation because monism is not true. Beckett cannot believe the monist story and cannot make himself believe the monist story. He cannot make himself believe the monist story not because he cannot tell himself a lie but because at the moment when the dualist story is abandoned and the monist story is inhabited instead, the monist story becomes the content of a disembodied dualist consciousness.

An alternative and more effective way of answering the question of why Beckett is not a monist is simply to look at propaganda for a monist theory of mind. Here is William James in confident mood, expounding the advantages of having a soul that is at home in the world:

> The great fault of the older rational [i.e., Cartesian] psychology was to set up the soul as an absolute spiritual being with certain faculties of its own by which the several activities of remembering, imagining, reasoning, and willing etc. were explained . . . But the richer insight of modern days perceives that our inner faculties are adapted in advance to the features of the world in which we dwell, adapted, I mean, so as to secure our safety and prosperity in its midst.[2]

Three.

There have been plenty of people who have themselves experienced Beckett's plight, which can be roughly expressed as the plight of existential homelessness, and have felt it to be a tragic plight or an absurd plight or a plight both tragic and absurd at the same time. In the latter half of the nineteenth century there were many people who, *pace* William James, suspected either that the high civilization of the West had taken an evolutionary turn that was leading it to a dead end, or that the future belonged not to the reflective, hyperconscious, alienated 'modern' type of human being but to the unreflective, active type, or both. Cultural pessimism of this kind was still very much alive as Beckett grew up. Fascism, whose apogee he was fated to live through and suffer under, glorified the instinctive, unreflective, active type and stamped its heel on sickly, reflective types like him.

What had arrived to concentrate the minds of Zola and Hardy and Huysmans and people like them was the theory of biological evolution, which by the end of the century had been taken in and absorbed by most people who liked to think of themselves as modern. There was a continuum of life forms that linked bacteria at the one end to *Homo sapiens* at the other. But there were also phyla that terminated, became extinct, because over-adapted. Could it be that the huge brain of *Homo sapiens*, developed to bear the weight of so much consciousness, was an over-adaptation, that mankind was doomed to go the way of the dinosaurs, or if not mankind in toto then at least the hyper-reflective Western bourgeois male?

Four.

What is missing from Beckett's account of life? Many things, of which the biggest is the whale.

'Captain Ahab, I have heard of Moby Dick,' says Starbuck, the mate of the *Pequod*. 'Was [it] not Moby Dick that took off thy leg?'

'Aye, Starbuck,' says Captain Ahab, 'it was Moby Dick that dismasted me.' For that 'I'll chase . . . that white whale . . . over all sides of earth, till he spouts black blood and rolls fin out'.

But Starbuck is dubious. I joined this ship to hunt whales, he says, not to pursue vengeance – 'vengeance on a dumb brute . . . that simply smote thee from blindest instinct. To be enraged with a dumb thing, Captain Ahab, seems blasphemous'.

Ahab is unswayed. 'All visible objects . . . are but as pasteboard masks,' he says, offering a philosophical account of his vendetta against the white whale. 'But in each event – in the living act, the undoubted deed – there, some unknown but still reasoning thing puts forth the mouldings of its features from behind the unreasoning mask. If man will strike, strike through the mask! How can the prisoner reach outside except by thrusting through the wall? To me, the white whale is that wall, shoved near to me.'[3]

Are our lives directed by an intelligence, malign or benign; or on the contrary is what we go through just stuff happening? Are we part of an experiment on so grand a scale that we cannot descry even its outlines, or on the contrary is there no scheme at all of which we form a part? This is the question I presume to lie at the heart of *Moby-Dick* as a philosophical drama, and it is not dissimilar to the question at the heart of Beckett's *oeuvre*.

Melville presents the question not in abstract form but in images, in representations. He can do it no other way, since the question offers itself to him in a singular image, the image of blankness, of no-image. Whiteness, says Ishmael the narrator, in a chapter entitled 'The Whiteness of the Whale', is 'the intensifying agent in things the most appalling to mankind'; his mind throws up a picture of an all-white landscape of snow, of 'dumb blankness, full of meaning'.[4]

The question offers itself in images. Through images, even blank images, stream torrents of meaning (that is the nature of images). One image: the white wall of the cell in which we find ourselves imprisoned, which is also the white wall constituted by the huge forehead of the whale. If the harpoon is cast, if the harpoon tears through the wall, into what does it tear?

Another image: the whale, huge in its rage, huge in its death-agony. In the world of 1859, the white whale is the last creature on earth (on God's earth? perhaps, perhaps not) whom man, even man armed for battle, goes forth to confront with fear in his heart.

A whale is a whale is a whale. A whale is not an idea. A white whale is not a white wall. If you prick a whale, does he not bleed? Indeed he does, and by the barrelful, as we read in chapter 61. His blood cannot be escaped. His blood bubbles and seethes for furlongs behind him, till the rays of the sun, reflected from it, redden the faces of his killers. It turns the sea into a crimson pond; it doth the multitudinous seas incarnadine.

In their white cells, Beckett's selves, his intelligences, his creatures, whatever one prefers to call them, wait and watch and observe and notate.

All white in the whiteness of the rotunda . . . Diameter three feet, three feet from ground to summit . . . Lying on the ground two white bodies . . . White too the vault and the round wall . . . all white in the whiteness . . .[5]

All known all white bare white body fixed one yard legs joined like sewn. Light heat white floor one yard square never seen. White walls one yard by two white ceiling . . .[6]

Why do these creatures not grasp their harpoon and hurl it through the white wall? Answer: Because they are impotent, invalid, crippled, bedridden. Because they are brains imprisoned in pots without arms or legs. Because they are worms. Because they do not have harpoons, only pencils at most. Why are they cripples or invalids or worms or disembodied brains armed at most with pencils? Because they and the intelligence behind them believe that the only tool that can pierce the white wall is the tool of pure thought. Despite the evidence of their eyes that the tool of pure thought fails again and again and again. You must go on. I can't go on. Go on. Try again. Fail again.

To Melville the one-legged man who trusts himself to the harpoon-thrust, though the harpoon fails him too (to the harpoon is knotted the rope that drags him to his death), is a figure of tragic folly and (maybe) tragic grandeur, à la Macbeth. To Beckett, the legless scribbler who believes in pure thought is a figure of comedy, or at least of that brand of anguished, teeth-gnashing, solipsistic intellectual comedy, with intimations of damnation behind it, that Beckett made his own, and that even became a bit of a reflex with him until the late dawning he underwent in the 1980s.

But what if Beckett had had the imaginative courage to dream up the whale, the great flat white featureless front (*front*, from Latin *frons*, forehead) pressed up against the fragile bark in which you venture upon the deep; and behind that front, the great, scheming animal brain, the brain that comes from another universe of discourse, thinking thoughts according to its own nature, beyond malign, beyond benign, thoughts inconceivable, incommensurate with human thought?

Five.

Try again.

A being, a creature, a consciousness wakes (call it that) into a situation which is ineluctable and inexplicable. He (she? it?) tries his (her? its?) best to understand this situation (call it that) but never succeeds. In fact, the very notion of understanding a situation becomes more and more opaque. He/she/it seems to be a part of something purposive, but what is that something, what is his/her/its part in it, what is it that calls the something purposive?

We make a leap. Leave it to some other occasion to reflect on what this leap consisted in.

A being, a creature, one of those creatures we, whoever we are, call an ape (what his/her/its name for himself/herself/itself is we do not know; we are not even sure that he/she/it has the concept of a name; call him/her/it 'It' henceforth; we may even need to question the concept of having a concept before we are finished) – It finds itself in a white space, in a situation. It seems to be part of something purposive; but what?

Before its eyes are three black plastic tubes a metre long and nineteen millimetres in diameter. Below each of the tubes is a small wooden box with an open top and a door that is closed but can be opened.

A nut is dropped (we pause to note this 'is dropped', which seems to have no subject, no agent – how can that be? – before we go on) into the third tube (one–two–three: can we assume the concept of the count, can we assume right and left?). If the being, the creature, the ape, It, wants the nut (always, in these stories of bizarre situations to which you awake, it comes down to something edible), It must open the correct box, where the correct box is defined as the box containing the nut.

The nut is dropped into the third tube. It chooses a box to open. It opens the third box, and lo and behold, there is the nut. Greedily It eats the nut (what else is there to do with it, and besides, It is starving).

Again the nut is dropped into the third tube. Again It opens the third box. Again the box contains a nut.

The nut is dropped into the second tube. Has It been lulled by habit into thinking the third box is always the lucky box, the full box? No: It opens the second box, the box directly beneath the second tube. There is a nut in it.

The nut is dropped into the first tube. It opens the first box. The nut is in it.

So tube one leads to box one, tube two to box two, tube three to box three. All is well so far. This may be an absurdly complicated way of feeding a being, an appetite, a subject, but such appears to be the way things work in the present universe, the white universe in which It finds itself. If you want a nut, you must take care to watch into which tube it is dropped, and then open the box below.

But ah! the universe is not so simple after all. The universe is not as it may appear to be. In fact – and this is the key point, the philosophical lesson – the universe is never as it appears to be.

A screen is introduced: It can still see the top ends of the tubes, and the bottom ends, but not the middles. Some shuffling takes place. The shuffling comes to an end, and everything is as it was before, or at least seems to be as it was before.

A nut is dropped into the third tube. It, the creature, opens the third box. The third box is empty.

Again a nut is dropped into the third tube. Again It opens the third box. Again it is empty.

Within It, within Its mind or Its intelligence or perhaps even just Its brain, something is set in motion that will take many pages, many volumes to unravel, something that may involve hunger or despair or boredom or all of these, to say nothing of the deductive and inductive faculties. Instead of these pages and volumes, let us just say there is a hiatus.

It, the creature, opens the second box. It contains a nut. It makes no sense that it should be there, but there it is: a nut, a real nut. It eats the nut. That's better.

A nut is dropped into the third tube. It opens the third box. It is empty. It opens the second box. It contains a nut. Aha!

A nut is dropped into the third tube. It opens the second box. It contains a nut. It eats the nut.

So: the universe is not as it was before. The universe has changed. Not tube three and box three but tube three and box two.

(You think this is not life, someone says? You think this is merely some thought experiment? There are creatures to whom this is not just life but the *whole* of life. This white space is what they were born into. It is what their parents were born into. It is what their grandparents were born into. It is all they know. This is the niche in the universe in which they are evolved to fit. In some cases, this is the niche in which they have been genetically modified to fit. These are *laboratory animals*, says this someone, by which is meant animals who know no life outside the white laboratory, animals incapable of living outside the laboratory, animals to whom the laboratory, while it may look to us like white hell, is the only world they know. End of interjection. Go on.)

Again there is an episode of something being shuffled behind the screen, which It is not allowed to watch.

A nut is dropped into the third tube. It, the creature, opens the second box. It is empty. It opens the third box. It is empty. It opens the first box. It contains a nut. It eats the nut.

So: no longer three and three, no longer three and two, but three and one.

Again, shuffling.

A nut is dropped into the third tube. The creature opens the first box. It is empty.

So: after each shuffling, everything changes. That seems to be the rule. Three and three, then shuffling, then three and two, then shuffling, then three and one, then shuffling, then three and – what?

It, the creature, is doing its best to understand how the universe works, the universe of nuts and how you lay your hands (your paws) on them. That is what is going on, before our eyes.

But is that truly what is going on?

Six.

Something opens and then almost immediately closes again. In that split second a revelation takes place. It is trying to be understood (language creaks under the strain) how the universe works, what the laws are.

Someone is dropping nuts into tubes, and doing so not idly (not like a bored god) but with a goal in mind: to understand how my mind works, and more specifically to understand the limits of my mind. Can I link one with one, two with two, three with three? If I can, can I link three with two, two with one, one with three? If I can, how long before I can learn instead to link three with two, two with two, one with two? And how long thereafter before the penny drops and I link each episode of invisible shuffling of tubes with a revolution in the laws by which the universe works?

This is not a meaningless universe, that is, it is not a universe without rules. But getting to understand the rules of the universe counts for nothing, in the end. The universe is interested not in what you can understand but at what point you cease to understand. Three with three and two with two and one with two, for instance: will you be able to understand *that*?

Let us call him God or Godot, the little God. How much can this God, with his nuts and tubes and boxes, find out about me, and what if anything will be left that he cannot know? The answer to the first question may not be knowable, though it does seem to depend on how tireless his interest in me may be, on whether he may not have better things to do with his time. The answer to the second question is clearer: he can never know what it is to be me.

God thinks I spend my time waiting for him to arrive with his apparatus for testing my limits. In a sense he is right: I am in the cage in which, as far as I know, I was born. I cannot leave, there is nothing for me to do but wait. But I am not seriously waiting for God. Rather I am occupying time while I wait for him. What God does not understand is this 'not seriously' with which I wait for him, this 'not seriously' which looks like a mere adverbial, like 'patiently' or 'idly' – I am patiently waiting for God, I am idly waiting for God – not a major part of the sentence, not the subject or the predicate, just something that has casually attached itself to the sentence, like fluff.

God believes I am a body and a mind, miraculously conjoined. With my body I eat the nut. Something happens, and the nut, either the idea of the nut or the fact of the nut in the stomach, triggers a thought: *Nut good. More nut. Understand one-two-three, get more nut.* It amuses God to think that is what happens, to think that the miracle (that is to say the trick) of conjunction allows him to use a nut to get the mind to work. God reflects in passing that conjoining a body with a mind was one of his more inspired ideas, his more inspired and funniest. But God is the only one who finds it funny. The creature, It, I, the laboratory animal, does not find it funny, except in a grim Beckettian way, because the creature, It, I, does not know it is a body and a mind conjoined. *I think, therefore I am*: that is not what It thinks. On the contrary, it thinks, *I am! I am! I am!*

Go on.

Seven.

In the year 1937 the University of Cape Town in South Africa advertised a vacancy for a lecturer in Italian. Applicants should hold at least an honours degree in Italian, said the advertisement. The successful candidate would spend most of his time teaching Italian for beginners. Perks would include six months of sabbatical leave every three years, and a contribution toward the expense of travel, by ocean liner, to and from the old country.

The advertisement appeared in the *Times Literary Supplement*, where it was seen by T. B. Rudmose-Brown, Professor of Romance Languages at Trinity College, Dublin. Rudmose-Brown promptly contacted one of the better students to have graduated from his department and suggested that he apply.

The student in question, S. B. Beckett, by then thirty-one years old, followed Rudmose-Brown's suggestion and sent in an application. Whether the application was seriously intended we do not know. We know that at the time S. B. Beckett had ambitions to be a writer, not a language teacher. On the other hand, what writing he did brought in no money; he was living off handouts from his brother. So it is not inconceivable that penury might have forced his hand. It is not inconceivable that, if offered the job, he might have knuckled down and made the journey to the southernmost tip of Africa, there to instruct the daughters of the merchant class in the rudiments of the Tuscan tongue and, in his spare time, loll on the beach. And who is to say that among those daughters there might not have been some sweet-breathed, bronze-limbed Calypso capable of seducing an indolent Irish castaway who found it hard to say no into the colonial version of wedded bliss? And if, furthermore, the passage of the years had found the erstwhile lecturer in Italian language advanced to a professorship in Italian, perhaps even a professorship in Romance Languages (why not? – he was, after all, the author of a little book on Proust), what reason would he have had to abandon his insular paradise and set sail again for Ithaca?

The laconic letter of application S. B. Beckett wrote in 1937 has survived in the University of Cape Town archives, together with the letter Rudmose-Brown addressed to the selection committee in support of his candidacy, and an attested copy of the testimonial he had written when Beckett graduated from Trinity College in 1932. In his letter Beckett names three referees: a doctor, a lawyer and a clergyman. He lists three publications: his book on Proust, his collection of stories (which he cites as *Short Stories* rather than by its proper title, *More Pricks Than Kicks*), and a volume of poems.

Rudmose-Brown's testimonial could not be more enthusiastic.

He calls Beckett the best student of his year in both French and Italian. 'He speaks and writes like a Frenchman of the highest education,' he says. 'As well as possessing a sound academic knowledge of the Italian, French and German languages, he has remarkable creative faculty.' In a PS, he notes that Beckett also has 'an adequate knowledge of Provençal, ancient and modern'.

One of Rudmose-Brown's colleagues at Trinity College, R. W. Tate, adds his support. 'Very few foreigners have a practical knowledge of [Italian] as sound as [Beckett's], or as great a mastery of its grammar and constructions.'

Regrettably, the dice did not fall in Beckett's favour. The lectureship went to a rival whose research interest was the dialect of Sardinia.

Eight.

Why does the title 'Franz Kafka, PhD, Professor of Creative Writing, Charles University, Prague' raise a smile to our lips, when the title 'Saul Bellow, BA, Professor of Social Thought, University of Chicago' does not?

Because Kafka does not fit, we say. True, artists do not easily fit or fit in, and, when they are fitted in, fit uncomfortably. (Such a short word, *fit*, three letters, one syllable, yet with such unexpected reaches.) But Kafka, we feel, exhibits misfit of a higher order than other artists. Kafka is the misfit artist himself, the angel Misfit. He would fit no better behind a lectern than behind the counter of a butcher shop, or punching tickets on a tram. And what would Professor Kafka teach, anyway? How not to fit in? How to make a living as a specialist in not fitting in, as one can make a living as a specialist in not eating?

Yet the fact is that Kafka was a perfectly competent insurance adjuster, respected by his colleagues at the Workmen's Accident Insurance Company, 7 Pořič St, Prague, where he was employed for many years. Do we perhaps underestimate Kafka – underestimate his competence, his versatility, his ability to fit in? Are we misled, perhaps, by the famous photographs of the man, with the brilliant, dark eyes that seem to bespeak piercing insight into realms invisible and to hint that their owner does not belong in this world, not wholly?

What of Beckett? Should we smile at the thought of Samuel Barclay Beckett, BA, MA, Professor of Romance Languages, University of Cape Town?

It helps to be lean, and Beckett was as lean as Kafka. It helps to have a piercing gaze, and Beckett had his own variety of piercing gaze. Like photographs of Kafka, photographs of Beckett show a man whose inner being shines like a cold star through the fleshly envelope. But soul can shine through flesh only if soul and flesh are one. If soul and flesh belong to distinct realms, and their conjunction is an everlasting mystery, then no photograph will ever tell the truth.

19. Late Patrick White

One.

Patrick White is, on most counts, the greatest writer Australia has produced, though the sense in which Australia produced him needs at once to be qualified: he had his schooling in England, studied at Cambridge University, spent his twenties as a young man about town in London, and during the Second World War served with the British armed forces.

What Australia did provide him with was fortune, in the form of an early inheritance – the White family were wealthy graziers – substantial enough for him to live an independent life.

The nineteenth century was the heyday of the Great Writer. In our times the concept of greatness has fallen under suspicion, especially when attached to whiteness and maleness. But to call Patrick White a Great Writer – specifically a Great Writer in the Romantic mould – seems right, if only because he had the typically great-writerly sense of being marked out from birth for an uncommon destiny and granted a talent – not necessarily a welcome one – which it is death to hide, the talent in his case consisting in a heightened power to see through appearances to the truth behind them.

White's sense of being special was closely tied to his homosexuality. He did not contest the verdict of the Australia of his day that homosexuality was 'deviant', but took his deviance as a blessing as much as a curse: 'I see myself not so much a homosexual as a mind possessed by the spirit of a man or woman according to the actual situations or [sic] the characters I become in my writing . . . Ambivalence has given me insights into human nature denied, I believe, to those who are unequivocally male or female'.[1]

The award of the Nobel Prize in 1973 took many by surprise, particularly in Australia, where White was looked on as a difficult writer with a mannered, unnecessarily complex prose style. From a European perspective the award made more sense. White stood out from his anglophone contemporaries in his familiarity with European modernism (his Cambridge degree was in French and German). His language, and indeed his vision of the world, was indelibly marked by an early immersion in expressionism, both literary and pictorial. His sensibility was always strongly visual; he often remarked that he wished he could have been a painter.

White's art education began in London in the 1930s, at the hands of the expatriate Australian painter Roy de Maistre, through whom he met Francis Bacon. Both de Maistre and Bacon, and other artists too, went into the making of Hurtle Duffield, the artist hero of *The Vivisector* (1970), the novel in which, late in his career, White explores what it might be like to be a painter, the kind of painter to whom art is a way to the truth.[2]

Hurtle Duffield is born into a poor working-class family, and to all intents and purposes sold by his father to a wealthy Sydney family, the Courtneys, who detect something exceptional in the boy. They are not mistaken. Hurtle Duffield, later Hurtle Courtney, later Hurtle Duffield again, is a genius of the archetypal Romantic type: a loner, driven to create by an inner demon, a maker of his own morality, prepared to sacrifice everything and everyone at the altar of his art.

At the age of sixteen Hurtle flees the threatening advances of his stepmother, enlists in the army, and goes off to the Western Front. After the war he spends a hand-to-mouth year in Paris steeping himself in the new European art, then returns to Australia and settles on the fringes of Sydney, living in seclusion, painting. Over the years he builds up a reputation among the Sydney cognoscenti, and is able to move to a large old house in the city.

Though rendered in the fullest detail, the life of Duffield up to this point is only a preliminary to the phase of his life that truly concerns White: the phase from his mid-fifties until his death, when all the options on offer have been explored, the pattern of his life has been established, and the true struggle can begin between himself and God. Duffield's vision of God is a bleak one: God is the great Vivisector, who for his own inscrutable purposes flays and tortures us while we still breathe.

The Vivisector is held together not by plot – its plot is rudimentary – but by its close focus on Duffield's evolution as an artist and a man, by the power of White's prose, and by a set of thematic motifs that are enunciated and then repeatedly returned to, in the process accreting meaning, much as a sketch is gradually reworked into a painting. Vivisection is one such motif. For God turns out to be not the only vivisector. As his prostitute lover comes to realize, Duffield uses women for experimental purposes. To get at the truth inside her, she says, he is prepared to turn a woman into 'a shambles'. Then 'out of the shambles he paints what he calls his bloody work of art!'[3]

Sex is evisceration; painting is disfigurement. Working on a self-portrait, Duffield feels as if he is slashing at the canvas, and at his own face, with a razor.

Rhoda Courtney, Hurtle's adoptive sister, has a deformity, a hump on her back, that evokes fascinated horror in him. From a single remembered glimpse of Rhoda naked he paints her in the posture of a priestess, and returns to the painting at intervals throughout his life to consult it and find new meaning in it. He and she end up living in the same house, held together by a force of love indistinguishable from exasperation and hatred, both suffering, as Rhoda recognizes, from something incurable that goes deeper than her deformity or Duffield's solitariness, some special vision of the darkness at the end of the tunnel that renders them unfit for ordinary life.

The great challenge that faces White in *The Vivisector* is to get the reader to believe that Duffield's paintings are as disturbing and even overwhelming as he, White, wants them to be. To an extent he can achieve this by recording their impact on strangers, in particular the Sydney art establishment and the nouveau-riche patrons who buy the paintings. But the procedure is fraught with ambivalence, since it is precisely these people who are the target of his most scathing satire. If their lives are false through and through, how can their aesthetic judgment be trusted? Finally, White can meet the challenge of making Duffield's genius credible only by pouring his very considerable resources as a writer into translating the paintings into the medium of words. Duffield's consuming struggle to turn his vision into marks on the canvas is rendered in prose that itself bears the marks of a struggle to convert paint into text.

There is of course something absurd at the core of the entire enterprise of embodying a metaphysical vision in a series of paintings whose sole mode of being is as words on the page. If the vision belonged to a poet rather than a visual artist the problem would not arise. To get us to believe in his hero Yuri Zhivago, Boris Pasternak has merely to write authentic poetry and attribute it to Zhivago. Why did White set himself an impossible task?

The answer to this question must have something to do with White's sense of himself as a painter manqué, a man with a painterly vision of the world though none of the painter's skills. At a deeper level, it must have had something to do with the particularity of painting, with the simple fact that a painting must always exceed any translation of it into words. If we could achieve in words all that we can achieve with paint, we would not need painting.

Like Alf Dubbo, the Aboriginal painter in *Riders in the Chariot*, Duffield is not a man of ideas. When he tries to express himself in words, the words feel inauthentic, as though forced out of him by a ventriloquist. White's visionaries in general think intuitively rather than abstractly; if his painters can be said to think at all, they think in paint. In the kind of painting that Duffield does, figurative expressionism tending more and more toward the abstract, the movement of the hand *is* the way in which the painter thinks.

In a letter written in 1968, while he was still working on *The Vivisector*, White mentions, not entirely seriously, that he fears the book will be received by the public as 'Sex Life of Famous

Painter'.[4] Hurtle Duffield does not have an extensive sex life – his main sexual activity is masturbation – but it is extreme, the sex life of a man who uses women as a stimulus to epiphany. The two women with whom he has extended relationships both die, and the accusation made by an old friend that he is responsible is not without foundation. He has, so to speak, ridden them to death in an effort to transmute into artistic truth the transports of ecstasy he has shared with them, transports that, as he looks back, strike him as sometimes depraved.

The unexpected turn to lyricism in the paintings of the next-to-last phase of Duffield's career – a lyricism that some of Sydney's cognoscenti find cloying – is largely an after-effect of the affair he has with a thirteen-year-old girl, Kathy Volkov, for whom White draws – a little too closely at times – on Vladimir Nabokov's Lolita. By a strange kind of incestuous autogenesis, their intercourse, rather than getting Kathy pregnant, turns her into the child he has not had, his masterpiece and (in the medium of music) heir, in contrast to the two dead women, his failures. And Kathy is not ungrateful: 'It was you who taught me how to see, to be, to know instinctively,' she will write, looking back on their liaison. (p. 539)

As for Duffield's very last phase, in which, semi-paralysed, past sex, he is tended by a faithful boy (shades of Tolstoy's *The Death of Ivan Ilyich*), this is dominated by the unfinished painting in which he comes closest to realizing his vision of God: a simple painting in indigo, the word INDIGO itself an anagram swollen with cryptic meaning.

The Vivisector has many failings. There are stretches where White writes at less than white heat (one thinks here of the entire Kathy Volkov episode). The repeated assaults on the hypocrisy and pretentiousness of Sydney high society can grow wearisome. But the weaknesses of the book pale by comparison with what it achieves. In Hurtle Duffield, White found a way of giving body to a conception of the artist – and therefore of himself – as megalomaniac, certainly, but also as Luciferian hero, as – to quote his own epigraph from Rimbaud – 'the great Accursed One', and of doing so with just enough mockery, just enough exposure of the chaos in which the artist lives, inner and outer, to make the portrait compelling.

In her study of Patrick White and his place in the Australian art scene, Helen Verity Hewitt observes that, at just the time when White was writing *The Vivisector*, the kind of painting that Hurtle Duffield does was becoming passé. The watershed date was 1967, when the work of a new generation of American artists was put on display in Sydney and Melbourne in an exhibition seen by huge numbers of people. The revolution in sensibility represented by this new work was enthusiastically endorsed by younger Australian practitioners. 'Human feeling, expressionism and spiritual quests were seen by the new "internationalists" as embarrassing and gauche . . . Hard-edge, minimal and colour-field painting stressed the autonomy of the art object and its divorce from any notions of self-expression'.[5]

1967 was also the year when the Art Gallery of New South Wales held a major retrospective of the work of Sidney Nolan. White was overwhelmed by the sweep of Nolan's achievement as revealed in the exhibition, which seemed to him 'the greatest event – not just in painting – in Australia in my lifetime'. He drew on it for the retrospective of Duffield's work near the end of *The Vivisector*. He also sent Nolan the novel in draft, asking him to report candidly 'how close or remote I am from the workings of a painter's mind'.[6] Nolan thus had solid grounds for believing that Duffield was modelled on him.

It was not only in painting that, as the 1960s drew to an end, a changing of the guard took place. Much as the cohort of artists – Nolan, Albert Tucker, Arthur Boyd, John Perceval – who had imported German and French expressionism into Australian art in the immediate post-war years and, along with the more senior William Dobell, had become the public face of Australian painting, were now being supplanted by a new generation with new metropolitan models, so White, likewise formed in important respects by European expressionism, and likewise in the 1960s the representative, even the colossus, of Australian literature, was about to be relegated to a back shelf by a reading public enthusiastic for new writers from Latin America, India, and the Caribbean. The book White was working on in 1967, the book that became *The Vivisector*, was thus fated to be an elegy not only for the school of painting represented by Duffield but also for the school of writing represented by White himself.

Two.

The Vivisector was the eighth of the eleven big novels that White published between 1939 and 1979. In the remaining years of his life, up to his death in 1990, he produced stories, plays, and memoirs, but no fiction on the previous grand scale. His health was declining; he doubted he had the staying power, or indeed the will, to bring off a substantial new work.

To an inquiry from the Australian National Library as to his plans for the disposition of his papers, he responded: 'I can't let

you have my papers because I don't keep any.' As for his manuscripts, he said, these were routinely destroyed once the book
had appeared in print. 'Anything [that is] unfinished when I die
is to be burnt,' he concluded.[7] And indeed, in his will he
instructed his literary executor, his agent Barbara Mobbs, to
destroy whatever papers he left behind.

Mobbs disobeyed that instruction. In 2006 she committed the
surviving papers, a surprisingly large cache packed in thirty-two
boxes, to the library. Researchers, including White's biographer
David Marr, have been busy with this *Nachlass* ever since.
Among the fruits of Marr's labours is *The Hanging Garden*, a
50,000-word fragment of a novel that White commenced early
in 1981 but then, after weeks of intense and productive labour,
abandoned.

Marr has high praise for this resurrected fragment: 'A masterpiece in the making,' he calls it. (p. 30) One can see why.
Although it is only a draft, the creative intelligence behind the
prose is as intense and the characterization as deft as anywhere in
White. There is no sign at all of failing powers. The fragment,
constituting the first third of the projected novel, is largely
self-contained. All that is missing is a sense of where the action
is leading, what all the preparation is preparatory to.

After the initial burst of activity White never returned to *The
Hanging Garden*. It joined two other abandoned novels among
the papers that Mobbs was instructed to destroy; it is not inconceivable that these too will be resurrected and offered to the
public at some future date.

The world is a richer place now that we have *The Hanging Garden*. But what of Patrick White himself, who made it clear that

he did not want the world to see fragments of unachieved works from his hand? What would White say of Mobbs if he could speak from beyond the grave?

Perhaps the most notorious case of an executor countermanding the instructions of the deceased is provided by Max Brod, executor of the literary estate of his close friend Franz Kafka. Kafka, himself a trained lawyer, could not have spelled out his instructions more clearly:

> Dearest Max, My last request: Everything I leave behind me . . . in the way of notebooks, manuscripts, letters, my own and other people's, sketches and so on, is to be burned unread and to the last page, as well as all writings of mine or notes which either you may have or other people, from whom you are to beg them in my name. Letters which are not handed over to you should at least be faithfully burned by those who have them. Yours, Franz Kafka.[8]

Had Brod done his duty, we would have neither *The Trial* nor *The Castle*. As a result of his betrayal, the world is not just richer but metamorphosed, transfigured. Does the example of Brod and Kafka persuade us that literary executors, and perhaps executors in general, should be granted leeway to reinterpret instructions in the light of the general good?

There is an unstated prolegomenon to Kafka's letter, as there is in most testamentary instructions of this kind: 'By the time I am on my deathbed, and have to confront the fact that I will never be able to resume work on the fragments in my desk drawer, I will no longer be in a position to destroy them.

Therefore I see no recourse but to ask you act on my behalf. Unable to compel you, I can only trust you to honour my request.'

In justifying his failure to 'commit the incendiary act', Brod named two grounds. The first was that Kafka's standards for permitting his handiwork to see the light of day were unnaturally high: 'the highest religious standards', he called them. The second was more down to earth: though he had clearly informed Kafka that he would not carry out his instructions, Kafka had not dismissed him as executor, therefore (he reasoned) in his heart Kafka must have known the manuscripts would not be destroyed. (pp. 173, 174)

In law, the words of a will are meant to express the full and final intention of the testator. If the will is well constructed – that is to say, properly worded, in accordance with the formulaic language of testamentary tradition – then it will be a fairly mechanical task to interpret the will: we need nothing more than a handbook of testamentary formulas to gain unambiguous access to the intention of the testator. In the Anglo-American legal system, the handbook of formulas is known as the rules of construction, and the tradition of interpretation based on them as the plain-meaning doctrine.

However, for quite a while now the plain-meaning doctrine has been under siege. The essence of the critique was set forth over a century ago by the legal scholar John H. Wigmore:

The fallacy consists in assuming that there is or ever can be some one real or absolute meaning. In truth, there can only be some person's meaning; and that person, whose meaning the law is seeking, is the writer of the document.[9]

The unique difficulty posed by wills is that the writer of the document, the person whose meaning the law is seeking, is absent, inaccessible.

The relativistic approach to meaning enunciated by Wigmore has the upper hand in many jurisdictions today. According to this approach, our energies ought to be directed in the first place to grasping the anterior intentions of the testator, and only secondarily to interpreting the written expression of those intentions in the light of precedent. Thus rules of construction can no longer be relied on to provide the last word; a more open attitude has come to prevail toward admitting extrinsic evidence of the testator's intentions. In 1999 the American Law Institute, in its Restatement of Property, Wills and Other Donative Transfers, went so far as to declare that the language of a document (such as a will) is 'so colored by the circumstances surrounding its formulation that [other] evidence regarding the donor's intention is *always* [my emphasis] relevant'.[10] In this respect the ALI registers a shift of emphasis not only in United States law but in the entire legal tradition founded on English law.

If the language of the testamentary document is always conditioned by, and may always be supplemented by, the circumstances surrounding its formulation, what circumstances can we imagine, surrounding instructions from a writer that his papers be destroyed, that might justify ignoring those instructions?

In the case of Brod and Kafka, aside from the circumstances adduced by Brod himself (that the testator set unrealistic standards for publication of his work; that the testator was aware that his executor could not be relied on), there is a third and more compelling one: that the testator was not in a position to understand the broader significance of his life's work.

Public opinion is, I would guess, solidly behind executors like Brod and Mobbs who refuse to carry out their testamentary instructions on the twofold grounds that they are in a better position than the deceased to understand the broader significance of the work, and that considerations of the public good should trump the expressed wishes of the deceased. What then should a writer do if he truly, finally, and absolutely wants his papers to be destroyed? In the reigning legal climate, the best answer would seem to be: Do the job yourself. Furthermore, do it early, before you are physically incapable. If you delay too long, you will have to ask someone else to act on your behalf, and that person may decide that you do not truly, finally, and absolutely mean what you say.

The Hanging Gardens is the story of two European children evacuated for their safety to Australia during the Second World War. Gilbert is British, sent away to escape the bombing of London. Eirene is the child of a Greek father and an Australian mother. During their first night together the children, whose ages are not given but who must be eleven or twelve, share a bed. In Eirene there begins to grow an obsession with Gilbert in which inchoate sexual stirrings are mixed with an obscure realization that they are not just fellow aliens in a new land but two of a kind, brought together by fate. Of Gilbert's feelings for Eirene we know less, in part because he is trapped in boyish male disdain for girls, in part (one guesses) because realization of her place in his life was intended to come later, in the body of the book that never got to be written.

After a year or two in foster care, the children are separated. Though Eirene broods on memories of their time together, they have no further contact. The fragment ends in mid-1945, with victory in Europe and the prospect that the two children will be returned to their native countries.

Greece and Australia constitute the poles between which Eirene moves. Having just begun to get a feel for Greek politics and her parents' position in Greek society, she must now navigate the very different Australian system, where she will be looked down on as a 'reffo' (refugee) and stigmatized, because of her dark skin, as a 'black'. At school, her precocious acquaintance with Racine and Goethe will count against her: anti-egalitarian, un-Australian. But spiritual meanness of the Australian variety, though amply exhibited, is not the real focus of White's concern in *The Hanging Garden*.

Several other motifs are sounded in the fragment but then hang in the air with little indication of how he meant to develop them. The most intriguing of these concerns *pneuma*, a word that Eirene remembers from the island in the Cyclades where she spent a year with her father's family – an 'old' family, anti-monarchist. *Pneuma*, she informs Gilbert, cannot be explained in English, but obscurely she feels it is a force or spirit watching over the pair of them.

Pneuma is indeed one of the more mysterious forces in early Greek religion, and then in the religion of the early Christians. Issuing from deep in the earth, *pneuma* is what the oracle at Delphi inhales to give her the power of prophecy. In the New Testament it is the wind that is also the breath of God.

The wind [*pneuma*] blows where it wishes and you hear the sound of it, but do not know where it comes from and where it is going; so it is with everyone who is born of the Spirit [*pneuma*].[11]

Similarly, Jesus breathes on his disciples and says, 'Receive the Holy Spirit [*pneuma*].'[12]

White clearly intends *pneuma* to be more than a mere marker of Eirene's Greek origins. He may well have intended it to fore-shadow the breath or spirit that speaks through the artist, thereby hinting at what the future would hold for his two characters.

White had a deep attachment to Greece, principally through Manoly Lascaris, whom he met and fell in love with in Alexandria during the war, and with whom he came to share the rest of his life. His 1981 memoir *Flaws in the Glass* includes a lengthy record of their travels in Greece. For a period, he writes, he was 'in the grip of a passionate love affair, not so much with Greece as the idea of it'. He and Lascaris even considered buying a house on Patmos. 'Greece is one long despairing rage in those who understand her, worse for Manoly because she is his, as Australia is worse for me because of my responsibility.' It is possible that through Gilbert (standing in for himself) and Eirene (standing in for Lascaris) he hoped, in *The Hanging Garden*, to explore more deeply feelings of despairing rage at a beloved country (Australia on the one hand, Greece on the other) that has fallen into the hands of a brash, greedy, nouveau-riche class.[13]

To a friend at school, Eirene confides that what she seeks above all in life is love, but more specifically 'transcendence'. In the flat light of Australia there is no place for the transcendent ('Australians are only born to live'); but in Greece she had intuitions

almost in my cradle, anyway from stubbing my toes on Greek stones, from my face whipped by pine branches, from the smell of drying wax candles in old mouldy hillside chapels ... Mountain snow stained with Greek blood. And the *pneuma* floating above, like a blue cloud in a blue sky.[14]

Intimations such as these, hinting that she is in the world to show us how to transcend the world, mark Eirene as one of White's elect, along with Voss and the four Riders in the Chariot and Arthur Brown in *The Solid Mandala* and Hurtle Duffield in *The Vivisector*: outsiders mocked by society yet doggedly occupied in their private quests for transcendence, or, as White more often calls it, the truth.

20. Patrick White, *The Solid Mandala*

Patrick White's first novel, *Happy Valley*, appeared in 1939, in London, and won praise from the critics. In Australia it had a more guarded reception: it misrepresented country life, said reviewers, and its style was unnecessarily difficult. His second novel, *The Living and the Dead* (1941), came out first in the United States, where his publisher was prepared to back him strongly, seeing in him presciently an heir to the great English-language modernists: Joyce, Lawrence, Faulkner. The book was ignored in Australia.

The indifference with which his third novel, *The Aunt's Story* (1948), was received plunged White into gloom, and for years he gave up writing. Then, after what seems to have been a mystical illumination, he began work on *The Tree of Man* (1955).

The feeling for the Australian landscape that he there rediscovered in himself did not extend to Australian society. He was dismayed by the pressure toward conformity, by a spirit of prudishness expressed in a rigid censorship system and a general policing of morals, by the single-minded immersion of the middle class in the pursuit of money. *Riders in the Chariot* (1961), in which a small company of artists and visionaries is subjected to the malevolent small-mindedness and xenophobia of the suburbs, expressed in extreme form his alienation from the social world.

The loneliness and suffering of the artist, reviled or perse- cuted or ostracized for telling truths that the multitude cannot bear, is a recurrent theme in White's work. *Voss* (1957), the novel for which he became best known, embodies the Romantic myth by which he lived and from which he drew sustenance. Johann Ulrich Voss, explorer by vocation, ventures into the forbidding interior of the Australian continent; in the course of suffering and dying there, he gains visionary insight into the mysteries not only of the land but of human existence, and of the human heart.

It was hardly to be expected that an artist who saw himself as marked out for a lonely, higher destiny would be taken to the bosom of an Australia that prided itself on its egalitarian ethos. White's achievements were not recognized at home, nor indeed in Britain, where the complex music of his prose and the mystical bent of his thought were alien to the modest domestic realism of post-war British fiction. In the United States, however, *The Tree of Man*, *Voss*, and *Riders in the Chariot* secured his reputation as an Antipodean William Faulkner.

The studied coolness with which White's writing was received at home underwent some change in the 1960s, as Australia began to shake off its sense of cultural inferiority and, in the arts, to assert a degree of independence from Britain. *Riders in the Char- iot* was widely read; from then on, White would be grudgingly admired if not loved.

At this very point in White's career, however, influential crit- ics, particularly within the academy, began to lose interest in him. To Marxists he stood for elitist high art; to cultural mate- rialists he was too much of an idealist; feminists felt he was a misogynist; to postcolonial critics he was too wedded to European canons and too little concerned with the advancement of Australia's Aboriginal minority; while to postmodernists he was simply a belated modernist. By the end of the century, ten years after his death, he was little read in schools and universities; his name had faded from the national consciousness.

Yet Patrick White remains, on most counts, the greatest writer Australia has produced. All of his novels from *The Aunt's Story* onward are fully achieved works, with no weak link in the chain. He himself nominated *The Aunt's Story, The Solid Mandala* (1966), and *The Twyborn Affair* (1979) as his best. *Voss* was not on his list, perhaps because he was sick of being identified as Patrick White, author of *Voss*.

It is hard to think of a more unappealing character than Waldo Brown in *The Solid Mandala*. Waldo is envious and spiteful and vain. Convinced he is an unrecognized literary master, a genius in hiding, he is nevertheless too idle or too timorous to sit down and write the masterpiece he believes lies in embryo within him. Everything in life that is bountiful or generous he regards with suspicion or contempt. Concerned to present himself to the world as a figure of rectitude and authority, he has no idea that people regard him as a figure of fun. Although the actual physical being of women repels him, he deigns to offer his hand in marriage to a girl, and is then bewildered when she turns him down. Not for a minute does he entertain the thought that he may be homosexual. His obsessive sexual imagination finds its most natural expression in masturbation.

Waldo is very much the child of his parents, embodying the worst features of both: his mother's social snobbery, his father's sterile relationship with books. After reading Dostoevsky's *The Brothers Karamazov*, his father burns it. He does not explain why, but we infer that it threatens to undermine the neat, rational model of the universe he has adopted from his British upbringing. Waldo thoroughly approves of his father's action.

As a child Waldo is clever in a conventional sort of way, whereas his twin brother Arthur is so backward in class (aside from his inexplicable gift for numbers) that he has to be removed from school. It is accepted in the Brown family that Arthur cannot cope with the world and needs to be protected. On Waldo falls the duty of protecting him, a duty he performs resentfully. To him, Arthur is a sort of club foot he is doomed to drag around after him. As a grown man he has fantasies of murdering Arthur: once he is rid of the incubus of his twin, he tells himself, he will be released into a life of comfort and pleasure in which his superior gifts will be recognized and rewarded. Yet he and his brother continue to sleep in the same bed in the miserable little house their father built in the remoter suburbs of Sydney.

The climax of *The Solid Mandala* (the conclusion of Part Three) arrives when the twins are well into their sixties. Forced to confront the fact that he has been living a lie, that he is no genius, that if there is a genius or at least a creative force in the family it is Arthur, Waldo launches himself upon his brother. Between the two there occurs what is either an embrace or a wrestling contest, in which Arthur participates in a spirit of love, Waldo in a spirit of hatred. Locked to his twin, Waldo dies.

At one level *The Solid Mandala* is a perfectly realistic story of the intimate lives of two brothers of very different psychological make-up, children of British immigrants who never quite find their feet in Australia. Patrick White was a critic and indeed a satirist of many aspects of Australian society, in particular of its hostility to the life of the mind. He had a sharp eye for significant detail and a sharp ear for speech; he had read Charles Dickens and knew how to use Dickens's technique of building comic characters out of little mannerisms and verbal tics. *The Solid Mandala* can be read as a closely rendered account of the fate of a certain kind of middle-class family in the evolving social environment of twentieth-century Australia. Mr Brown, father of Waldo and Arthur, adopts enthusiastically one of the founding truisms of national Australian mythology: that Australia is a country without shadows. Much of Patrick White's *oeuvre*, including *The Solid Mandala*, is concerned to make the shadows in and over Australia visible. Read in this way, as a corrective to Australian cheeriness, *The Solid Mandala* is a very dark book indeed, driven only, it would seem, by disgust and despair.

But White had greater ambitions for the book, as any attentive reader must soon become aware. It is no accident that he makes his Brown brothers twins. To the sterile rationalism of Waldo is opposed the inarticulate metaphysical yearning of Arthur. To Waldo's prim, fearful attitude toward the body and its appetites is opposed Arthur's often clumsy urge to touch people. (Arthur remains a virgin to the end, yet he enjoys a range of close and indeed intimate friendships with women: in White's world, women tend to be more in tune with their instincts and intuitions than men are.) To Waldo's fastidious verbal art (so fastidious that he can barely put pen to paper) is opposed Arthur's sensuous, pleasurable hand-work with dough and cream. Waldo thinks of himself as an intellectual, but his mind is closed: Arthur is the one who, driven by the urge to know, pores over the great books of humankind. Far from being copies of each other, the twins are as opposite as can be, yet are held together by fate and by deep-lying forces within them.

There were two writers whom White was reading closely as he worked on *The Solid Mandala*. One was the Dostoevsky of *The Brothers Karamazov*. The other was Carl Jung.

The Brothers Karamazov overwhelmed White, as it overwhelms most of its readers. But the subjects that Dostoevsky takes up in the book, chief among them the human drive – a drive that may be obeyed or may be denied – toward a God who may or may not answer, may or may not exist, are subjects that White too felt compelled to address, in one work after another, to the extent that one can say that, in *The Solid Mandala* in particular, White writes in dialogue with Dostoevsky.

White's relation to Jung is quite different. He plunders Jung's writings – which are inter alia a treasure house of arcane knowledge – for insights that he can use in his story of Waldo and Arthur. In Jung he found the following passage, which he allows Arthur to discover and meditate on during one of his visits to the municipal library: 'As the shadow continually follows the body of one who walks in the sun, so our hermaphroditic Adam, though he appears in the form of a male, nevertheless always carried about with him Eve, or his wife hidden in his body'.[1]

Arthur immediately (and correctly) identifies himself with the hermaphroditic Adam, but then (mistakenly) tries to identify his hidden Eve with one or other of the women he is close to. It is not White's manner to make use of symbols in a strict, unambiguous manner, but Arthur might be better advised to look to his twin as his true Eve. For at its most abstract level *The Solid Mandala* is a book about the human psyche, and in the human psyche, as White sees it, the two warring principles, called by some the conscious and the unconscious, by others the male and the female, by yet others the moist and the dry, are in fact protean in the guises they can assume.

Though Waldo has been instructed that he is his brother's protector, Arthur sees their relationship quite differently. It is he, Arthur, who must protect Waldo: Waldo is lost in the world of his reading and lacks the suppleness needed to cope with the real world. Unlike Waldo, Arthur performs his protective duty with love, from the moment when, at school, he appears like a flaming angel to rescue Waldo from the boys who are tormenting him until the last day of their life together, when he comes to the chilling realization that despite all his efforts he has failed to save Waldo from himself – that Waldo has irredeemably become a Dostoevskian lost soul.

Coming across the word *totality* while he is still an adolescent, Arthur innocently asks his father what it means. Trapped in his narrow rationalism, Mr Brown is unable to explain. Yet unbeknown to himself, Arthur has the answer in his pocket. A mandala (the word comes from Sanskrit) is an ancient emblem of the universe, of totality. It consists of a square, whose four sides are identified with four gods or universal forces, enclosed within a circle. Among the glass marbles that Arthur owns are four mandalas, spherical rather than circular and therefore solid. At the heart of each is a mystic or mysterious design. His favourite marble has a knot at its heart.

(*To lose one's marbles* is a common idiom meaning to lose one's mind. It is a central irony of the book that Arthur, the person who is in all quarters thought to have lost his marbles, has been in possession of them all the time.)

Part of Arthur's life-quest is to identify the four persons (the four avatars of the divine) to whom the four mandalas by right belong. Waldo, as it turns out, is not one of the four; but the Browns' nearest neighbour on Terminus Road is. Mrs Poulter embodies much of White's mystical materialism: an ordinary Australian-born working-class woman, entirely unintellectual, without any pretensions, she lives close to the earth; in her hands the most mundane daily tasks, like fetching water or preparing food, become sacraments. In one of the great scenes of the book, Arthur dances the golden mandala for Mrs Poulter (for, as he has learned from his reading, the mysteries can more easily be explored through the physical, intuitive, non-rational medium of dance than through the rational medium of language).

The dance scene, which shows White at the peak of his powers as an artist in prose, establishes Arthur as the true spiritual hero of the book but also exposes a tragic paradox for White himself, namely that the art he practises will not take him to the heart of the mystery of life. It is not the writer but the dancer, the holy fool whose dance can only be danced, cannot be done in words except from the outside, who leads us and shows us the way. Odious as Waldo may be, it is Waldo not Arthur who in this book stands for the writer, that is, for Patrick White. It is no accident that the next novel White published, *The Vivisector*, has as its central character not a writer but a painter, whose art becomes more and more insane and antisocial as he grows older, more and more an exploration of enigmatic shapes and forms lying deep in his psyche.

After the discovery of Waldo's stinking, mutilated corpse and the collapse of the house of Brown, Arthur makes a last appeal for help, offering himself to Mrs Poulter as the son she never had, even though he is in fact older than she. In an ideal world Mrs Poulter would accept the gift, for she belongs among the elect, the handful of people in the book whose souls are not closed to the divine. But in the world we have, as she knows and Arthur knows too, that is not possible, not *realistic*. So we are left with the hope that in 'Peaches-and-Plums', the euphemistically named institution for the insane to which he will be committed, Arthur will be received with the loving care that he deserves – that all God's creatures deserve. But that too is not a realistic hope.

21. The Poetry of Les Murray

One.

In 1960 a bulky anthology titled *The New American Poetry* was published in the United States under the imprint of Grove Press. It contained samples of the work of some forty poets, most of them young, unknown outside the circumscribed world of poetry readings and little magazines. As a guide to a new generation of American poets it was unreliable: among the rising stars it missed out were Galway Kinnell, W. S. Merwin, Sylvia Plath, Adrienne Rich, and Richard Wilbur. But covering the field was never the intention of its editor, Donald M. Allen. Rather, Allen wanted to showcase a surge of new writers who were not interested in the kind of poem – the compact, well-crafted, personal lyric – favoured in the New Critical schoolroom, who on the contrary, in sprawling verses, preferred to denounce the military-industrial complex or sing the body electric or report visions of the Buddha in the supermarket.

Grove Press could not have guessed at the impact the book would have. *The New American Poetry* both captured and helped to create the spirit of the 1960s. In its first decade it sold 100,000 copies; in 1999 – by which time half the young rebels it had announced were in the grave – it could be republished as a classic.

The new wave took some years to reach the Antipodes. When the anthology did wash ashore in Sydney, it was impounded by a customs service charged with protecting the morals of a notably prim public (Joyce's *Ulysses* could not be openly sold in Australia until 1953). Once it was released and absorbed, however, its effects were far-reaching. The Australian body poetic divided in two, enthusiasts for the New Americans clustering under the umbrella of the magazine *New Poetry*, while doubters migrated to *Poetry Australia*, edited (from 1973) by Les A. Murray, a poet with, by then, two books of verse to his name.

Though not unreceptive to American examples – his early poems owe a clear debt to Robert Frost – Murray was hostile to modernism in most of its manifestations. The examination he gave to the poets in Allen's book was of the most cursory kind. In Gary Snyder, for instance, he claimed to detect the 'almost affectless equanimity of the uprooted modern person' – about as thorough a misreading of Snyder as is possible.[1] But Murray was using Allen's poets only as stand-ins for a larger and vaguer target: the modernist sensibility, the modernist world view. Modernists, in his dismissive diagnosis, wrote out of a 'pathological state [of] depression'.[2] 'Modernism's not modern: its true name's *Despair*'.[3]

As an antidote to modernist despair, Murray recommended a dose of Australian verse of the kind popular in the late nineteenth century. To back up this prescription he went on to produce his own anthology, *The New Oxford Book of Australian Verse*, in which convict ditties, drinking songs, and anonymous ballads were strongly represented, as well as Aboriginal songs in translation.

Murray's wholesale rejection of modernism may seem to mark

him as simply an isolated provincial conservative swimming against the tide of the times. But there was more substance to his response than that. For a poet to repudiate newfangled foreign fashions and stand up instead for a home-grown tradition that celebrated the life of the mounted frontiersman or his outlaw cousin the bushranger was, in its Australian context, a clear political statement. In agitation for union of the six British colonies in an Australian federation – as came to pass in 1901 – the lone horseman in the bush had been used as an icon of national identity. 'The narrow ways of English folk / Are not for such as we; / They bear the long-accustomed yoke / Of staid conservancy,' wrote A. B. ('Banjo') Paterson, much-loved poet of the bush. 'We must saddle up and ride / Towards the blue hill's breast: / And we must travel far and fast / Across their rugged maze.'

In truth, even in Paterson's time there was more than a little idealization in the picture of Australians as restless frontier spirits: by 1900 a majority were settled in towns and cities (compared with thirty-five per cent in the United States). But in pitting the ballad tradition against the modernists, Murray was calling on Australian poetry to follow its own native course and foster its own native values, which would include an optimistic expansiveness that turned its back on both the 'narrow ways' of the old Mother Country and the cramped despair of the modernists, and a no-nonsense egalitarianism, suspicious of all pretensions, including intellectual pretensions. (Of the three rallying cries of modern democratic revolutions, *Égalité* has always had more resonance in Australia than *Liberté*.)

Curiously, lone horsemen are pretty much absent from Murray's own poetry. For him the totemic beast has been not the horse but the cow, which stands for domesticity rather than solitude, settlement rather than exploration. One of his most ambitious poems, the sequence 'Walking to the Cattle Place' (1972), traces the line of descent of Australian cattle farming back to the cattle cultures of ancient India and Grecian Boeotia. Boeotia, sneered at by its rival, Athens, as rustic and unsophisticated, is elected by Murray as his spiritual birthplace, a shining example of a decentralized, rurally based polity.

If the good people of rural New South Wales (where Murray hails from) are the Boeotians, and Murray is their Hesiod, then the Athenians are represented by the Sydney intelligentsia. 'The educated caste,' writes Murray, 'has been able to free itself from the older [land-owning] Establishment and become a dominating, oppressing power in its own right,' conducting all-out war on 'vernacular Australia', vernacular Australia being the

> republic . . . inherent in our vernacular tradition, which is to say in that 'folk' Australia, part imaginary and part historical, which is the real matrix of any distinctiveness we possess as a nation, . . . the Australia of our deepest common values and identifications.[4]

One of the weapons used by the intelligentsia against rural white Australians, says Murray, is to stigmatize them as 'bigoted, conservative, ignorant, despoilers of the environment, a doomed, obsolete group'.[5] The term he uses for the process of putting down a despised class is *relegation*. The cultural war waged by the intelligentsia on the values of rural white Australians is only one instance of a wider process of relegation or banishment practised by the post-Enlightenment West against older, unenlightened cultures, including Australian Aboriginal culture.

Thus, in the choice for or against modernism, what is at stake in Murray's eyes is not just the survival in Australia of simple, humane, communal, old-fashioned country values but, more widely, the survival worldwide of a way of life thousands of years old. Murray's conservatism is defined by his defence of this traditional way of life.

Two.

Murray likes to present himself as an outsider to urban networks of cultural power. This is not an accurate picture. Murray is in fact a considerable intellectual and, until his midlife move back to his rural birthplace of Bunyah, NSW, was a substantial presence in the public arena. A polyglot with a degree in German literature, he was employed for years by the Australian National University as a translator, with responsibility for all the Germanic and Romance languages. As an essayist and anthologist he advanced a powerful if idiosyncratic reading of the Australian poetic tradition from its colonial beginnings. As editor of *Poetry Australia* and as poetry consultant to a major publisher he was also, to a degree, able to steer Australian poetry along the course he wanted it to take.

In spite of his modest origins, his gifts were recognized early: among his patrons were such important literary figures as Kenneth Slessor and A. D. Hope. Called upon as an unofficial adviser by Gough Whitlam, prime minister of Australia from 1972 to 1975, Murray helped devise a system of financial support for the arts, a system that might properly be called enlightened and that Murray himself has benefited from.

Though he has at various times held university fellowships, Murray has little good to say about universities, particularly about what goes on in the literature classroom. Academic literary critics are, to him, heirs of an Enlightenment hostile to the creative spirit. Behind its mask of the disinterested pursuit of knowledge, he sees the Enlightenment itself as a cabal of rootless, disaffected *clercs* scheming to grasp power, usually by controlling the fashion for what may or may not be said in public ('political correctness'). Universities have been turned by the Enlightenment into 'humiliation mills' that grind out generations of students ashamed of their social origins, alienated from their native culture, recruits to a new metropolitan class whose Australian manifestation Murray dubs 'the Ascendancy', evoking the Protestant landowning class which for centuries dominated public life in Ireland. In Murray's hands the term is meant to capture the 'foreign-derived oppressiveness' of the new class but also its *'arriviste*, first-generation flavour'. The Ascendancy is 'the natural upper class of a socialist world order'; holding a university degree is the modern equivalent of being a landowner.[6]

Universities offer people a chance to improve themselves; to the extent that self-improvement includes moving up the social ladder universities can be accused of fostering inequality. Self-improvement was certainly what, back in 1957, Sydney University offered Les Murray, son of a struggling tenant farmer. The young man's response to the offer was confused. He missed classes, failed examinations, dropped out to lead a vagrant life, yet finally returned to complete his degree. In Murray's own account of that period of his life, he took only what he wanted from the university – the resources of its library – while resisting its more insidious sociopolitical project. But the very vehemence of his polemic against higher education suggests a supplementary reading: that the young man was as much attracted as repulsed by the promise that submission to the rituals and mysteries of the academy would allow him to shed his origins and be reborn declassed.

Three.

The self-authored myth of how Murray of the many wiles evaded the Enlightenment, resisted the lures of the Ascendancy, fought off the modernists, travelled the world, saw many sights, and returned at last to his own Ithaca forms the backbone of a not inconsiderable *oeuvre*: a 500-page *Collected Poems* (2002) plus several later books of poetry; two novels in verse; and a body of essays on literary and political subjects.

Certain themes in this myth stand out for the importance Murray attaches to them or – what amounts to the same thing – for the part they play in his work. The principal of these is Bunyah as the Great Good Place. Another is the theme of the poisoned childhood: from being belittled and punished as a child, Murray learned to despise and punish himself, his self-loathing rising to a peak at high school, where he was taunted for being fat and given the nickname Bottom. Another is the inherited (genetic) curse, manifesting itself both in inconsiderate, even cruel treatment of those around him ('autism') and in spells when he is not himself, is out of his mind, in the grip of depression, a.k.a. the black dog. A fourth theme is vocation: after marrying a Catholic and converting from the rigid

Presbyterianism into which he was born, he discovered how to serve God by being his poet-priest. 'Prose is Protestant-agnostic,' he writes, 'but poetry is Catholic: / poetry is presence.'[7]

These four themes are interlinked, as they are linked with Murray's wider social and political views. From having it drummed into him as a child that he was wicked, unlovely, and undesirable, Murray grew into a man torn between shame (at himself, at his origins) and anger against those who dared to jeer at him or at what he called 'my people'. This anger comes out most nakedly in the *Subhuman Redneck Poems* of 1996, whose very title is a challenge. Here is Murray on Ascendancy high culture:

> It's my mission to irritate the hell out of the eloquent who would oppress my people, by being a paradox that their categories can't assimilate: the Subhuman Redneck who writes poems.[8]

And again:

> Most Culture has been an East German plastic bag
> pulled over our heads, stifling and wet,
> we see a hotly distorted world
> through crackling folds and try not to gag.[9]

Four.

Over the years, Murray has written numbers of poems that are in one way or another of Aboriginal inspiration. Some explore the history of settler-Aboriginal contact; some are based on Aboriginal song forms; some use Aboriginal personae to express an Aboriginal consciousness. The most ambitious of these works is 'The Buladelah-Taree Holiday Song Cycle', a sequence of thirteen poems celebrating the Christmas period when city folk return to the country to join in family reunions and renew the bond with their natal earth. This song cycle, composed in long lines with a dactylic pulse, shows – triumphantly, I would say – how a modern poet working at a high creative pitch can celebrate the values of ordinary folk while remaining accessible to the ordinary reader.

Murray has written at length about the composition of his song cycle and his debt to the traditional poetry of the Wonguri-Mandjikai people of Arnhem Land in northern Australia, whose Song Cycle of the Moon Bone, he says, stunned him when he first read it. 'It may well be the greatest poem ever composed in Australia.' He praises R. M. Berndt, its translator, for finding a language in tune with

the best Australian vernacular speech . . . It has perhaps been the tragedy, the sickness, of poetry here [in Australia] that it has so rarely caught precisely that tone, and that our audiences have been trained not to expect it from us.[10]

Reiterating his criticism of an arriviste Australian intelligentsia that has cut itself off from the people, he proceeds to make a contentious sociological claim:

[In the mid-twentieth century] the Aborigines were partly a people, partly a caste, partly a class, though really that last term is inaccurate: they were actually part of a larger class of the rural poor, and it is still often more useful to see them in that light than in currently fashionable radical-racialist terms. We, my family, were in the same class ourselves.[11]

On the Murrays he observes:

I suppose we were heirs to the unadmitted guilts of the white conquest of Australia, though I don't remember our being conscious of them at all. Perhaps we were too poorly educated . . . They may be no more than an outgrowth of learned liberalism, or a residue of childhood fears. Really, I am not at all sure about white conquest-guilt; it may be no more than a construct of the political Left, that great inventor of prescriptive sentiments and categories.[12]

Murray's assimilation of the white rural poor with the people whose lands they took over; his reluctance to, in the parlance of today, 'say sorry' for the historic crimes of colonialism ('You can't go apologizing for things you [sc. personally] didn't do,' he objected in a 2001 interview); and, not least, his use ('appropriation') of Aboriginal cultural forms without the permission of their ancestral guardians have all been controversial.[13]

In response to criticism, Murray has distanced himself from an individualism that looks down on communal forms and a cosmopolitanism that denigrates local attachments. He has asserted in their place a colour-blind Australian nationalism that encompasses a Romantic belief in culture springing organically from the native soil:

> I am grateful beyond measure to the makers and interpreters of traditional Aboriginal poetry and song for many things, not least for showing me a deeply familiar world in which art is not estranged, but is a vital source of health for all the members of a community . . . Aboriginal art has given me a resort of reference and native strength, a truly Australian base to draw on against the constant importation of Western decays and idiocies and class consciousness.[14]

Five.

In essays written in the 1980s, Murray gives a striking phenomenological account of the experience of reading poetry. Less convincingly, he goes on to make claims for the importance of poetry to our psychic health. The experience of reading a 'real' poem, Murray says,

> is marked by a strange simultaneity of stillness and racing excitement. Our mind wants to hurry on and have more and more of it, but at the same time it is held by an awe which yearns to prolong the moment and experience it as timeless. We only half-notice, consciously, that our breathing has tightened and altered, submitting to commands from beyond ourselves . . . We may say that the poem is dancing us to its rhythm, even as we sit apparently still,

reading it. It is, discreetly, borrowing our body to embody itself.[15]

The poem itself is a paradoxical entity, both finite and inexhaustible:

Each interpretation we put upon the poem will wear out in time, and come to seem inadequate, but the standing event of the poem will remain, exhausting our attempts to contain or defuse it.[16]

Drawing upon popular psychology, Murray identifies the lately evolved human forebrain as the site of waking consciousness, while the older, reptilian brain is responsible for dreams. A 'real' poem, being both truly thought and truly dreamed, represents 'wholeness of thinking and of life'. It 'enacts this wholeness and draws us into it, so as to promote and refresh our own [wholeness]'.[17]

This approach to the defence of poetry, though not unusual in itself, seems curious in the light of Murray's strictures on modernism. For the conception of the poem as a timeless object that invites yet exhausts interpretation reminds one of nothing so much as the poem as verbal icon (William K. Wimsatt) or as well-wrought urn (Cleanth Brooks). In fact, Murray's poetics sits very well with the blend of English psychological empiricism and German idealist aesthetics that made up American New Criticism; and many of his poems themselves profit from the kind of close analytical reading practised in the New Critical classroom.

New Criticism was notoriously unhelpful in the reading of

'primitive' poetry like the Moon Bone Cycle, or poetry in the line of Walt Whitman or Charles Olson – the line followed in Allen's *New American Poetry*. It is to Murray's credit as a poet that his own more expansive work leaves his theorizing well behind. One of the chief Australian values that he celebrates is sprawl. Sprawl is to Murray what loafing is to Whitman: an at-easeness in the world that upsets the tidy minds of school-teachers and urban planners. 'Reprimanded and dismissed / [sprawl] listens with a grin and one boot up on the rail / of possibility.'[18]

Six.

In an unpublished letter quoted by his biographer Peter Alexander, Murray describes his poetry-writing as 'quasi-priestly work' done in imitation of Christ ('It's His life as I can live it by my efforts').[19] In this respect Murray harks back to the poet-priest Gerard Manley Hopkins, to whom he owes more than one debt.

Paul Kane, who has written the best study we have of poetry in Australia, traces Murray's views on poetry and religion back to Rudolf Otto (1869–1937), whose book *Das Heilige* (1917), translated as *The Idea of the Holy*, Murray read during his student years; and, behind Otto, to the philosopher Jakob Friedrich Fries (1773–1843), who posited a faculty of *Ahndung* (surmise, presentiment) that allows human beings direct cognition of the divine. It is via this unorthodox branch of Kantian philosophy, Kane suggests, that Murray's thinking about the poetic vocation ought to be approached.[20]

In a number of important poems from the early 1980s,

Murray explores the state of mind (or of spirit) in which the poet makes contact with the divine. The key terms here are *grace* and *equanimity*, abstractions to which his poems essay to give body. The poem 'Equanimity' – which in its very tone is a model of even-spiritedness – concludes with a suggestion to us his readers that if we find the spiritual state of equanimity as difficult to grasp via the rational intellect as it is hard to achieve by an effort of the will, we may find it

more natural to look at the birds about the street, their life
that is greedy, pinched, courageous and prudential
as any on these bricked tree-mingled miles of settlement,
to watch the unceasing on-off
grace that attends their nearly every movement,
the same grace moveless in the shapes of trees
and complex in our selves and fellow walkers: we see it's
    indivisible
and scarcely willed. That it lights us from the
    incommensurable
we sometimes glimpse, from being trapped in the point
(bird minds and ours are so pointedly visual):
a field all foreground, and equally all background,
like a painting of equality. Of infinite detailed extent
like God's attention. Where nothing is diminished by
    perspective.[21]

We should not be dismayed, suggests Murray, by the elusive, flickering, on-off quality of our contact with the numinous. Rather, we should learn to wait with equanimity – as poet or as believer – for the next flash of grace. Poetic insight and revelation are both, by their nature, 'intermittent, / as the action of those birds – crested pigeon, rosella parrot – / who fly with wings shut, then beating, and again shut'.[22]

Seven.

Murray has written poems that belong on any list of the best ('classic') Australian verse; some of these have been around long enough to seep into the national consciousness. Among them are the ruminative sequence 'Walking to the Cattle Place' (1972) and the celebratory 'Buladelah-Taree Holiday Song Cycle' (1977); 'Equanimity' and the pair of philosophical essay-poems 'On Interest' (all 1983); numbers of more intimate pieces like 'Evening Alone at Bunyah' (1969) or 'The Tin Wash Dish' (1990); the virtuoso 'Translations from the Natural World' (1992), showing off Murray's uncanny power to enter into animal minds; and 'Dog Fox Field' (1990), about the extermination of the feeble-minded under the Nazis.

The verse novel *Fredy Neptune* (1998) occupies an uneasy place in Murray's output. On the model of Voltaire's *Candide*, it takes its German–Australian hero Fredy Boettcher, an innocent with physical powers approaching the superhuman, on a tour of world history from 1914 to 1945. As a country boy continually stigmatized for his Germanness, Fredy is an obvious stand-in, if not for Murray himself then for the stigmatized self in which Murray has at times felt trapped.

The versifying in *Fredy Neptune* is consistently lively, and there are plenty of striking incidents, but Murray's skills as a storyteller are limited, and what may be intended as picaresque quickly degenerates into just one thing after another. Murray himself has hinted that the novel is best read side by side with the *Redneck* poems, that is to say, as a cathartic exercise in getting a weight of resentful rage off his chest.

None of the poems I have singled out as among Murray's best dates from later than 1992. Since that date he has – aside from the *Collected Poems* of 2002 – published several collections of – in my view – lesser poems. Under the title *Killing the Black Dog* (1997) he has also published a memoir of his long struggle with depression. The memoir comes with a combative afterword, dated 2009, in which he rehashes old but evidently not forgotten quarrels with 'official' Australian culture, condemned for orchestrating media campaigns against him and more generally for being out of touch with public sentiment.[23]

The time has perhaps come for Les Murray to let go of old grudges. He has received many public honours and is widely acknowledged to be the leading Australian poet of his generation. His poems are 'taught' in schools and universities; scholars write learned articles about them. He claims that he is read more abroad than at home. This may or may not be so. But even if it were true, he would not be the first writer to suffer such a fate. It is a better fate than not being read at all.

22. Reading Gerald Murnane

Between 1840 and 1914 Ireland emptied itself of half of its population. As many as a million died of starvation, but most who departed their native land departed in hope of a better life elsewhere. Though North America was the favoured destination, over 300,000 went in search of that better life in Australia. By 1914 Australia had a stronger ethnic Irish presence than any country in the world bar Ireland itself.[1]

The community life of Irish Australians centred, not unnaturally, on the Catholic Church. Until the mid-twentieth century the church in Australia was an extension of the Irish Church; only with the arrival after the Second World War of waves of immigrants from Catholic southern Europe, bringing with them their own rituals and folk-ways, did it begin to lose its predominantly Irish complexion.

Strict on obedience to doctrine and on outward forms of observance, suspicious of the modern world and its allures, the church in Australia concentrated its energies on keeping its flock from straying, doing its best to make sure that every child of a Catholic family received a Catholic schooling. Gerald Murnane, born in 1939, was one of the beneficiaries of this policy. From *Tamarisk Row* (1974) onward, in a solid body of fiction and non-fiction,

Murnane has recorded the impact of an Irish-Australian Catholic education on a male child whose character and family background are so close to his own that only a Murnanian spirit of scrupulousness prevents one from calling this child his younger self. Among the residues of that education have been, on the one hand, an unquenched belief that there is another world beyond this one, and, on the other, ingrained feelings of personal sinfulness.

Murnane's belief in another world needs to be qualified at once. Although, after high school, he took the first steps toward entering the priesthood, he soon abandoned the idea and indeed gave up religious observance for good. The belief he has retained is therefore philosophical rather than religious in nature, though no less strong for that. As for access to that other world – a world distinct from our own and in many ways better than it – this is gained neither by good works nor by grace but by giving the self up to fiction.

When it comes to sinfulness, the boy we meet in Murnane's books – the boy I will eschew calling the young Murnane – has all the frustrated curiosity about sex that one might expect in a child brought up in a community where impure deeds are inveighed against from the pulpit, yet in such clouded terms that what such deeds may actually consist in remains a puzzle. In a revealing episode related in *Barley Patch* (2009), the boy waits up until the household is asleep, then steals out of bed to explore a dolls' house belonging to his girl cousins that he has been forbidden to touch, linked in his subconscious mind (I use the term 'subconscious mind' provisionally – see Murnane's strictures below) not only with the girls' private parts but with the tabernacle where the ceremonial vessels of the Mass are kept. By moonlight he peers through the tiny window, longing to reach in a finger and touch the mysteries inside yet fearful of leaving some guilty trace behind.[2]

How the male gets into the female is only one of the many mysteries that this child faces. In his naive cosmology, God the Father is at best a remote presence. Presiding over his destiny instead is a figure he calls the Patroness, a composite of the Virgin Mary and his own mother in her youth. 'The very purpose of her existence,' he records, 'was to remain aloof from me and so to provide me with a task worthy of a lifetime of effort: the simple but baffling task of gaining admission to her presence.'[3] A need to offer up to the female principle some strenuous act of penance becomes one of the deeper motives in Murnane's writing, animating his novel *Inland* (1988) in particular.

As a writer, Murnane is anything but a naive, straightforward realist. Putting down on paper what an Irish Catholic upbringing was like in Australia circa 1950 is only a fraction of his ambition. As he makes abundantly clear, his boy hero, who while venerating his Patroness also tries to get his cousins to take off their knickers in the toolshed, has a twofold existence, both the everyday world he shares with us and in a quite other world that is nonetheless in a not easily explained way part of our own.

In this connection Murnane likes to quote a gnomic observation attributed to Paul Eluard: 'There is another world but it is in this one'.[4] For the reader of Murnane's fiction, grasping just how the other world relates to this one is the main obstacle to understanding what Murnane is up to, or believes himself to be up to.

Thus: Is the boy about whom Murnane writes to be understood as a figure in his imagination? Is there a site, loosely to be called an imaginary world, where all the personages in

Murnane's fictions have their existence; and when Murnane (or the fictional being 'Murnane') writes of another world that is in this one, does he have nothing more unusual in mind than the world held in the imagination of his authorial self?

Of himself, his mind, and the power of that mind to conjure beings who do not 'really' exist, Murnane has the following to say:

> He had never been able to believe in something called his unconscious mind. The term *unconscious mind* seemed to him self-contradictory. Words such as *imagination* and *memory* and *person* and *self* and even *real* and *unreal* he found vague and misleading, and all the theories of psychology that he had read about as a young man begged the question of *where* the mind was. For him, the first of all premises was that his mind was a place or, rather, a vast arrangement of places.[5]

He fills out his scheme of the mind – or rather, of his own mind, since he is not interested in generalities – as follows:

> In his fifties, he . . . had come to believe that he was made up mostly of images. He was aware only of images and feelings. The feelings connected him to the images and connected the images to one another. The connected images made up a vast network. He was never able to imagine this network as having a boundary in any direction. He called the network, for convenience, his mind.[6]

The activity of writing, then, is not to be distinguished from the activity of self-exploration. It consists in contemplating the sea of internal images, discerning connections between them, and setting these connections out in grammatical sentences ('There is nothing in the world so complex that it cannot be expressed in grammatical sentences,' writes Murnane or 'Murnane', whose views on grammar are firm, even pedantic).[7] Whether connections between images lie implicit in the images themselves or are created by an active, shaping intelligence; what the source is of the energy (the 'feelings') that discerns such connections; whether that energy is always to be trusted – these are questions that do not interest him, or at least are not addressed in a body of writing that is rarely averse to reflecting on itself.

In other words, while there is a Murnanian topography of the mind, there is no Murnanian theory of the mind worth speaking of. If there is some guiding, shaping force behind the fictions of the mind, it can barely be called a force: its essence seems to be a watchful passivity.

As a writer, Murnane is thus a radical idealist. His fictional personages or 'image-persons' (*character* is a term he does not use) have their existence in a world much like the world of myth, purer, simpler, and more real than the world in which their mundane avatars are born, live, and die.[8]

For readers who, despite Murnane's best efforts, cannot tell the difference between image-persons and figments of the human imagination, it may be best to treat Murnane's theorizing – which extends into the very texture of his fiction – as no more than an elaborate way of warning us not to identify the storytelling *I* with the man Gerald Murnane, and therefore not to read his books as autobiographical records, accountable to the same standard of truth as history is. The *I* who tells the story will be no less a constructed figure than the actors in it.

With David Malouf (born 1934) and Thomas Keneally (born 1935), Gerald Murnane belongs to the last generation of writers to come to maturity in an Australia that was still a cultural colony of England, repressed, puritanical, and suspicious of foreigners. Of that generation, Murnane has been the least obedient to received norms of realism and the most open to outside influence, whether from Europe or from the Americas.

Between 1974 and 1990 Murnane published six books. Among these, *The Plains* (1982) and *Inland* (1988) are usually read as novels, though they lack many of the standard features of the novel: they have no plot worth speaking of, and only the most desultory narrative line; their personages have no names and few individuating characteristics. *Landscape with Landscape* (1985) and *Velvet Waters* (1990) are, more recognizably, collections of short fictions, some showing the imprint of Jorge Luis Borges. Murnane is conspicuously absent from the list of Australian writers who have answered the call to celebrate or interrogate Australianness: one of the pieces in *Landscape with Landscape* is a satirical commentary, not entirely successful, on this call.

After 1990, according to his own account, Murnane gave up writing fiction. In a preliminary note to *Invisible Yet Enduring Lilacs* (2005) he writes: 'I should never have tried to write fiction or non-fiction or anything in-between. I should have left it to discerning editors to publish all my pieces of writing as essays.' Both *Lilacs* and the book that followed it, *Barley Patch*, are, loosely speaking, collections of essays. *Barley Patch*, the more substantial of the two, comprises recollections of Murnane's family, childhood, and early manhood; reflections on his career as a writer, including his decision to give up fiction; explorations of his own practice as a writer; an outline of his philosophy of fiction; and synopses of abandoned projects – synopses so detailed and well developed that they threaten to become works of fiction themselves.

As a child, Murnane recalls, he loved to read because reading allowed him to wander freely among fictional personages and stare openly at (fictional) women. In real life staring was proscribed; surreptitious spying became his secret sin. He longed to meet a girl who would be curious enough about him to spy on him. To spark the curiosity of girls he would ostentatiously ignore them and occupy himself in writing. All the time he yearned for 'some layer of the world far beyond my own drab layer [where] it might have been possible sometimes to follow one's own desires without incurring punishment'.[9]

He entered his twenties (he continues in straight autobiographical vein) 'lack[ing]the skills that enabled most other young men of my age to acquire steady girlfriends or even fiancées and wives'. At weekends he met with other lonely, sex-starved young Catholic men to drink beer and talk about girls. For the rest he holed up in his room, writing.[10]

His decision to devote himself to writing instead of furthering his education was greeted with disapproval from his family; after his first book came out he was disowned by a favourite uncle. To fortify his resolve he recited to himself, like a mantra, Matthew Arnold's poem 'The Scholar Gypsy', which celebrates a life of solitary intellectual endeavour. For an income, he told himself, he would bet on the horses.

Looking back, he wonders how he could have wasted three decades of his life making up fictions. He entertains several hypotheses, none entirely serious. One is that, fearful of travel, he needed to invent a world beyond his small corner of Victoria.

When he gave up fiction-writing, Murnane informs us, he also gave up reading new books, devoting himself instead to the writers who meant the most to him, chiefly Marcel Proust, Emily Brontë, and Thomas Hardy. During the years left to him, he resolves, he will occupy himself with the 'mental entities' who have visited him in the course of a lifetime; he will 'contemplate those images and yield to those feelings that [comprise] the lasting essence of all my reading and my writing'. These images will be tirelessly rearranged and remapped, so that his works of fiction can eventually be viewed as a set of variations, chapters in a single lifelong task. The example of Proust is clear.[11]

Fascination with the image clusters in his mind leads Murnane to explore how memory works. He reads books on mnemonics, including Frances Yates's *The Art of Memory*; he even invents a system of his own based on horse racing and jockeys' colours. What interests him most are what (if he did not abhor the notion of the unconscious) he might call unconscious associations: the way the word *hiatus*, for example, brings to his mind 'a grey-black bird struggling against winds high in the sky'.[12]

Images in his memory trouble his waking hours, will not go away, until he can slot them into an image network. The qualities of these images – their associations, their emotional coloration – engage him more deeply than their overt content.

His fictions are, fundamentally, explorations of the qualities of images. He has little interest in where in his life experience these images originate, that is to say, no wish to subordinate them to the seeming real.

The most difficult pages of *Barley Patch* concern the status of the 'other' world where fictional beings live. Although such beings may depend on one or other author to write them into existence, they ultimately escape or exceed authorial control. Their interior lives are all their own; in some cases their author fails to grasp who they truly are.

An important stage in a life of writing is attained, Murnane continues, when the writing self is able to graduate from merely observing and reporting on inner images to sharing an image life with image persons in the other world. Readers of the right kind may be brought or swept along too, into a realm where they or their image selves rub shoulders with fictional beings.

Too sketchy and eccentric to constitute a proper metaphysics of fiction, these pages are better read as the poetic credo of a writer who at one point goes so far as to posit that the 'real' (mundane) world and the real (ideal) world maintain themselves in a tension of erotic reciprocity, each holding the other in existence:

Being no more than the conjectured author of this work of fiction, I can have come into existence only at the moment when a certain female personage who was reading these pages formed in her mind an image of the male personage who had written the pages with her in mind.[13]

There will be readers who will dismiss Murnane's dual-world

system as idle or fanciful theory-spinning, and perhaps go on to say that it shows he is all intellect and no heart. Murnane indirectly addresses this criticism when, in *Barley Patch*, he tells the story of his last visit to a beloved uncle dying of cancer – the same uncle who had cut ties with him when he decided to become a writer. The two spend their last hour together in a typically male Australian way: warding off any display of sentiment, discussing horse racing. After which Murnane leaves the hospital room, finds a private place, and weeps.

His uncle was right, Murnane reflects afterwards: there was no need for him to waste his life writing. Why then did he do it? The answer: without writing he 'would never be able to suggest to another person what I truly felt towards him or her'.[14] That is to say, only by telling a story of a man who appears to have no feelings but privately weeps, addressing the story, elegiacally, to one who can no longer hear it, is he able to reveal his love.

Murnane's writing, from *Inland* onward, reflects continually on this difficult personal fate. On the one hand, being a writer has set him further and further apart from human society; on the other hand, it is only through writing that he can hope to become human. The elegiac tone that marks his later work comes from the realization that he is what he is, that in this life there will be no second chance, that only in the 'other' world can he make up for what he has lost.

Barley Patch concludes with a summary of one of the fiction projects Murnane abandoned in the 1970s. Its hero is a young man who is awkward with girls, thinks of entering the priesthood, and so forth – a young man much like his historical self. Then abruptly he abandons the summary, realizing he has resumed writing, albeit in précis form, the work he had resolved to give up.

In *Inland,* which can loosely be labelled fiction as *Barley Patch* can loosely be labelled essays, we are back in the schooldays of the young Murnane (the young Murnane self). At the age of eleven he is joined in his class by a girl whom he names simply 'the girl from Bendigo Street'.[15] The two become close companions, even soulmates, until they are sundered by a family move and never meet again.

No word of love passes between them. However, through an intermediary the boy inquires whether the girl likes him, and is told that she likes him 'very much'.[16]

This unrealized love from thirty years ago is revisited by the older Murnane (the older Murnane self). *Inland* is a letter to the girl from Bendigo Street: a declaration of love; a lament over a lost opportunity; but also – and here we touch on a motive force that is harder to pin down – an act of atonement.

The transgression for which *Inland* is meant to atone is not visible in the story of the youthful pair, but seems part of the constitution of the Murnane self who figures as writer of the book. *Inland* tries to give substance to this obscure originary sin by situating it in an overt work of fiction, and thus – in Murnane's metaphysical system – making it real.

The fiction that Murnane invents is a complicated piece of work, so complicated that following its ins and outs will defeat many first-time readers. One of the seminal books for Murnane has been *People of the Puszta,* a novel exploring rural life in Hungary published in 1936 by Gyula Illyés (1902–83). Illyés records an episode from his childhood on a country estate: the young daughter of a neighbour, raped by one of the stewards, drowned herself, and he saw the corpse. The dead girl became an inspiration to him, 'an angel of defiance and revolt' in his later struggles to put an end to the abuse of powerless serfs by the rural gentry.[17]

This tragic story, alluded to repeatedly in Murnane's *oeuvre*, comes most strongly to the fore in *Inland*, where responsibility for the girl's death is taken on by an unnamed Hungarian landowner. This person narrates the early episodes of the book and is one of the avatars of Murnane-the-writer. His confession, expressed in the most veiled of terms, takes the form of an essay contributed to a journal called *Mainland* published by the Institute of Prairie Studies in Ideal, South Dakota, and edited by Anne Kristaly, one-time beloved of the landowner. Anne Kristaly, Hungarian by birth, is now married to a jealous Scandinavian who does his best to block communications between the two.

The story of this trio – landowner, Anne Kristaly, husband – complicated by metafictional by-play and parodies of Hungarian authors like Sándor Márai (Murnane reads Hungarian and is familiar with Hungarian literature), takes up the first fifty pages of the book and is its least successful part. After fifty pages, the Hungarian plains and the Institute of Prairie Studies are abandoned. Murnane, as it were, takes a deep breath and plunges into the long contrapuntal composition that constitutes the rest of the book, the most ambitious, sustained, and powerful piece of writing he has to date brought off.

The underlying narrative is about the eleven-year-old boy and the girl from Bendigo Street, their friendship and their parting, and of the man's later attempts, Orpheus-like, to summon her back, or if not her then her shade, from the realm of the dead and the forgotten. Woven into this narrative are a number of motifs whose common element is resurrection: the violated serf girl who returns as an angel of defiance; the lovers in *Wuthering Heights* united beyond the grave (*Inland* concludes with the famous last paragraph of Emily Brontë's novel); the great recuperative vision experienced by Marcel in *Time Regained*; and verses from the Gospel of Matthew that foretell the second coming of Christ.

The horizons of the boy in *Inland*, defined by the state of Victoria where he dwells, may be narrow, but the inversion of seasons between northern and southern hemispheres, consequent upon the axial tilt of planet Earth, turns out to be of profound concern to him. As Messiah, Jesus prophesied that the world would soon end but then comforted his followers by telling them to watch the fig tree: when the grey branches showed shoots of green (that is, when spring was in the offing), he would return. Obedient to Rome as ever, the boy's parish priest follows the northern calendar; thus even as he preaches on the text from Matthew and exhorts his congregation to watch, as if from the depths of winter, for the first shoots of the fig tree, the heat of midsummer is already upon them.

The obvious lesson to draw is that the church should adapt its mode of teaching to the realities of Australia. The lesson the young Murnane draws, however, is that there are two calendars operating simultaneously, two world-times, and that unless he can find a way of living according to both, superimposing the one upon the other, he will not be saved.

Once again we see reality being bent to fit a dual-world system. We sympathize with the plight of a boy caught in a trap of his own fashioning only because of the power of the writing in which his story is told. The emotional conviction behind the later parts of *Inland* is so intense, the somber lyricism so moving, the intelligence behind the chiselled sentences so undeniable, that we suppress the impulse to smile, forgive the boy his imagined sins, and allow the peasant girl from Hungary and the girl from Bendigo Street to shine their benign radiance on us from a world beyond that is somehow also this world.

On every day while I was writing on [these] pages, I thought of the people referred to or named in the book with the word for *grassland*[i.e., *puszta*]on its cover.

At first while I was writing I thought of those people as though they were all dead and I myself was alive. At some time while I was writing, however, I began to suspect what I am now sure of. I began to suspect that all persons named or referred to in the pages of books are alive, whereas all other persons are dead.

When I wrote the letter which was the first of all my pages, I was thinking of a young woman who was, I thought, dead while I was still alive. I thought the young woman was dead while I remained alive in order to go on writing what she could never read.

Today while I write on this last page, I am still thinking of the young woman. Today, however, I am sure the young woman is still alive. I am sure the young woman is still alive while I am dead. Today I am dead but the young woman remains alive in order to go on reading what I could never write.[18]

23. The Diary of Hendrik Witbooi

One of the overarching themes of modern southern African history is the spread of European settlement into the interior of the continent. Starting from the Dutch settlement at the Cape of Good Hope, colonists pushed northward and eastward in a process that went on from the mid-seventeenth century until the turn of the twentieth century, taking them far beyond the borders of the present Republic of South Africa.

Expansion toward the east brought the settlers into conflict with Bantu-speaking peoples; northward expansion brought them into conflict with the far less numerous Khoisan. It was on the northern frontier that the Witbooi dynasty emerged, of which Hendrik Witbooi (1830–1905) was to become the pre-eminent member.

As Dutch-speaking farmers moved northward toward the Gariep (Orange) River, they took over the pasturage and watering places of Khoi pastoralists and reduced those who did not flee to the status of serfs. Since the capacity of the authorities in the Cape to exercise their powers at a distance was severely limited, the northern frontier had become a haven for runaway slaves and other escapees from the law, who coalesced into armed bands living by hunting, plundering, and cattle-rustling. These bands were in time joined by numbers of disaffected Khoi serfs. Soon they were making regular raids into the lands of the Nama across the Gariep. By the early nineteenth century a half-dozen such bands had established themselves north of the river in Great Namaqualand, the Namaland of present-day Namibia, and were penetrating further north into Hereroland.

In relation to the indigenous Nama and Herero peoples, these raiders behaved as colonizers in much the same way that the Dutch Boers behaved elsewhere on the frontier. By dint of superior military technology (firearms, horses) and organization (the so-called commando system) they broke the power of the tribal owners of the land. They established their hegemony, exacted tribute, and destroyed indigenous culture, imposing new codes of language, dress, and behaviour.

A key fact about these colonists – known as Oorlams to distinguish them from the Dutch on the one hand and the tribal Khoi on the other (the origin of the word *Oorlam* is uncertain) – is that, in the terminology of nineteenth-century racial science, they were 'mixed'. In culture they are hard to distinguish from 'white' Boers (they spoke Dutch, they wore European-style clothes); but then, the Boers of the frontier had adopted so many of the elements of migratory native pastoralism that their way of life had become as much African as European.

In the Oorlam colonization of Namaland, the numbers of people involved were, by today's standards, tiny. A typical Oorlams band would consist of no more than a few hundred people, including women and children; while the entire indigenous Nama population was of the order of 10,000 souls. Between Oorlams and the subjected Nama concubinage and marriage took place; in photographs taken in the 1880s, it is hard to detect any physical difference between the two, though certain Oorlams, like the group that settled around Rehoboth, the so-called Basters, continued to assert their European descent.

The Oorlam invasion brought the peoples of southern Namibia into the modern world. In the case of the Nama, it destroyed their traditional culture, imposing a new economy which turned out to be unsustainable and bringing about the impoverishment of their land. In the case of Hereroland, Oorlam overlordship was less secure and the impact on Herero institutions correspondingly less severe. Both the Nama and the Herero had over the centuries evolved flourishing and stable cattle-based economies for which the key skills lay in providing pasturage and water for their beasts. The economy of the Oorlams, which formed part of a larger frontier economy that brought in manufactured goods from the Cape, as well as luxury items (sugar, alcohol, coffee), and – crucially – arms and ammunition, was likewise based on cattle. For their side of the trade, however, the Oorlams relied less on the rearing of their own stock than on stock-raiding or – what amounts to the same thing – exacting tribute in the form of livestock. As young Nama men were drawn into the exciting life of the Oorlam militias, the old cattle-tending skills of the Nama grew to be despised, and as these skills were lost the sizes of the herds declined. To make up for falling revenues, the Oorlams turned their energies to commercial hunting, first for the trade in ivory, later for ostrich feathers; but within another generation the game was hunted out too.

The semi-legendary founder of the Witboois was Kido (Cupido) Witbooi, who led his people across the Gariep into Namaland. Kido was succeeded by his son Moses. Moses was murdered in 1886 and his place as *kaptein* (chieftain, military leader) of the Witboois usurped. The usurper was challenged and killed by Hendrik Witbooi, grandson of Kido, who thus became *kaptein*.

Born in 1830, Hendrik Witbooi (or, to give him his Nama name, /Khobesin) was, by the standards of the day and of his people, well educated. He could read and write Dutch; he had a more than passing knowledge of history, as well as of manual trades like carpentry; while with the missionary Johannes Olpp he had studied the Bible. Whereas to other indigenous leaders church affiliation seems more often than not to have been a means to an end (the missions provided an entry point into the colonial trade network and more generally into the Western knowledge system), Witbooi took the Bible seriously and had a sense of himself as a visionary leader of his people on the model of Moses. His literary style shows the influence of his Bible reading.

Witbooi's *Dagboek* (*Diary*) consists of a large leather-bound journal purchased from a stationer in Cape Town. Some 189 pages are covered in the handwriting of Witbooi himself and of various scribes and secretaries. The text, consisting mostly of copies of correspondence relating to the affairs of the Witboois, is written in Cape Dutch; the spelling of words is sometimes phonetic. Witbooi clearly intended it to constitute the annals of his reign. This unique document was taken as booty during a German raid in 1893 and found its way to the Cape archives. A transcript was published in Cape Town in 1929.[1] There is no evidence that Witbooi continued with his diarising after 1893.

The *Diary* opens in 1884, with the Witboois locked in armed struggle with the Herero. In these early entries, Hendrik

Witbooi's pleasure in a life of skirmishing and cattle-raiding comes across clearly. Indeed, but for an unforeseen irruption of history one might have predicted for him the life of a typical Oorlam *kaptein*, competing for wealth and power with other Oorlam groups, with the Herero, and with the indigenous Nama: a charismatic leader with a core of able-bodied men with guns and horses under his command, and a group of families under his protection who owed him their loyalty.

In fact, however, the fate of Witbooi and his people was decided from afar. Since 1870 the European powers had been blocking the import of Prussian goods, and pressure was mounting in Prussia to find markets elsewhere. In 1882 the German trader Adolf Lüderitz established a station at what is now Lüderitz Bay on the Namibian coast, and appealed to Berlin for official backing. Chancellor Bismarck acceded. From his fellow European powers he demanded and obtained control, in the form of a protectorate ('German South-West Africa'), over the hinterland of this trading post. Thus Germany acquired its first overseas colony, 835,000 square kilometres in extent. Other colonial claims soon followed: in Togo, Cameroon, Tanganyika, Samoa.

Bismarck himself was not in favour of a full-blown takeover of the new territory, which would have entailed the creation of a local administration and, eventually, the building of expensive infrastructure for settlement. His intention, rather, was to grant charters on the Lüderitz model that would allow private entrepreneurs to exploit the territory. But colonialism has a dynamic of its own. Under Bismarck's more ambitious successor, German expeditionary forces followed the German flag, and then German settlers arrived to occupy the land wrested by those forces from the native peoples. Within twenty years the southern half of South-West Africa had been subdued, with great brutality and loss of life, and its peoples had lost their land and their cattle. On 29 October 1905 Hendrik Witbooi died of wounds received while fighting the Germans. The site of his grave, somewhere near Vaalgras, is unknown. There is a memorial to him in Gibeon, the main settlement of the Witboois.

After Hendrik's death the demoralized Witboois sued for peace. However, sporadic resistance against the Germans continued until 1907, when the last of the guerrilla leaders, Jakob Morenga, was shot by British colonial police near Upington in the Cape Colony.

In hindsight we can see that if the peoples of the territory had come together early to resist the colonizers, they might have been able to make the enterprise too expensive for Germany to sustain. They were, after all, experienced in small-scale warfare; they were armed with Western weapons and knew the terrain as the Germans did not. Regrettably, however, inter-group feuding continued unabated, and was exploited by the Germans to split the opposition. Indeed, between 1894 and 1904 the Witboois contributed fighting men to various German campaigns against the Herero. The last-ditch uprising of 1904, initiated by Samuel Maharero and joined belatedly by the aged Witbooi, though widely supported, was doomed to fail against the superior forces that the Germans had by then assembled.

Not the least attractive feature of Witbooi's letters, both to his German foes and to traditional rivals like Samuel Maharero, is their antique courtesy. Witbooi adhered to a code of honour which included doing no violence to women and children, treating prisoners humanely, and giving the enemy dead a decent burial. It also included not attacking until first attacked (though

Witbooi is sometimes driven to tortuous feats of sophistry to prove he was not the aggressor).

Because an officer's code of honour was important to his concept of soldiering, he was shocked by the attack on his base at Hoornkranz in 1893, when German soldiers deliberately slaughtered women and children. A similar contempt for African life, backed by pseudo-Darwinian racial science, which classified the Khoisan, including the Nama, as one of the inferior races, was exhibited in the course of the suppression of the 1904 uprising. General Lothar von Trotha, who led the German forces, arrived in South-West Africa with a well-merited reputation for ruthlessness gained in campaigns in China and Tanganyika. He was by no means ashamed of the barbarities he practised. '[Africans] submit only to force,' he wrote. 'To exercise such force with undisguised terrorism [*Terrorismus*] and even with atrocities [*Grausamkeit*] has been and is my politics [*Politik*]. I destroy rebellious tribes with streams of blood and streams of money.'[2]

Witbooi's illusion that European military officers adhered to a code of chivalry had been encouraged by his dealings with Major Theodor Leutwein, the most humanly attractive of the series of German commanders whom he faced on the battlefield. The letters exchanged between the two have an old-world charm: 'My dear Captain,' writes Leutwein on 8 July 1894, 'I am not planning to open hostilities before the contractually agreed date [of 1 August]. Your people may come and go in your camp without fear of harassment, as well as visit my own men. [However] from 1 August we will be at war . . . I will first send you notice of the commencement of hostilities. Until such time I shall not shoot.'[3]

After the above-mentioned hostilities had commenced, and

after Witbooi had been forced into retreat, he writes as follows to Leutwein: 'My dear Friend, I received your letter [of 4 September] on the run and note that you are willing to negotiate. I agree to a ceasefire . . . I shall reply to your letter from the waterhole. Be patient . . . It would be best for you to await my reply at Naukluft . . . In good hope and with friendly greetings, Your Friend Captain Hendrik Witbooi.' (pp. 144–5)

But his gentlemanly relations with Leutwein should not create the impression that Witbooi was naive about the realities of war. On the contrary, he was a canny political operator and a gifted guerrilla commander who used the mobility of his forces and the marksmanship of his men to compensate for their small numbers (his forces never numbered more than six hundred, and were usually much smaller). The bitter quality of Witbooi's wit was probably lost on Major Curt von François, Leutwein's predecessor and the officer responsible for the atrocities at Hoornkranz: 'I beg you again, dear Friend,' he writes to François on 24 July 1893, 'to send me two cases of Martini Henry cartridges so that I can fight back . . . Give me arms, as is customary among great and courteous nations, so that you may conquer an armed enemy: only thus can your great nation claim an honest victory.' (pp. 120–1)

Witbooi's letters rise to eloquent heights in his denunciation of the concept of land ownership that the new colonizers seek to impose. 'This part of Africa is the territory of Red chiefs,' he writes in 1892 to a fellow *kaptein*.*

---

* In Witbooi's racial typology, the Oorlams and the Nama belong together as Red peoples, as distinct from the Blacks (the Herero) and the Whites (Boers, British, Germans).

We are one of colour and custom. We obey the same laws, and these laws are agreeable to us and to our people; for we are not severe with each other, but accommodate to each other, amicably and in brotherhood . . . [We] do not make prohibiting laws against each other, concerning water, grazing, or roads; nor do [we] charge money for any of these things. No, we hold these things to be free to any traveller who wishes to cross our land, be he Red, or White, or Black . . . But with White people it is not so at all. The White men's laws are quite unbearable and intolerable to us Red people; they oppress us and hem us in in all kinds of ways and on all sides, these merciless laws which have no feeling or tolerance for any man rich or poor. (pp. 80–1)

To Witbooi, the liberty he fights for is no abstract idea but a deeply felt freedom to ride and hunt where you will, to move your cattle from pasturage to pasturage according to the season, and sometimes perhaps to practise your skills as a cattle-rustler. In other words, he wants to preserve into the twentieth century an attractive way of life, semi-nomadic but ultimately parasitic. 'It is neither a sin nor crime for me to want to remain the independent chief of my country and people,' he writes defiantly to Leutwein in 1894. 'If you want to kill me for this without any fault of mine, there is no harm done, nor is it a disgrace: I shall die honestly for that which is my own.' (p. 140) Part of the pathos of his position is that the way of life in whose defence he is prepared to die had become economically unsustainable: even if there had been no German invasion, it would soon have had to come to an end.

It is a blessing that Witbooi did not live to see the fate of his Red people under the German heel. Like the Herero, they lost their firearms, their cattle, and their land. New laws were brought in to proscribe 'vagabondage' (i.e., nomadism) and turn them into a labour force for the new German settler class, whose number had by 1913 climbed to 15,000. Of the survivors of the great uprising, some were transported to remote German colonies, others confined in concentration camps. In the most notorious of these camps, on Shark Island in Lüderitz Bay, 1,032 of the 1,795 inmates perished within a year, of cold and illness.

Of all Herero and Nama prisoners, forty-five per cent died in captivity. Between 1904 and 1911 the Herero population declined from 80,000 to 15,000, the Nama ('Red') population from 20,000 to 10,000. It is hard not to see the camps as part of a programme whose goal first became apparent in the sequel to the Battle of Waterberg, when Trotha drove the remnants of the Herero fighting force, together with their women and children, into the Omaheke desert to perish of thirst. Defeating the Herero on the battlefield, and subsequently the Nama too, was, it turned out, only a first step in a larger and more sinister project: genocide.

In 2004, at an event marking the centenary of the 1904 uprising, a spokesperson for the German government delivered to the Namibian people a carefully worded speech that included a *'Bitte um Vergebung'* (plea for forgiveness) for German crimes but avoided the word *Entschuldigung* (apology). 'The atrocities committed at that time would today be called genocide [*Völkermord*],' she said, 'and nowadays a General von Trotha would be prosecuted and convicted.'[4]

Notes and References

1. Daniel Defoe, *Roxana*

1. Hippolyte Taine, *Histoire de la littérature anglaise* (Paris, 1863), vol. 3, pp. 266–7.
2. Daniel Defoe, *Roxana: The Fortunate Mistress*, ed. David Blewett (London: Penguin, 1982), pp. 105, 243.
3. Aristotle, *Nichomachean Ethics*, part 3, chapter 1.

2. Nathaniel Hawthorne, *The Scarlet Letter*

1. Nathaniel Hawthorne, Preface to 1851 edition of *Twice-Told Tales*.
2. Nathaniel Hawthorne, 'The Custom-House', in *The Scarlet Letter*, eds. Sculley Bradley et al. (New York: W. W. Norton, 1978), p. 11.
3. Review by Arthur Cleveland Coxe, reproduced in Hawthorne, *The Scarlet Letter*, eds. Bradley et al., p. 257.
4. Henry James, *Hawthorne*, ed. Tony Tanner (New York: Macmillan, 1967), p. 109.
5. Edgar Allan Poe, review (1847) of *Twice-Told Tales* and *Mosses from an Old Manse*, reproduced in James McIntosh, *Nathaniel Hawthorne's Tales: Authoritative Texts, Backgrounds, Criticism* (New York: W. W. Norton, 1987), pp. 333–4.
6. Herman Melville, 'Hawthorne and his Mosses' (1850), reproduced in McIntosh, p. 341.

3. Ford Madox Ford, *The Good Soldier*

1. Ford Madox Ford, *The Good Soldier*, in *The Bodley Head Ford Madox Ford*, ed. Graham Greene (London: The Bodley Head, 1962), vol. 1, p. 42.
2. Gustave Flaubert, *Madame Bovary*, trans. Paul de Man (New York: W. W. Norton, 1965), p. 250.

4. Philip Roth's Tale of the Plague

1. Albert Camus, *The Plague*, trans. Stuart Gilbert (London: Penguin, 1948), p. 252.
2. Philip Roth, *Nemesis* (New York: Houghton Mifflin, 2010), pp. 118, 75.
3. Sophocles, *Oedipus the King*, in *Complete Greek Tragedies: Sophocles I*, trans. David Grene (Chicago: University of Chicago Press, 1954), line 1,415.
4. Philip Roth, *Indignation* (New York: Vintage, 2008), p. 12.
5. Philip Roth, *Everyman* (New York: Vintage, 2006), p. 180.

5. Johann Wolfgang von Goethe, *The Sorrows of Young Werther*

1. *Goethes Werke*, ed. Erich Trunz (Munich: Beck, 1951–68), vol. 6, p. 521.
2. Thomas Mann, 'Goethes "Werther"', in Hans Peter Herrmann (ed.), *Goethes 'Werther': Kritik und Forschung* (Darmstadt: Wissenschaftliche Buchgesellschaft, 1994), p. 95.
3. Johann Wolfgang von Goethe, *Dichtung und Wahrheit: The Autobiography of Johann Wolfgang von Goethe*, trans. John Oxenford, 2 vols. (London: Sidgwick & Jackson, 1971), vol. 2, p. 212.
4. *Goethes Werke*, ed. Trunz, vol. 6, p. 522.
5. Johann Wolfgang von Goethe, *Erotic Poems* (London: Oxford University Press, 1988), p. 125 (my translation).
6. *Conversations with Eckermann*, 2 January 1824.
7. Thomas Mann, 'Goethes "Werther"', in Herrmann (ed.), p. 101. Charlotte Kestner's letter is quoted in Thomas Mann, *Lotte in Weimar*, trans. H. T. Lowe-Porter (London: Secker & Warburg, 1947), p. 330.
8. Mann, *Lotte in Weimar*, pp. 280–1, 25.

9. Johann Wolfgang von Goethe, *The Sorrows of Young Werther*, trans. David Constantine (Oxford: Oxford University Press, 2012), p. 103.

10. Ehrhard Bahr, 'Unerschlossene Intertextualität: Macphersons "Ossian" und Goethes "Werther"', *Goethe-Jahrbuch* 124 (2007), p. 179.

11. Quoted in Dafydd Moore, 'The Reception of *The Poems of Ossian* in England and Scotland', in Howard Gaskill et al. (eds.), *The Reception of Ossian in Europe* (London: Continuum, 2004), p. 31.

12. John Dryden, 'On Translation', in Rainer Schulte and John Biguenet (eds.), *Theories of Translation* (Chicago: University of Chicago Press, 1992), p. 26.

13. Henry Crabb Robinson, *Diary*, vol. 2 (1889), p. 432.

14. Goethe, *Dichtung und Wahrheit*, vol. 2, pp. 110, 208.

15. Goethe, *The Sorrows of Young Werther*, trans. Constantine, p. 5; *The Sorrows of Werter*, trans. Daniel Malthus (London, 1787), p. 1.

6. Translating Hölderlin

1. Michael Hamburger, *Collected Poems 1941–1983* (Manchester: Carcanet, 1984), p. 21.

2. Friedrich Hölderlin, *Gedichte*, ed. Jochen Schmidt (Frankfurt: Deutscher Klassiker Verlag, 1992), p. 217.

3. Quoted in David Constantine, *Hölderlin* (Oxford: Clarendon Press, 1988), p. 34.

4. Quoted in Constantine, *Hölderlin*, p. 20.

5. Quoted in Friedrich Hölderlin, *Selected Poems*, trans. J. B. Leishman (London: Hogarth Press, 1944), p. 12.

6. Quoted in Stephan Wackwitz, *Friedrich Hölderlin* (Stuttgart: Metzler, 1985), p. 25.

7. Quoted in Constantine, *Hölderlin*, p. 169.

8. Quoted in Hölderlin, *Selected Poems*, trans. Leishman, p. 23.

9. Constantine, *Hölderlin*, p. 110.

10. Friedrich Hölderlin, *Hyperion and Selected Poems*, ed. Eric L. Santner (New York: Continuum, 1990), p. 130.

11. Friedrich Hölderlin, *Sämtliche Werke*, vol. 6/1, ed. Adolf Beck (Stuttgart: Kohlhammer, 1954), p. 297.

12. Quoted in Constantine, *Hölderlin*, p. 270.

13. Constantine, *Hölderlin*, p. 305.
14. Quoted in Ulrich Häussermann, *Friedrich Hölderlin in Selbstzeugnissen und Bilddokumenten* (Hamburg: Rowohlt, 1961), p. 166.
15. Friedrich Hölderlin, *Poems and Fragments*, trans. Michael Hamburger (London: Routledge, 1966), p. 239.
16. Martin Heidegger, *Poetry, Language, Thought*, trans. Albert Hofstadter (New York: Harper & Row, 1971), p. 93.
17. Martin Heidegger, *Existence and Being*, trans. Werner Brock (London: Vision, 1949), p. 311. The lines are from the poem 'Rousseau'. Cf. Hölderlin, *Poems and Fragments*, trans. Hamburger, p. 181.
18. 'Idea for a Universal History', in Immanuel Kant, *Political Writings*, ed. Hans Reiss, trans. H. B. Nisbet (Cambridge: Cambridge University Press, 1970), p. 52.
19. Humboldt is quoted in Joachim Wohlleben, 'Germany 1750–1830', in K. J. Dover (ed.), *Perceptions of the Ancient Greeks* (Oxford: Blackwell, 1992), p. 195.
20. Hölderlin, *Poems and Fragments*, trans. Hamburger, p. 325.
21. Friedrich Hölderlin, *Sämtliche Werke*, vol. 4, ed. Friedrich Beissner (Stuttgart: Kohlhammer, 1961), p. 221.
22. Hölderlin, *Sämtliche Werke*, vol. 6/1, ed. Beck, pp. 425–6.
23. Hölderlin, *Sämtliche Werke*, vol. 4, ed. Beissner, pp. 150–1.
24. Hölderlin, *Poems and Fragments*, trans. Hamburger, p. 505.
25. 'The Only One', in Hölderlin, *Poems and Fragments*, trans. Hamburger, p. 537.
26. *Hymns and Fragments by Friedrich Hölderlin*, trans. Richard Sieburth (Princeton: Princeton University Press, 1984), p. 249.
27. Michael Hamburger, *String of Beginnings: Intermittent Memoirs 1924–1954* (1973) (London: Skoob Books, 1991), p. 118.
28. Preface (1966) to Hölderlin, *Poems and Fragments*, pp. x, xi.
29. Michael Hamburger, 'Hölderlin ins Englische übersetzen', in Christophe Fricke and Bruno Pieger (eds.), *Friedrich Hölderlin zu seiner Dichtung* (Amsterdam: Castrum Peregrini, 2005), p. 130.
30. Preface (1966) to Hölderlin, *Poems and Fragments*, p. xii.
31. *Hymns and Fragments*, trans. Sieburth, p. 111.

7. Heinrich von Kleist: Two Stories

1. Heinrich von Kleist, *The Marquise von O— and Other Stories*, trans. David Luke (London: Penguin, 1977), p. 114. Luke's translation of 'Michael Kohlhaas' is used throughout.
2. Thomas Mann, 'Preface', *The Marquise von O— and Other Stories*, trans. Martin Greenberg (London: Faber, 1960), p. 14.
3. Heinrich von Kleist, 'On the Gradual Formulation of Thoughts while Speaking', in *Selected Prose*, trans. Peter Wortsman (New York: Archipelago, 2010), pp. 255–63.
4. Quoted in Mann, 'Preface', trans. Greenberg, p. 20.
5. Kleist, 'The Marquise of O-', in *Selected Prose*, trans. Wortsman, p. 121.
6. Quoted in Nancy Nobile, *The School of Days: Heinrich von Kleist and the Traumas of Education* (Detroit: Wayne State University Press, 1999), p. 148.

8. Robert Walser, *The Assistant*

1. Quoted in George C. Avery, *Inquiry and Testament* (Philadelphia: University of Pennsylvania Press, 1968), p. 11.
2. Quoted in K.-M. Hinz and T. Horst (eds.), *Robert Walser* (Frankfurt a/Main: Suhrkamp, 1991), p. 57.
3. Quoted in Mark Harman (ed.), *Robert Walser Rediscovered* (Hanover and London: University Press of New England, 1985), p. 206.
4. Quoted in Idris Parry, *Hand to Mouth* (Manchester: Carcanet, 1981), p. 35.
5. Quoted in Peter Utz (ed.), *Wärmende Fremde* (Bern: Peter Lang, 1994), p. 64. See also Katharina Kerr (ed.), *Über Robert Walser* (Frankfurt a/Main: Suhrkamp, 1978), bd. 2, p. 22.
6. Robert Walser, *Gesammelte Werke*, ed. Jochen Greven (Frankfurt a/Main: Suhrkamp, 1978), bd. X, p. 323.
7. Robert Walser, *The Assistant*, trans. Susan Bernofsky (New York: New Directions, 2007), pp. 178–9.

9. Gustave Flaubert, *Madame Bovary*

1. Review dated 4 May 1857, in Gustave Flaubert, *Madame Bovary: Backgrounds and Sources*, ed. and trans. Paul de Man (New York: W. W. Norton, 1965), p. 325.
2. Letter of 26 July 1852, in *The Letters of Gustave Flaubert, 1830–1857*, ed. Francis Steegmuller (London: Faber, 1979), p. 166.
3. Review dated 18 October 1857, in Flaubert, *Madame Bovary*, ed. and trans. de Man, p. 340.
4. Letter of 23 December 1853, in *Letters*, ed. Steegmuller, p. 203.
5. Letter of 14 August 1853, in *Letters*, ed. Steegmuller, p. 195.
6. Letter of 4 September 1852, in *Letters*, ed. Steegmuller, p. 169.
7. Letter of 9 December 1852, in *Letters*, ed. Steegmuller, p. 173.

10. Irène Némirovsky, Jewish Writer

1. Irène Némirovsky, *A Life of Chekhov*, trans. Erik de Mauny (London: Grey Walls Press, 1950), p. 71.
2. Olivier Philipponnat and Patrick Lienhardt, *La Vie d'Irène Némirovsky* (Paris: Grasset, 2007), p. 403.
3. Irène Némirovsky, *Suite Française*, trans. Sandra Smith (New York: Vintage, 2007), Appendix I, p. 376.
4. Philipponnat and Lienhardt, *La Vie*, p. 347.
5. Jonathan Weiss, *Irène Némirovsky: Her Life and Works* (Stanford: Stanford University Press, 2007).
6. Quoted in Alan Astro, 'Two Best-Selling French Jewish Women's Novels from 1929', *Symposium* 52/4 (1999), pp. 241 ff.
7. Irène Némirovsky, *Les Biens de ce monde* (Paris: Albin Michel, 1947), p. 319.
8. Irène Némirovsky, *Les Chiens et les loups* (Paris: Albin Michel, 1940), p. 200. The title carries a double meaning: *entre chien et loup* is the hour of twilight.
9. Némirovsky, *Les Chiens et les loups*, p. 150.
10. Némirovsky, *Suite Française*, p. 348.
11. Michael Marrus and Robert Paxton, *Vichy France and the Jews* (New York: Basic Books, 1981), p. 366.
12. Irène Némirovsky, *Le Vin de solitude* (Paris: Albin Michel, 1935), p. 17.

13. Némirovsky, *Le Vin de solitude*, p. 281.
14. Némirovsky, *Le Vin de solitude*, pp. 301–2.
15. Elisabeth Gille, *Le Mirador* (Paris: Stock, 2000), p. 421.

11. Juan Ramón Jiménez, *Platero and I*

1. Juan Ramón Jiménez, *Platero and I*, trans. William and Mary Roberts (New York: New American Library, 1956), p. 78.

12. Antonio Di Benedetto, *Zama*

1. Antonio Di Benedetto, *Zama*, trans. Esther Allen (New York: New York Review Books, 2016), p. 15.
2. Jorge Luis Borges, 'The Argentine Writer and Tradition', trans. James Irby, in *Labyrinths* (New York: New Directions, 1962), pp. 184-5.
3. Quoted in Steven Gregory and Daniel Timerman, 'Rituals of the Modern State,' *Dialectical Anthropology* 11 (1986), p. 69.
4. Eduardo Luis Duhalde, *El estado terrorista argentino* (Barcelona: Argos/Vergara, 1983), pp. 155-9. Duhalde is not to be confused with Eduardo Alberto Duhalde, president of Argentina 2002-3.
5. Quoted in Natalia Gelós, *Antonio Di Benedetto Periodista* (Buenos Aires: Capital Intelectual, 2011), p. 66.
6. Quoted in Liliana Reales, ed., *Antonio Di Benedetto: Escritos periodisticos* (Buenos Aires: Adriana Hidalgo, 2016), pp. 45-6.

13. Leo Tolstoy, *The Death of Ivan Ilyich*

1. Leo Tolstoy, 'Master and Man', in *The Death of Ivan Ilyich and Other Stories*, trans. Richard Pevear and Larissa Volokhonsky (London: Vintage, 2009), p. 244.
2. Quoted in Henri Troyat, *Tolstoy*, trans. Nancy Amphoux (New York: Octagon, 1980), p. 485.
3. Tolstoy, *The Death of Ivan Ilyich*, in *The Death of Ivan Ilyich and Other Stories*, trans Pevear and Volokhonsky, p. 44.

14. On Zbigniew Herbert

1. *The Collected Poems 1956–1998*, ed. and trans. Alissa Valles (New York: Ecco Press, 2007). All passages quoted are from this volume.

15. The Young Samuel Beckett

1. *The Letters of Samuel Beckett, Volume 1: 1929–1940*, eds. Martha Dow Fehsenfeld and Lois More Overbeck (Cambridge: Cambridge University Press, 2009), p. 53, hereafter cited as *Letters*.
2. Quoted in Brigitte le Juez, *Beckett before Beckett*, trans. Ros Schwartz (London: Souvenir Press, 2008), p. 19.
3. *Letters*, p. 99. *Poena* (Latin), punishment.
4. James Knowlson, *Damned to Fame* (New York: Simon & Schuster, 1996), p. 92.
5. Quoted in *Letters*, p. 511, note 9.
6. The notebooks for the Johnson play are preserved at the University of Reading. The surviving dramatic fragment has been published in Samuel Beckett, *Disjecta: Miscellaneous Writings and a Dramatic Fragment*, ed. Ruby Cohn (New York: Grove Press, 1984).
7. Arnold Geulincx, *Ethics, with Samuel Beckett's Notes*, trans. Martin Wilson, eds. Hans von Ruler, Anthony Uhlmann, and Martin Wilson (Leiden: Brill, 2006).
8. Quoted in Knowlson, *Damned to Fame*, p. 171.
9. Quoted in Mary Jacobus, *The Poetics of Psychoanalysis* (Oxford: Oxford University Press, 2005), p. 180.
10. Wilfred Bion, *Attention and Interpretation* (London: Tavistock, 1970), pp. 55–6.

16. Samuel Beckett, *Watt*

1. *The Letters of Samuel Beckett, Volume 1: 1929–1940*, eds. Martha Dow Fehsenfeld and Lois More Overbeck (Cambridge: Cambridge University Press, 2009), pp. 15, 55.
2. *Letters 1929–1940*, p. 518; *The Letters of Samuel Beckett, Volume 2: 1940–1956*, eds. George Craig, Martha Dow Fehsenfeld, Dan Gunn and Lois More Overbeck (Cambridge: Cambridge University Press, 2011), p. 48.
3. Samuel Beckett, *Watt* (New York: Grove, 1959), p. 254.
4. René Descartes, *Philosophical Works*, trans. Elizabeth Haldane and G. R. T. Ross (Cambridge: Cambridge University Press, 1969), vol. 1, p. 92.

5. See C. J. Ackerley, *Obscure Locks, Simple Keys: The Annotated Watt* (Tallahassee: JOBS Books, 2005), p. 84.

17. Samuel Beckett, *Molloy*

1. Samuel Beckett, *Molloy. Malone Dies. The Unnamable* (London: Calder, 1959), p. 176.

18. Eight Ways of Looking at Samuel Beckett

1. First published in 1959, this essay forms part of *Samuel Beckett: A Critical Study* (Berkeley: University of California Press, 1968).
2. William James, *Psychology (Briefer Course)* (1892) (Cambridge, Mass.: Harvard University Press, 1984), p. 11.
3. Herman Melville, *Moby-Dick*, chapter 36.
4. Melville, *Moby-Dick*, chapter 42.
5. 'Imagination Dead Imagine', *Samuel Beckett: The Grove Centenary Edition* (New York: Grove Press, 2006), vol. 4, p. 361.
6. 'Ping', *Samuel Beckett: The Grove Centenary Edition*, vol. 4, p. 371.

19. Late Patrick White

1. Patrick White, *Flaws in the Glass* (London: Cape, 1981), pp. 80, 154.
2. Duffield was 'a composite of several [painters] I have known, welded together by the one I have in me but never became'. White, *Flaws in the Glass*, p. 151.
3. Patrick White, *The Vivisector* (London: Penguin, 1970), p. 248. I have regularized White's spelling.
4. Patrick White, *Letters*, ed. David Marr (Sydney: Random House, 1994), p. 327.
5. Helen Verity Hewitt, *Patrick White, Painter Manqué* (Melbourne: Miegunyah Press, 2002), p. 82.
6. White, *Letters*, ed. Marr, p. 321.
7. David Marr, 'Patrick White: The Final Chapter', *The Monthly*, April 2008, p. 30.
8. Max Brod, Epilogue to *The Trial*, trans. Willa and Edwin Muir, in Franz Kafka, *Collected Novels* (London: Penguin, 1988), p. 173.

9. John H. Wigmore, *Evidence in trials at common law*, § 2462, at 198 (James H. Chadbourn, ed., 1981).

10. Quoted in Richard F. Storrow, 'Judicial discretion and the disappearing distinction between will interpretation and construction', *Case Western Reserve Law Review* 56 (2005), p. 71.

11. John 3:8 (New American Standard Bible).

12. John 20:22.

13. White, *Flaws in the Glass*, pp. 175, 201.

14. Patrick White, *The Hanging Garden* (New York: Picador, 2012), pp. 152, 208, 195, 196, 197.

20. Patrick White, *The Solid Mandala*

1. Patrick White, *The Solid Mandala* (London: Penguin, 1969), p. 281.

21. The Poetry of Les Murray

1. Les Murray, *The Paperbark Tree: Selected Prose* (Manchester: Carcanet, 1992), p. 33.

2. Quoted in Paul Kane, *Australian Poetry: Romanticism and Negativity* (Cambridge: Cambridge University Press, 1996), p. 199.

3. Quoted in Peter Alexander, *Les Murray: A Life in Progress* (Melbourne: Oxford University Press, 2000), p. 56.

4. Murray, *The Paperbark Tree*, pp. 48, 47, 46.

5. Murray, *The Paperbark Tree*, p. 73.

6. 'Humiliation mills' quoted in Peter Pierce, 'Les Murray's "Narrowspeak"', in Laurie Hergenhan and Bruce Clunies Ross, *The Poetry of Les Murray: Critical Essays* (Brisbane: University of Queensland Press, 2001), p. 83. 'The Ascendancy', etc.: Murray, *The Paperbark Tree*, p. 48.

7. Les Murray, *Collected Poems* (Melbourne: Black Inc, 2006), p. 341.

8. Quoted in Alexander, *Les Murray*, p. 73.

9. Murray, *Collected Poems*, p. 424.

10. Murray, *The Paperbark Tree*, p. 90.

11. Murray, *The Paperbark Tree*, p. 72.

12. Murray, *The Paperbark Tree*, pp. 72–3.

13. Interview with John Kinsella, *Meanjin* 2001/2, p. 158.

14. Murray, *The Paperbark Tree*, pp. 96–7.
15. Murray, *The Paperbark Tree*, p. 259.
16. Murray, *The Paperbark Tree*, p. 260.
17. Murray, *The Paperbark Tree*, p. 260.
18. Murray, *Collected Poems*, p. 183.
19. Alexander, *Les Murray*, p. 107.
20. Kane, *Australian Poetry*, chapter 11.
21. Murray, *Collected Poems*, pp. 179–80.
22. Murray, 'Poetry and Religion', *Collected Poems*, p. 265.
23. Les Murray, *Killing the Black Dog: A Memoir of Depression* (New York: Farrar, Straus & Giroux, 2009), p. 32.

22. Reading Gerald Murnane

1. See R. F. Foster, *Modern Ireland 1600–1972* (London: Allen Lane, 1988), pp. 323, 324; David Fitzpatrick, *Oceans of Consolation* (Melbourne: Melbourne University Press, 1995), p. 6.
2. Gerald Murnane, *Barley Patch* (Champaign: Dalkey Archive Press, 2011), pp. 27, 127.
3. Murnane, *Barley Patch*, pp. 129–30.
4. 'Il y a un autre monde mais il est dans celui-ci.' I am unable to confirm that Eluard is in fact the source. See Gerald Murnane, *Inland* (Champaign: Dalkey Archive Press, 2012), p. 103. The same line was used by Patrick White as an epigraph to *The Solid Mandala* (1974), his novel about a suburban visionary.
5. Gerald Murnane, *Emerald Blue* (Melbourne: McPhee Gribble, 1995), p. 87.
6. Murnane, *Emerald Blue*, p. 85.
7. Gerald Murnane, *Invisible Yet Enduring Lilacs* (Sydney: Giramondo, 2005), p. 181.
8. Gerald Murnane, *A History of Books*, (Sydney: Giramondo, 2012), p. 31.
9. Murnane, *Barley Patch*, p.126.
10. Murnane, *Barley Patch*, pp. 153, 157–9.
11. Murnane, *Barley Patch*, pp. 14, 85.
12. Murnane, *Barley Patch*, p. 204.
13. Murnane, *Barley Patch*, p. 170.
14. Murnane, *Barley Patch*, pp. 167–8.

15. Murnane, *Inland*, p. 98.
16. Murnane, *Inland*, p. 110.
17. Gyula Illyés, *Hungarian Review*, July 2011, p. 92.
18. Murnane, *Inland*, pp. 166–7.

23. The Diary of Hendrik Witbooi

1. *Die Dagboek van Hendrik Witbooi*. Foreword by Gustav Voigts (Cape Town: Van Riebeeck Society, 1929).
2. Quoted in Horst Drechsler, *Südwestafrika unter deutscher Kolonialherrschaft* (Berlin: Akademie Verlag, 1966), p. 180.
3. *The Hendrik Witbooi Papers*, ed. Brigitte Lau (Windhoek: National Archives, 1989), pp. 135–6. This edition includes a translation of the *Dagboek* by Annemarie Heywood and Eben Maasdorp.
4. www.windhuk.diplo.de/Vertretung/windhuk/de/03/Gedenkjahre_2004_2005/Seite_Rede_BMZ_2004-08-14.html.

Acknowledgments

(1) An earlier version appeared as an introduction to Daniel Defoe, *Roxana*, trans. Teresa Arijón (Madrid & Buenos Aires: El Hilo de Ariadna, 2014).

(2) An earlier version appeared as an introduction to Nathaniel Hawthorne, *La Letra Escarlata*, trans. José Donoso and Pilar Serrano (Madrid and Buenos Aires: El Hilo de Ariadna, 2013).

(3) An earlier version appeared as an introduction to Ford Madox Ford, *El buen soldato*, trans. Sergio Pitol (Madrid and Buenos Aires: El Hilo de Ariadna, 2015). Published in English in *The Best Australian Essays 2016*, edited by Geordie Williamson (Black Inc.).

(4) An earlier version appeared as a review of Philip Roth, *Nemesis*, in *New York Review of Books* 57/16 (28 October 2010).

(5) An earlier version appeared in *New York Review of Books* 59/7 (26 April 2012) as a review of Johann Wolfgang von Goethe, *The Sufferings of Young Werther*, trans. Stanley Corngold.

(6) An earlier version appeared as a review of Friedrich Hölderlin, *Poems and Fragments*, trans. Michael Hamburger, in *New York Review of Books* 53/16 (19 October 2006).

(7) An earlier version appeared as an introduction to Heinrich von Kleist, *La Marquesa de O. y Michael Kohlhaas*, trans. Ariel Magnus (Madrid and Buenos Aires: El Hilo de Ariadna, 2013).

(8) An earlier version appeared as an introduction to Robert Walser, *El ayudante*, trans. Juan José del Solar (Madrid and Buenos Aires: El Hilo de Ariadna, 2014).

(9) An earlier version appeared as an introduction to Gustave Flaubert, *Madame Bovary*, trans. Graciela Isnardi (Madrid and Buenos Aires: El Hilo de Ariadna, 2013).

(10) An earlier version appeared as a review of Irène Némirovsky, four novels, in *New York Review of Books* 55/18 (20 November 2008).

(11) An earlier version appeared as an introduction to Juan Ramon Jiménez, *Platero y yo* (Mexico: Lectorum, 2007).

(12) An earlier version appeared as a review of Antonio Di Benedetto, *Zama*, trans. Esther Allen (New York: New York Review Books, 2016), in *New York Review of Books* 64/1 (19 January 2017).

(13) An earlier version appeared as an introduction to Leo Tolstoy, *La muerte de Iván Ilich, Patrón y peón, Hadji Murat*, trans. Alejandro Ariel González (Madrid and Buenos Aires: El Hilo de Ariadna, 2014).

(14) An earlier version appeared in *New Walk* (Leicester) #2 (Summer 2011).

(15) An earlier version appeared as a review of Samuel Beckett, *Letters, 1929–1940*, in *New York Review of Books* 56/7 (30 April 2009).

(16) An earlier version appeared as an introduction to Samuel Beckett, *Watt*, trans. Cristina Piña (Madrid and Buenos Aires: El Hilo de Ariadna, 2015).

(17) An earlier version appeared as an introduction to Samuel Beckett, *Molloy*, trans. Roberto Bixio (Madrid and Buenos Aires: El Hilo de Ariadna, 2015).

(18) An earlier version appeared in *Borderless Beckett/Beckett sans frontières*, ed. Minako Okamuro et al. (Amsterdam: Rodopi, 2008).

(19) Drawn from an introduction to Patrick White, *The Vivisector* (New York: Penguin, 2008); and from a review of Patrick White, *The Hanging Garden*, in *New York Review of Books* 60/17 (7 November 2013).

(20) An earlier version appeared as an introduction to Patrick White, *Las esferas del mandala*, trans. Elena Marengo (Madrid and Buenos Aires: El Hilo de Ariadna, 2015).

(21) An earlier version appeared as a review of Les Murray, *Taller When Prone*, in *New York Review of Books* 58/14 (29 September 2011).

(22) An earlier version appeared as a review of Gerald Murnane, *Inland* and *Barley Patch*, in *New York Review of Books* 59/20 (20 December 2012).

(23) An earlier version appeared as an introduction to *Votre paix sera la mort de ma nation: Lettres d'Hendrik Witbooi* (Saint-Gervais: Passager clandestin, 2011).